THE LAND'S WILD MUSIC

THE LAND'S WILD MUSIC

ENCOUNTERS WITH

Barry Lopez, Peter Matthiessen,
Terry Tempest Williams,
& James Galvin

MARK TREDINNICK

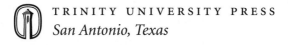 TRINITY UNIVERSITY PRESS
San Antonio, Texas

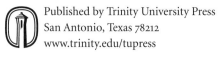
Published by Trinity University Press
San Antonio, Texas 78212
www.trinity.edu/tupress

Jacket design by Erin Kirk New
Book design by BookMatters, Berkeley, California
Cover illustration: *Strands of Gold* by Sheila Finch, courtesy of McLean Gallery, Malibu, California

⊗ The paper used in this publication meets the minimum requirements of the American National Standard for Information Sciences-Permanence of Paper for Printed Library Materials, ANSI Z39.48-1992.   .

Library of Congress Cataloging in Publication Data

Tredinnick, Mark.
The land's wild music : encounters with Barry Lopez, Peter Matthiessen, Terry Tempest Williams, and James Galvin / Mark Tredinnick.
    p.   cm.
SUMMARY: "A lyric reflection on the nature of landscape and its power to shape the lives and syntax of men and women. Examines the work of American writers Barry Lopez, Peter Matthiessen, Terry Tempest Williams, and James Galvin, looking at how their landscapes—the Cascades, Long Island, the Colorado Plateau, and the high prairies of the Rocky Mountains—have shaped them" —Provided by publisher.
Includes bibliographical references (p.   ).
ISBN-13: 978-1-59534-018-4 (pbk. : alk. paper)
ISBN-10: 1-59534-018-1 (pbk. : alk. paper)
ISBN-13: 978-1-59534-017-7 (alk. paper)
ISBN-10: 1-59534-017-3 (alk. paper)
1. American literature—20th century—History and criticism.   2. Landscape in literature.   3. Lopez, Barry Holstun, 1945– —Criticism and interpretation.
4. Williams, Terry Tempest—Criticism and interpretation.   5. Matthiessen, Peter Criticism and interpretation.   6. Galvin, James Criticism and inter-pretation.   7. Place (Philosophy) in literature.   8. United States—In literature.
9. Wilderness areas in literature.   10. Nature in literature.   11. Setting (Literature)   I. Title.
PS228.L36T74   2005
810.9'32'0904—dc22   2005016212

Printed in the United States of America
05   06   07   08   09 / 5   4   3   2   1

For Henry Thoreau, who came at the start,
and Henry Tredinnick, who came at the end

Contents

Acknowledgments

Although this book is the offspring of a sustained relationship with the keys of a laptop, it would not have come into being at all without the example, friendship, patience, and guidance of many other men and women, above all the writers I study here. I want to thank the choir of people and places whose song this book really is.

The Land's Wild Music began with Barry Lopez. Reading his work, which is everything (wise, lovely, humble, intimate, alive) I would wish prose to be, helped me recognize a calling, and it germinated the thought that became this critical journey that became, in time, this book. When it was little more than a thought, Barry helped me believe this project might be viable and someday bear fruit; he put me in touch with everyone I wished to meet; he helped secure me an invitation to a gathering of nature writers at Harvard, which became the starting point for my pilgrimage. Barry Lopez is a chapter in this book. More than that, he has been a friend and a teacher. And I count myself blessed.

The seminar I attended, thanks to Barry Lopez, at Harvard in October 2000 was "The Ecological Imagination: Reflections on Nature, Place, and Spirituality." Celebrating and exploring the contribution of nature writing to the resolution of the eco-spiritual crisis of our times, the seminar was hosted by Mary Evelyn Tucker and John Grim of Bucknell University as part of their ongoing Forum on Religion and Ecology. I thank them for including me in a rich conversation and for giving me a phrase—the ecological imagination—that helped me organize my thinking as I went.

One night in Moab, Utah, in the middle of my journey, Terry Tempest Williams said to me that, looked at one way, what I was doing was outrageous—inviting myself into the homes of a bunch of writers and talking with them about the way they work and live and write, and the way they love the landscapes from which their writing grows. Terry was right. And I am astonished and grateful that I found such a welcome from her and the other writers I visited—those whom I managed to fit into the book as well as those I didn't. For their generosity, hospitality, and candor I thank James Galvin, John Haines, Edward Hoagland, Bill Kittredge, Laurie Kutchins, William Lines, Barry Lopez, Peter Matthiessen, Richard Nelson, Michael Pollan, Carolyn Servid, and Terry Tempest Williams. And I thank their loved ones for putting up with the intrusion. I wanted to spend more time than I was able to with Pattiann Rogers and Wendell Berry, but I was helped along more than they realize by the moments and the correspondence we shared. Thanks, also, to Linda Hogan, Gary Snyder, and Mark Spragg.

Among the writers whose work did not make it into my book, I want particularly to acknowledge William J. Lines and Richard Nelson. They gave me more time, shared with me more conversation, and showed me more of their country—Vermont mountains and Alaskan waterways—than anyone. Richard Nelson, a wise, funny and civilized man, a brilliant storyteller and a fine writer, is, as Annie Dillard once remarked, "the nature writer the nature writers read." He should be here. I don't want you to think for a moment, mate, that I've left you out because you nearly got me killed in that wicked sea on Sitka Sound. The truth is, places can kill you. The truth is, you saved us both. The truth is, I couldn't find a way to do justice to everything you shared with me—above all your friendship. Don't worry—I'll get you next time.

Laurie Kutchins has been a victim of the erosion out of which this book shrank into what it needed to be. But I feel bad that I had to drop the chapter I wrote on her. Apart from the beauty of her own life and work, she shared with me some secrets about poetry, place, and listening, without which this book would be a shallower—as well as a smaller—thing. She guided me to the real world, where this book finishes up. So she is here, even though she is not.

Many others made me welcome, took care of me, challenged and inspired me during my travels: Jack Bennett and his family in Eugene; Erica Bleeg in Iowa City; Colleen Burke in Cambridge; Lyn Dalebout in Moose; John and Marilyn Daniel in Eugene; Martin Harrison in Darlinghurst; Gary Holthaus in Cambridge; Glen and Rhoda Love in Eugene; Melinda Mueller in Seattle; Martin Mulligan in Melbourne; Tina Richardson in Eugene; Kate Rigby in Melbourne; Eric Rolls and Elaine Van Kempen in North Haven; Carolyn Servid and Dorik Mechau in Sitka; Mark Spragg in Cody; Jan and John Straley in Sitka. Thanks to them, and to Lawrence Buell and Scott Russell Sanders, whom I met at Cambridge—for their words on that occasion, their scholarship and passion for the language of the land.

I wrote two chapters of *The Land's Wild Music* during a residency in Sitka, Alaska, courtesy of the Island Institute. Another chapter took shape during two short residencies at the Camden Head Pilot Station on the mid-north coast of New South Wales. To Carolyn Servid and Dorik Mechau and to Elaine Van Kempen and Eric Rolls—thanks for having me. *The Land's Wild Music* is a better thing than it might have been because of my spells in these beautiful places, and also because of opportunities that came my way to read from it and from the other book I was writing at the same time (*The Blue Plateau*) in Sitka and at the Iowa Writers' Workshop in 2002. I shared some thoughts about landscape witness at the *Ecology, Community, Culture* conference at the University of Queensland in June 2002, at the *Watermark Nature Writers' Muster* at Camden Haven in October 2003, at the *Sydney Writers' Festival* in May 2004, at *Songlines* in Katoomba in September 2004, and at the inaugural conference of ASLE-ANZ (the Association for the Study of Literature and the Environment-Australia and New

Zealand) at Monash University in April 2005. My book and I grew at these events.

Thanks to SueEllen Campbell, John Elder, Pete Hay, Scott Slovic, and John Tallmadge. Each of them read this work closely and guided its composition. Special thanks to John Cameron, writer, scholar, and sculptor of place, who schooled me and this book from start to finish. I received an Australian Postgraduate Award to write the dissertation from which this book grew. The University of Western Sydney helped fund two fieldtrips to the United States. I am grateful to the university (to John Cameron and Lesley Carbery in particular), and I am thankful for an education system in which it is still possible (though increasingly difficult) to get such support.

I owe a special debt to William Tydeman and Noel Parsons at Texas Tech University. Thank you both. George Thompson at the Center for American Places gave me somewhere to shelter in Nebraska when it was cold and my gas and my money were running low, and he always thought this book was a good idea. Both forms of his generosity made a difference.

I am honored to have Barbara Ras as my publisher. Nobody knows more about the literature of the land. No one has published so many good books of nature writing and ecocriticism. When it was almost too late, Barbara found my manuscript and fell for it. I will always be grateful for the email she sent me then. She understood my work better, almost, than I did; she helped me see what I could do better and what I could profitably lose; and she recruited the very best people to shape it into this thing you're holding now. At Trinity University Press, thanks also to Sarah Nawrocki and Lynn Gosnell. For making the book beautiful on the outside, I'm grateful to Erin Kirk New; for making it beautiful inside, I thank Bea Hartman and David Peattie. And thanks to Gerry van Ravenswaay for the index. Phillipa McGuinness at University of New South Wales Press has been a friend of this book, too. Thanks Pip. Thanks, as ever, to my agent, Fran Bryson, and her lieutenant, Liz Kemp.

Just when I thought I'd made this book the best thing I could make it, Anne Canright came along and showed me I was wrong. Anne's tough editing taught me more than I thought I needed to know about prose style. For making my book more like the thing I thought it already was, I thank her. I should add that any remaining failures are all my own work.

Though I traveled much and far to find the wild worlds of text and terrain that I speak of here, most of the time I worked at home, in the company of Maree, my wife. I thank her—for waiting for me to come home and trusting me to finish; for listening to my tales and enduring my rehearsals of strange arguments about arcane notions; for believing in my work and in me; for proofing earlier drafts of my manuscript when she had much better things to do; and for giving me, just as I finished the manuscript, the gift of our son Henry. (Books, it seems, take longer to make and to deliver than babies, and we've got ourselves a second son, Daniel, since I first thought I'd finished this book. But this is his brother's book—there will be another book for you, Daniel.)

I thank my older children, Michael and Louisa, for getting on with their lives so brilliantly while this study accreted in its slow fragments. I thank them for missing me, but not too much, while I was far away, and for asking now and then how I was going, as though they were really interested. Henry and Daniel I thank too, just for coming along and being so beautiful. If they ever read this book, they will know the work that made their father the man he was when they first met him.

I thank my parents, Bruce and Heather Tredinnick, for giving me a place on earth and raising me lovingly in it. Thanks for helping us try to do the same for our children (whom you are minding even as I write these words).

My ultimate debt, of course, is to the places I visited and the country I write. Without the land, there would be no words—there would be no wildness to write, no music to join.

To the places, then, of which the world is made, and all their wild musics. May we always hear them. May they always sing us; may we always sing them.

The Wild Music of Places

AN INTRODUCTION

The Blue Plateau, New South Wales

> If everything is vitally interconnected then the whole
> world is a poem, an enchantment simply awaiting
> notation . . .
>
> —Barry Hill, *Broken Song*

Barry Lopez came to my place in August 1998, and that's when all this
began.

Well, I guess it goes back as far as I do—further, in fact. But his
visit and the thoughts we exchanged in my cottage and out along the
cliff walk above these orange scarps, about prose and place, about
calling, about the meteorology and geomorphology of one's writing—
that's where this book got started. That's when this journey began
that has taken me far from my home in this Australian plateau, deep
into the homelands and books of these four writers, in pursuit of the
ideas Barry and I woke that day; that has carried me home again, a
changed man, ready to write the book of home, *The Blue Plateau*, I
had just started when Barry Lopez called.

Two years later, one afternoon in August 2000, I sat at the kitchen
table in Katoomba, rereading Barry Lopez's *Of Wolves and Men*.
Winter's last westerlies were still troubling the trees outside, and not
a thing was still along the ridgetop. The timber house groaned about
me. It swayed imperceptibly in a stiff-jointed, desultory dance with the

1

afternoon. But it was staying where it was for now, which was good for me. Things were stiller at the table, but the day's animated weather was not stopping at the walls and windows. My fingers were moving fast along the lines of type; my mind was finding its way across the topography of the text, moving in the contours of the country of the mind that made it, going the way the author's fingers went, making the pattern of sounds that compose his text.

Something had led me back to Lopez's book; and something made me turn back to the epigraphs on its opening pages. One comes from Henry Beston's nature writing classic, *The Outermost House.*

> We need another and a wiser and perhaps a more mystical concept of animals. . . . In a world older and more complete than ours they move finished and complete, gifted with extensions of the senses we have lost or never attained, living by voices we shall never hear. They are not brethren, they are not underlings; they are other nations, caught with ourselves in the net of life and time. (1928, 24–25)

The second epigraph Lopez takes from a long essay by Michel de Montaigne, "The Defense of Raymond Sebond," written around 1575. Here is some of it:

> Presumption is our natural and original disease. The most wretched and frail of all creatures is man, and withal the proudest. He feels and sees himself here lodged in the dirt . . . in the lowest story of the house . . . and yet in his imagination he places himself above the circle of the moon, bringing heaven under his feet.
>
> By the vanity of the same imagination he equals himself to God, attributes to himself divine faculties, and withdraws and separates himself from all other creatures; he allots to these, his fellows and companions, the portion of faculties and power which he himself thinks fit.
>
> How does he know, by the strength of his understanding, the secret and internal motions of animals, and from what comparison between them and us does he conclude the stupidity he attributes to them? (Montaigne 1958, 330–31)

I had read *Of Wolves and Men* without ever noticing these words. Finding them now, I experienced one of those moments, heavy with recognition of truth, light with joy, when one of the circles that shapes a life comes almost to completion.

Moving to the study and sitting at my desk, I pulled my edition of *The Complete Essays of Montaigne* from where it sits, its spine facing me where I write. I found the essay in Book Two, first published in 1580. Lopez has found the heart of the essay, which is fearsomely long. I sped through it over the next half hour. It is an elegant, rigorous, and passionate argument against the arrogance of humanity's conventional habit—even then—of elevating itself above the rest of the living world. It is an essay on the sentience of the nonhuman world, even perhaps on the sacredness and mystery of living things. Montaigne was, of course, a nobleman who retired from public life to reflect and write at his estate in the Dordogne. Images from the land about him accompany many of his thoughts in the long essay, along with quotations from the classical sages—Lucretius, Plato, Virgil, Ovid, Euripides.

The circle that rounded itself in this discovery was a circle of calling. I am here in a sandstone plateau, above a valley made by the Kedumba Creek, to write, to reflect on the nature of things—on the nature of nature, really; on the nature of this place on earth. I would like every thought of mine to grow from the life of the place, for my writing to be an act of presence here, enlivened by the place to which it gives some witness. I came, though, to this country and to this sense of my calling as a writer by a path that wandered and took no pattern until I read Montaigne some years ago and recognized the kind of writing I felt born to attempt. Like Montaigne, I have felt called to turn words—as musical and meaningful, as engaging and exact as I can manage—to the task of discovering and speaking for the actual lives we—we and all the other living things—lead on this earth. When I read Montaigne, and then found my way to other essayists—E. B. White, Aldous Huxley, many others—I felt that I had stumbled on a tradition and a form—the essay, I mean—that I could write within. It seemed like something I could do; it even seemed like a way of using words and of seeing the world that I had been drawn to all my life.

And it did not take me long, reading the best essays, to come upon Barry Lopez, Wendell Berry, Annie Dillard, Richard Nelson, Ted Hoagland, and Terry Tempest Williams—the nature writers. Reading them led me to reread some of the place-oriented books that had moved me in earlier days: Karen Blixen's *Out of Africa* and Gavin Maxwell's *Ring of Bright Water*, from way back in my childhood. Much of the best essay writing—the loveliest and the wisest prose, the most humane, the most hopeful and real, the writing that carried on what Montaigne had begun—was being turned out, I realized, by writers whose subject was the land, by men and women under the influence of the sky and the whole more-than-merely-human world about them.

I was living at this time in Balmain, an old working-class neighborhood across the water from the city, loud with the noise of cargo and traffic. City buildings filled my window, beyond the scarlet bottlebrush. My reading among the nature essayists grounded my sense of vocation more deeply and precisely, and it reawakened in me a lifetime's longing to live in country, to put down roots in unpaved earth and live and write what the landscape bestowed on me.

So, in time, I came to Katoomba and to the idea of a book of this place, a cycle of essays in the nature-writing tradition, but growing out of sandstone, shaping itself like silvertop ash in the vivid air of ridge and valley country—*The Blue Plateau*. Montaigne and nature writing brought me as much as the country itself. And on the second day of our moving into the timber bungalow beside Banksia Park, Barry Lopez came to visit. I had interviewed him by phone some months earlier for a piece I was writing on his new collection of essays, *About This Life* (1998). Later, in August, he came to Sydney for some readings and publicity, after talking at the Melbourne Writers' Festival. And so, I invited him to Katoomba for a day, and he came. We walked out along a path with which I have become intimate now, and we looked out across the valley to Mount Solitary as the light fell. "We have come at just the right time," he said.

Lopez inscribed my copy of *About This Life* with some words of thanks for the conversations we shared in these mountains and the hope that we might continue them. Two years later—shortly after my epiphany inside the windblown house—I flew out for the McKenzie River in Oregon to continue that conversation with him, the start of a journey of conversations that this book charts. I have Lopez's book here on my desk now. It stands in a long row beneath the windowsill, flanked by Terry Tempest Williams and Michel de Montaigne.

My belated discovery—inside this wind, inside this shaking house, inside this other book of Lopez's—of that passage from Montaigne moved me with a sense of calling confirmed. It was not just the weather that stirred me, though it was *also* the weather. For it felt like the whole place was shaking me, making sure I noticed how my own work had its origins not just here, but in a tradition these other writers carried on, and in the path my life had already taken to get me here. Looking hard at the world had led Montaigne, so long ago, to thoughts much like those I had come to this place to consider. These thoughts belong to the tradition of nature writing, too, which I had come here to practice and reflect upon. The wind and the place, Montaigne and Lopez sent me back to that barely begun book of my own, an essay that was trying to sing this country, to tell it like it is. (As I write the final draft of this introduction today, that other book, *The Blue Plateau*, sits beside me, a finished manuscript.) My sense is that if it's any good, *The Blue Plateau* will have about it something of the life and character of this very landscape.

Before I turned to writing, I published books. Among the books I published in those years were William Lines's *Taming the Great South Land*, George Seddon's *Searching for the Snowy*, and Tom Griffiths's *Secrets of the Forest*, three works of nonfiction, of powerful prose, that explore the land and mankind's connection to it on this continent. These were books I took to, in whose creation I participated closely. They are important books for reasons that have nothing to do with me, being made by the intelligences of those three authors. But I loved those books in a quite unreasonable way; and they were all of them strange to me—and to the market. No one, including me, knew quite what to make of them—books of considered and lyrical prose treating with the land. I can see now that my work on those books—commissioning and, to some small degree, shaping them—was part of how I found my way home to a literature of place; part of my journey to the sandstone country and Montaigne, Lopez, and nature writing.

One day I ran into Tom Griffiths in the State Library. He was pleased because *Secrets of the Forest* was about to come out in a new edition, coinciding with an exhibition in Melbourne celebrating the same mountain ash forests he explores in his book. He thanked me for championing the book the first time round. And he thanked me for my review of *About This Life*. Lopez, he said, was one of his favorite authors, an inspiration.

Such happenings are not mere coincidence. They articulate a pattern of meaningful connection. And it pays to notice them. I should not have been surprised, perhaps, to find Montaigne among the writers who influenced and anticipated Lopez, or to find Lopez among the writers who influenced the authors whose books I published and loved and in which I found my own future. For there is a way of writing about a place, in which the place itself—becoming part of you as you reach out into the world you witness—seems to participate. This is how Montaigne wrote, and many essayists have followed him, among them the nature writers. Donald Frame, who was Montaigne's biographer and translator, writes that the American transcendentalist Ralph Waldo Emerson found Montaigne's prose " 'wild and savory as sweet fern,' full of a 'sincerity and marrow,' that reaches to his sentences. 'Cut these words,' he wrote, 'and they would bleed; they are vascular and alive' " (Montaigne 1957, vii). Another scholar wrote of Montaigne: "Any one of his pages seems like the most fertile and wild of prairies, a 'free and untamed field': long, 'lusty' grasses, perfumes underneath the thorn, a mosaic of flowers, singing insects, streams beneath, the whole thing teeming and rustling. . . . Thought and image, with him, it is all one" (Sainte-Beuve, *Port-Royal*, 2:443–44, quoted ibid.).

I am very interested in prose that seems to sway like prairie grass and sing like insects and falling water. It is what this book is all about.

The Land's Wild Music

This book is a roving study of the literature of place. It is a meditation on the nature of places and the prose that witnesses them, on lyric apprehension and the ecological imagination.

There is a kind of literature that practices—that essays—ecological imagination, and we call it nature writing. Most of it is North American. In those books, most of them consisting of essays (lyric and personal), places come alive on the pages.

In Australia, where I live, there is no tradition yet of such writing. There is, of course, an indigenous culture of sacred geography, of sacramental custodianship, made in painting and songline, dance and story, and it is already millennia old. Any literature we may make in these late days can hardly hope to embody the same intimacy with—and intonation of—the land as indigenous mythology and ceremony do. Yet it might shape a whitefella dreaming; it might fashion and sustain a new kind of reconciliation between latecoming Australians and these mysterious geographies, and among all of us who now share this landmass. I believe a literature of place, ecologically imagined and written in the landscapes' own vernacular, is emerging now out of the engagement of writers with the plight and wisdom of the country's first peoples. For theirs is a culture, as I understand it, grounded in, at its heart a celebration of, an enacted belonging in, the land—or, as indigenous people here say, using the colonizers' tongue (and in the process colonizing it), in *country*.

I should say a thing or two about that word *country*, for I will be using it in this book. Many Australians these days, indigenous and nonindigenous, use this word when talking about geography, place, and human belonging. And it is a good, rich word. I would like to throw it into our conversation. It means something close to *land*, as Barry Lopez, for example explores that word in his essay "Landscape

and Narrative" (1989, 61–71): the local ecology; the set of relationships between lifeforms and landforms that are alive in this particular ecosystem. But *country* unambiguously includes human inhabita-
tion and belonging—it even includes a sense of human stewardship,
kinship to place, and practical reverence for a particular geography—
as *land* does not always. Let me quote the Australian poet and critic
Martin Harrison on the point: "One thing indeed that sets Australian
work apart is a prevalent sense that 'country' (definitely not country-
side, nearly yet not quite what Americans and Europeans call land and
landscape) is something you are part of, something which changes
your senses of self and placement and which requires a change in
envisioning if you are to see it and understand it. Land, in other words,
is active and malleable; it can also be oneiric and ancestral" (2004, 54).

Harrison goes on to add that in white consciousness and in white
poetry in Australia concerned with questions of belonging to place, a
sense of one's country is necessarily "disjunctive" or even "subjunc-
tive," by which he means that it doubts itself. "Country," he writes,
"does not easily offer back a comfortable image of white . . . presence" (ibid.). How can one claim to belong in, or to hear, a place that
was for so long the site of belonging of a people you have evicted? How
can one claim kinship with a place one has come to so freshly by
means of such violent dispossession (enacted by one's forebears), by
means also of technological interventions that have caused the land
such grief? How can one, as a European, ever claim to be *of* one's particular country? Ecological imagination of country is, Harrison feels,
bound to be conflicted and its expression in works of literature contingent and uneasy. A certain subjunctivity becomes us here, as white
men and women, he implies. But it has also, I would add, disabled us
in our attempts to know and express where we find ourselves. We
inherit from indigenous cultures, in other words, an understanding of
and a longing for the kind of identification with place that they know
and express in their art and mean when they speak of their *country;*
but we, if we are nonindigenous, don't feel entitled to claim the places
we find ourselves in, find ourselves falling for. *Country* when I speak

it contains this anxiety and longing, this aspiration and bow of respect to the continent's first peoples. I speak of my country subjunctively.

I use *country* in this book to mean the land about one, including its human histories and human presence. Because I share the unease of my fellow European artists about one's own claim to belonging, I leave open the question of whether I—or, in their own landscape, any of the writers I deal with here—can claim to be a part of the place we find ourselves in, feel responsible for, and wish to render into a work of art. I use *country*, then, almost interchangeably with *land*, but I mean to imply (in a way that the words *land* and *landscape* do not always) human presence within a place as a necessary part of what that place is and how it got to be that way.

Perhaps it is this deep unease about our human and our personal place within *country* that has kept our places from us European-Australians—or kept them out of our writing, in prose especially. For so far we Europeans have not managed much ecological imagination. Only rarely have we found a way to catch the lyrics of the country itself in works of literature—as they are caught and expressed in all the ancient languages and dances that colonization and English have done so much to ruin. We have not composed a literature of place in which the Australian geographies sing.

So, as I sat to attempt such a thing myself—my own landscape memoir, *The Blue Plateau*—I got to wondering how a man such as I, the grandson of a Methodist minister, the descendant of Cornish and German settlers, speaking English in a colonized landscape, might write a work of literature worthy of my own home ground. Wondering, in this way, I did not stay seated long. Instead—and perhaps it was one of those distractions from the task at hand for which writers are notorious—I set off to explore such a literature in a place where in modern times it has mostly found voice, where it is already old: the United States of America. I went seeking not a North American vernacular but the deeper ground from which a vernacular literature of country might grow—a writer's imaginative engagement with whatever it is that orders a place on earth. *The Land's Wild Music* tells the story of that journey and what it yielded. More broadly, *The Land's Wild Music* explores the nature of nature writing: the practices its writers follow to give expression to place, and the ways in which country might be said to find its way onto paper.

This book is a writer's road trip through the texts and home terrains of four North American writers of the natural world. It is the pilgrimage of an essayist and ecocritic through the words and worlds of Barry Lopez, Peter Matthiessen, Terry Tempest Williams, and James Galvin, a mobile apprenticeship in place and prose and witness. Here, I go traveling with writers in their native landscapes, exploring the practices of landscape witness, of ecological imagination, that they carry on there, and looking for the ways in which I might discern the wild structures, the coherent tendencies that go on composing and recomposing their homelands endlessly—that might also be at play in these writers' works. I talk with them about the business of writing the life of places. I take heed of the natural histories in which their works have arisen, looking for correlations between those physical terrains—the actual earth, the solid ground, to use Thoreau's phrase—and the terrain of these writers' words, wondering how the prose (and sometimes the poetry) may be said to be an expression of a writer's home ground.

I stepped out on this study hoping to understand a tradition of landscape-oriented writing to which I found myself called; to unearth what these writers and that tradition might teach me about how to know and how to write one's own country. And as I journeyed in the home country and the syntax of these four authors, I kept working on that landscape memoir of my own. I found that my writing changed. It slowed, deepened, fractured, and was remade by what I learned from these writers and their worlds—from the woods, the shoreline, the red desert, a mountain meadow, and Henry David's pond. *The Blue Plateau* is not the book it would have been without this journey, without those places. Nor am I the man.

The Land's Wild Music is, then, a natural history of the writing of four nature writers, an ecological imagining of their lives and works and places. But it is also a natural history of one writer's education in the wild and its writing, of his coming to belong on the earth and within a tradition that attempts a careful, shapely witness of the earth's places. It is an exploration of a calling.

How I Worked

"Great criticism doesn't commandeer its subjects," wrote Pulitzer Prize–winning critic Margo Jefferson recently, speaking of John Berger; "it collaborates with them" (2002, 31). Criticism demands detachment, but also, I think, a sympathetic understanding of the work and its creator; respect for that person's creativity; and knowledge that the work will always be a larger thing than any criticism can construe it as.

Mine is an inquiry begun out of passion and sympathy for the work of my subjects. Love stirred it. But critical thought accompanied it. Though mine is not the great criticism Jefferson had in mind, I have tried to collaborate with my subjects, as John Berger has done. I wanted to let these writers speak for themselves. I wanted to cast light on their places and their literary engagement with those places. I wished not to emaciate the lives and works of these writers under fierce and narrow critical scrutiny. As Martin Heidegger might say, I wanted to let these works, these words, these worlds be what they are. I wished to discover something within them, maybe answers to my questions, but not to commandeer them to my purpose.

Works of Nature

All artists who turn to a place, a scene, an encounter as their subject, want to transmute their subject and their experience of it into a piece of work that is in some sense flesh to their subject's flesh, or better, soul to its soul. They want, usually, to render its essence truthfully—unless their purpose is merely to express themselves. The love and wonder, or the horror and fear, that drew the writer or painter or musician to that vase of flowers, that town or valley or meadow, enjoins some kind of faithfulness in them, as a witness, toward the genius of the original. They will try to do the real world justice in art.

Usually this does not mean attempting some literal facsimile of the subject, an exact representation on canvas or paper. "I don't care so much," Vincent Van Gogh wrote to his brother in October 1885, "whether my color is exactly the same, as long as it looks beautiful on my canvas, as beautiful as it looks in nature" (letter 429). Nature can't paint in strokes, can't sculpt or write; but it can express itself. A nature writer, like any artist who turns to nature, tries, among other things, to catch the soul of that expression.

The world's forms and colors, patterns and shades, ecologies and weathers, act on human sensibility, sometimes, with a truth, a strangeness, and a necessity that many artists would like their art to embody, so that their work touches with a similar force those who meet it. An artist wants her work of art to feel like a work of nature—to feel as though it could not have been other than it is, and to feel like that bit of nature in particular. This may be especially the case for a writer who is concerned with nature itself. And it was the case for the great poet of nature (and human nature) Walt Whitman, according to his champion, John Burroughs:

> The image Walt Whitman seems generally to have in his mind is that of the Earth, "rolling, rolling, compact," and he aims to produce effects analogous to those produced by it; to address the mind as the landscape or the mountains . . . address it; not to excite admiration by fine and minute effects, but to feed the mind by exhibitions of power; to make demands upon it, like those made by Nature; to give it the grasp and wholesomeness which come from contact with realities; to vitalize it, by bringing to bear on it material forms. (Burroughs, "Notes on Walt Whitman as Poet and Person," [1857] 2001, 36)

Whitman, says Burroughs, wrote not just as an observer of nature but from inside it, "immersed in her." His poems "approximate to a direct utterance of Nature herself"; they amount to a "spiritual auracular analogy" of Earth herself, just here (ibid.). If an artist is humble, if his feet are on the ground, he knows that no words he may write, no lines he may draw, nothing he may make, will ever have such power or be so direct an utterance of an order larger than himself. Still, it is probably something he hopes for, even unconsciously: that his creation may participate in Creation itself. And when a writer's subject is a particular place, that writer, striving for authenticity in rendering it, may allow himself to hope that his work will strike a reader the same way the place struck the writer; that reading the words will feel like being in that place. Not *exactly* the same, mind you, not the same color necessarily; but as beautiful or fearful, as dense or empty or deep or cold. He hopes to write the nature of the place not from the outside, but from the inside; not as a visitor, but as a participant, an intimate—as though he were the place, writing.

What a nature writer sets about is far more, usually, than making a depiction of the natural world. What she is about is witness, of some kind, of a world larger than the merely human. But *what* does the nature writer witness—the place? herself in the place? the place in herself? And how does she perform that witness? What does she do in imagination and craft—the hard work, draft after draft—with what she makes of this place on earth, and what it makes of her? How does what she witnesses shape the artist she becomes? How does it shape the art she makes? How does the place a writer gives herself to, in intimate attention, shape the person she becomes and the prose she writes?

Those were the questions I had in mind when I set out. This book is what I came home with..

Lyric Apprehension of Place and Ecological Imagination

Because I work in prose myself, and because most nature writing takes place in essay form, *The Land's Wild Music* began life as a study of ecological literature in prose, of nature-writing *essays*. And to some extent that's what it remains—though what an essay really is, or can be, is something I discovered on the road. But it turns out my book is really a study of the lyric apprehension of place.

Barry Lopez wrote once that "the land is like poetry: it is inexplicably coherent, it is transcendent in its meaning, and it has the power to elevate a consideration of human life" (*Arctic Dreams*, 1986, 274). It is that coherence of places—almost inexpressible, never complete, and dependent on one's being present in the land for a bit—for which the lyricist of place reaches. Lyricism, I discovered, is less a way of turning out words than a way of being in the world—a way of moving, wide awake, somewhere on earth, within the lively, patterned materiality of a place-in-time. Sometimes it will be a poem the writer of lyric disposition makes in order to express his engagement in country; sometimes it will be a stretch of prose. As you will see, I've come to wonder whether landscape writing of the kind that stirs me might be understood as enacted, articulated *listenings*. Listenings to the reality of places implied by and manifest in what is observable in a place-in-time—the larger order that *almost* coheres in a place, that makes it what it is, but is never finished doing so.

The Musical Performance of Places

In his book *The Lie of the Land*, Australian cultural theorist Paul Carter encourages writers and readers and theorists to move beyond what he calls a visualist understanding of the poet's engagement with the world. There is, he argues, a dominant assumption at the heart of Western artistic theory and practice that a work of art aims to offer up a visual simulacrum of the object it engages with (1996, 5). Carter wants writers to renovate their art by reclaiming an older understanding of the writer's encounter with the world. He wants writers to engage with the world *metrically*—to remember the metrical qualities of places and the dynamic (that is, rhythmic and musical) qualities by which poetry does its deepest work (ibid., 331). A writer in this tradition—which is most clearly present in indigenous song and storytelling, though it has never, according to Carter, disappeared from Western artistic practice (think, in visual art, of Van Gogh's land-scapes)—attends to the "amplitude," the energetic quality of places. The writer in this tradition does not merely aim to *see* places (and let us see them, represented in her work): she aims to experience them through all her senses—in particular through hearing, since hearing discerns the vibrations, the movements of air that articulate the dyna-mism of places.

It is time, argues Carter, that more writers understood places as dynamic spaces, living and turbulent, never still and never finished becoming. Carter reminds us that landscapes are not just the visible entities we see, but also the soundscapes we hear. They include, of course, the community of living things present in a habitat: the trees, the birds, the mammals (including the humans), the insects and the microbes. A particular landscape is not only what we see and hear somewhere, however. It includes all the things that escape our notice—nearly everything, in short. A place includes the invisible things gath-ered somewhere (invisible because, like a bird beyond the next hill or the water moving in the aquifer, it remained out of sight; invisible because, like a microscopic organism, it is too small to make out with the naked eye; invisible because, like the air itself or infrared light, it is imperceptible to our eyes). A place includes, also, silent presences and processes (which Carter reminds us are rarely completely immo-bile): the rocks and the old lives fossilized within them, patterns of ero-sion, the memories and beliefs "enfolded" into places by human expe-rience (ibid., 331).

A landscape is what all these lives and forms amount to. And everything in a landscape is in motion, fast or slow; everything is engaged in interrelationship.

Think of places, Carter suggests, as entities composed of musical intervals, of turbulence and moving air; think of them as accreted, enfolded pasts and presents. Think of them as the sum of all the rela-tionships at play somewhere, seen and unseen, heard and unheard. Imagine places as expressions of curvilinear time. If places are to be reenvisioned in this way, a renewed kind of writing practice will be needed to express them. Write not to represent country, Carter urges. Write instead to articulate the dynamic reality of place; write as though performing a dance that responds to its rhythms (ibid.).

In Carter's view, it is the musical qualities of a piece of writing that best suggest the dynamic qualities of a landscape: the velocities of wind, orogeny, and erosion; the interplay of atoms within the cells of an old eucalypt; the swift flight of thornbill or flicker; the sound of the falling rain. A piece of writing reenacts the land in all its dynamism through its rhythm and roll, by playing out patterns of sound, through the shifting dance of tone and timbre—through its music (ibid., 13–14).

Nature is never still; and what we see is filled vibrantly with what we cannot see—atoms, geological movements, winds, seasons, sap, salt, microbes, thoughts of animals, rotation of leaves. Places are alive with movement and complexity. The characteristic interplay of biological and physical forces within a place is its identity—its soul, its personality, its lifeworld. It is what makes places live for us. Writing without an eye for movement (even if it is the slow erosion of a plain), without an ear for vibration (even the inaudible commotion of atoms within a grain of a rock,) or without a feeling for the gesture of things (the play of wind and light, the dance of trees in rain) will miss a place's self—its very nature.

In applying his thoughts to nature writing, I don't want to misrepresent Paul Carter. But I am indebted to him for opening my eyes and ears to the metrics of landscape and language, and for suggesting a set of ideas this book explores, notional answers to the questions I began with. In its lyric aspects—its music, its soundscape—a piece of writing may capture the nature of a place; it may even resemble the country it is born in. A work may give a musical impression of the complex life of a place. Through its rhythms, through everything about it that is more than merely literal, a piece of nature writing can move a reader as the place itself moves—and as it moved the writer.

Some writing sets places dancing, and sets readers dancing with them. This is the kind of writing I'm concerned with here.

Pilgrims' Progress: Ecocritical Narrative

This book is an act of ecocriticism. It is, in other words, an attempt at literary scholarship that takes nature seriously.

It proceeds by narrative, telling a story—though not always in a straight line and not always continuously; it makes its way in fragments—in episodes and excursions. It speaks in a human voice—mine, as it happens, for it is an essay. And it grounds itself within the natural histories it concerns. Ecocriticism has made a virtue of such techniques. "Ecocriticism without narrative," writes Scott Slovic, "is like stepping off the face of a mountain—it's the disoriented language of freefall" (1999, 37). Narrative that acknowledges the presence of the critic in the inquiry; that describes the relationship between critic, subject, and place; that explores specific geographical ground; and that favors the (intelligent) vernacular over the disembodied diction of conventional critical discourse—such writing is likely to engage its readers and, with luck, win their trust without compromising its critical integrity. It is also, in my case, more likely to disclose what really took place in my encounters with these writers, their country, and the country of their words. Such language, the phenomenologists would say, sings the lifeworld of the research experience. In collaboration with the texts and authors I study here, I have tried to speak, as they do, in what Slovic calls "the language of solid ground" (ibid., 34).

The Irish writer Tim Robinson once observed that a writer proceeds rather as a rock climber does up a rockface. The writer trusts the words he finds—their form, their shape and actuality, the fact that they come to hand—just as the climber trusts his holds. The writer trusts the feel of words and lets them lead him; he trusts the words the writing suggests, tries them, moves the way they lead. On the rockface and upon the page, theory helps, but it is the actual earth—the hold, the word that presents itself and seems right—that leads you on, that preserves you.

I have proceeded like this, I think: like a writer, like a climber, not like a traditional scholar. For the writer and the climber, the elegance and grace, the structure and arc of the traverse, the shape and rightness of the performance are what counts. The climbing itself is the point. The telling is what matters—not the conclusion, not the achievement of the summit, but the way you reached it. For the scholar, I think, the goal is different. The conclusion, not the experience, is the point; what is told is what matters in the end, rather more than the nature, the lyric, the emergent dance of the telling. On the other hand, I have attempted not merely an act of writing; I have attempted the kind of scholarship a writer attempts, a more disciplined, critical climb than I might otherwise have made.

There are tensions in such a narrative scholarship—between freedom and discipline, between lyric and narrative, between synthesis and analysis—and an ecocritic like myself risks a fall. I have slipped, but I have been climbing with ropes—braids of theory, wires of methodology—and colleagues (mentors, other scholars) at top and bottom. And I have made the top, grazed, but intact. What I have managed here is not quite so lyric a climb, nor so clean and compelling a conclusion as I might have hoped. But this is just an essay, just an attempt at something a little new. I seem to have reached an end, and I seem to have kept my balance. I am not the same man I was at the start. I have discovered things—a way of understanding how, for instance, in its lyric essence, in its *being*, in its distinctive patterns of sounds, a work of words may catch, perpetuate, and reverberate the lyric of a place on earth. I have discovered that the work of nature writing is not so much representation as lyric participation, a process of sustained rhythmic witness. And I have never stopped moving, from rockhold to rockhold; nor have I stopped being moved.

So maybe, after all, this is at once a scholarly and a writerly clamber, a theoretical and a narrative passage across stone. Maybe the way

I have gone about the climb will sustain the point I reach in the end; and maybe the way I get there is a dance worth dancing—or worth watching from a safe remove.

The Phenomenology of Nature Writing

This ecocritical dance with rock is also a reasoned phenomenological inquiry.

Maurice Merleau-Ponty felt that one could come to discern "the lifeworld" of things—of anything that appears to human conscious- ness—only if one attained a "wild," original, intuitive state of mind, orienting oneself to the phenomenal world (the "inherent essence of appearances") with an attitude unconstrained by human culture, lan- guage, thought, and presumption (Crotty 1996, 275; Stewart and Mickunas 1974, 3–4). The phenomenologist is supposed to take "a fresh and unprejudiced look" at "human experience in and of the world" (Moran and Mooney 2002, 1).

These phrases could just as neatly describe the disposition and purpose of the nature writer. Nature writing attempts a kind of wild being and wild writing. It listens to places and human experience within them, and it wants to honor the life it witnesses in the manner of its telling—as phenomenology does too. Like phenomenology, nature writing is a first-person enterprise (Crotty 1996, 272). Like phe- nomenology, nature writing seeks to sing, not merely to report on what it finds.

Phenomenology is a way of seeing, a methodology, a way of ori- enting oneself as an inquirer into human experience in and of the world. It demands attention—in contemplative mode—to appear- ances, that is, to phenomena, to the lifeworld of things themselves. What the phenomenological searcher is looking for is the nature and essence of things as they occur to human consciousness: the texture of experience and the meaning and order it implies. Phenomenology, at its beginnings, asked us to put aside presupposition in the looking. But it has come to acknowledge, since Heidegger, that no human inquiry can proceed free of presupposition. Hermeneutic phenomenology (to use two heavily polysyllabic words) asks the observer to circle back and forth between surprise (that is, wild witness) and presupposition; to reflect critically on the phenomenological data and on the presumptions you have "bracketed," while researching, in the light of appearances; and to propose an illuminating description built on that dance between witness and supposition.

This is what I have attempted here. What I have inquired *into* in this way is the inherent essence of nature writing—of the nature of writing, the nature of places, and the nature of the relationship between them.

I set out with suppositions and questions, but I tried to let myself be surprised. And I was. I tried to circle—another kind of dance, perhaps even a little rhythmic—between thesis and data, between idea and lifeworld, between abstraction and experienced actuality, backward and forward, in and out, trying my presuppositions against what I witnessed in a contemplative mode. I let my suppositions alter under that influence, and I tried not to let my theses distort my looking, so as not to miss the fullness and richness of the places I got to know, the reports and textured silences these writers gave me, my exploration of the country of their writing. This is how my writing proceeded. That is where this dance of inquiry went on—in my *writing* itself, where I learned many things I had not known at the start and which I didn't notice at the time in my "fresh and unprejudiced looking." What I have written is a description of what revealed itself in that circling mode, what I have made of it—and what it made of me.

It is a tenet of phenomenology that one cannot abstract one's conclusions from the *telling* out of which they are arrived at—or one can, but then the context, the narrative texture, the richness of the process of their coming into the world, will all be lost and one's conclusions will sound hollow. Phenomenology is essentially a *descriptive* mode of inquiry (Moran and Mooney 2002, 1). It seeks to illuminate and clarify the "structure and qualities" of things in themselves, as they are experienced, and it mistrusts reductive, purely causal explanations. I hope I have not, in my elaboration of these conclusions, emaciated the work of witness, the practice of lyrical being in the world that nature writing is. Elucidation—of the way a piece of prose can catch the lyric of a place, of the structures of texts and dynamics of the engagement of language with landscape—is my purpose here.

Back to the Places Themselves

The Land's Wild Music is a journey through the light, the wind, the rock, the water, sometimes the fire, that make the land that houses the writers who compose these lyrics of place. A fair bit of what I have learned about those writers I have learned from the places themselves. This book takes landscapes seriously. It reads the works of these writers as though the landscapes of which and in which they write might be worthy of regard in coming to an understanding of their works. It lets places throw light on the words composed within them.

1   *The Essential Prose of Things*

Where is the literature which gives expression to Nature?
—Henry David Thoreau, "Walking"

To feel and speak the astonishing beauty of things—
    earth, stone and water,
Beast, man and woman, sun, moon and stars—
. . . For man's half dream; man, you might say, is nature
    dreaming, but rock
And water and sky are constant—to feel
Greatly, and understand greatly, and express greatly,
    the natural
Beauty, is the sole business of poetry.
—Robinson Jeffers, "The Beauty of Things"

About the most obvious and least interesting thing you could say about nature writing is that it is writing about nature. I'd rather put it another way: Nature writing is literature that engages with the more than human realm. It's a literature—in its subject matter and its point of view—that is not *merely* human.

Lots of people—nature writers themselves, Ed Abbey, Henry Beston, John Hay, William Kittredge, Joseph Wood Krutch, Barry Lopez, Scott Russell Sanders, and Gary Snyder, among them; and scholars like Larry Buell, SueEllen Campbell, Thomas Lyon, Sherman Paul, Scott Slovic, and Frank Stewart—have thought hard and deep about the nature of the nature writing beast. These people have been my guides; and if you go to them, you'll find much that's worth knowing about this literature. Joseph Wood Krutch, for instance, typified nature writing as "*experience with* the natural world, as opposed, for example, to science writing, which is *knowledge about* natural phenomena" (quoted in F. Stewart 1995, 219). It is not merely a literature of nature appreciation. That's worth remembering.

I've come to a conclusion of my own, which I would put like this: The world that nature writing engages with is not bounded by society; it extends to the universe that came before, that goes beyond, that contains the human world. The world it deals with includes geology, weather, plants, animals, the lives of rivers, the fate of men and women somewhere among those other forms and forces of life (and death). It writes ecologies, not just societies. It writes the lives of men and women as though they were shaped by the landscapes and weathers, which they also shape; as though politics and love affairs and tragedies and wars, whatever else they may be, were aspects of the natural history of the world, with implications, large and small, for the whole of creation. Geologic time is what you hear ticking behind a work of nature writing. Natural history—Thoreau's actual earth—always has the bearing. It is the context—the imaginal ecology—out of which every sentence of every book of nature writing is written, no matter what that sentence speaks *about.*

But that kind of enterprise, that sense of geologic time, that feeling for the larger order of life, that placement of the present human moment in the broader scheme of things, you might tell me, is what the best literature, from the dawn of time, particularly poetry, has always attempted. And I would say you're right. But I would add that nature writing is the literature of our time—and it happens not just in essays, and its subject matter may be many things other than the natural history of a place—that most clearly perpetuates what Barry Lopez (see chapter 2) calls the ancient discourse of mankind: our attempt to know ourselves in this real world, our attempt to know the world and adapt to it and, where needs be, to adapt the world so that we might live well within it.

So, nature writing is, to use the jargon, biocentric (see Campbell 1996, 128; Sanders 1996, 189). It returns the natural order—all of it—to the ethical and aesthetic purview of mankind; and it returns mankind—all of us—to the natural world.

Places are what this literature writes; they are the stories it tells. Places and their people. The world is made of places; and it is through places that we know the world and know also who we are within it. Most nature writing describes the encounter of the writer, and of other human characters, with the actual world, with creation somewhere; it tries to render that meeting, that entering into the life of the wild world, in language that expresses the more than merely human (but also the human and, indeed, the personal) nature of that meeting. This literature is always *located*. It starts from the ground in one place on earth and resonates what wisdom and music it discerns there.

But giving us the place is not the whole point. The nature writer—if I may paraphrase Wallace Stegner—wants to explore who we are, as humans, because of where we are. By her witness of a place—by her noticing and writing—the nature writer is trying to know and elaborate the world differently. She is trying to discern and voice the realities that run through the nonhuman world, the world beyond our selves, *and* through the mind and body and very being of each of us humans; she is trying to discover the ways in which she—and by extension, all of us—belongs within the characteristic pattern of relationships that *are* the world just here.

But then again, what sets this literature apart is not so much what nature writing is about (the nature of places and who we are because of them) or the encounter it describes (my being in this place), as where it stands and speaks from. Nature writing stands *inside* nature— inside nature somewhere in particular—and looks at and listens to and speaks of a whole world of matters from there. It considers many things from nature's point of view—politics, aesthetics, language, authorship, morality, culture, humanity, and so on. It takes an ecological view of all things—not just landscape, but even authorship, selfhood, the source of language and meaning.

When the nature writer writes, she remembers the earth in every phrase and sentence. And that makes all the difference.

Theory asserts that men and women make meaning in the world;[1] nature writing senses that it is the land that gives rise to all meaning. The land *is*, and we are there within it, trying to perceive and understand and express it all greatly. Whatever it is we come to know, we learn by paying attention to the world; by listening to country. If we are truly wise, we will know that we know nothing more than the land has known since the start of things. Meanings dawn like days; neither will nor language makes them. But having listened and heard, we may speak of what we have come to know in writing that rings true to the land, to the patterns of the place in which that wisdom came to us. And if we were to do that, it would be nature that we'd be writing.

Scott Slovic broke new ground for nature writing and its study by considering it as a literature of human environmental awareness. In his essay "Nature Writing and Environmental Psychology" (1996) and in his book *Seeking Awareness in American Nature Writing* (1992), Slovic looks at "the interiority of outdoor experience" and suggests that nature writing explores not so much nature as the nature of human (environmental) awareness. Although mine is not, like Slovic's, an inquiry into consciousness, perhaps I am, from a different standpoint (not environmental psychology but phenomenology, linguistic and music theory, and literary composition), exploring pretty much the same relationship: that between the human mind (and the works it makes) and the nonhuman world—specifically, the nature writer's imaginative engagement with place. But my inquiry here is Slovic's turned inside out. What I'm interested in is the exteriority of the very indoor experience of writing authentic witnesses of place—that is, the ways in which place may be said to touch mind and, through it,

1. See SueEllen Campbell's fine essay on theory and ecology, "The Land and Language of Desire," in Glotfelty and Fromm 1996, 124–36. I use *theory* here as she does, meaning the various theoretical positions about text and textuality that can be grouped under the heading *poststructuralism*. As she puts it, "Theory sees everything as textuality."

text; to fashion diction and syntax, even awareness itself. Where Slovic was concerned with nature writing as a state of mind, as a way of being mindfully in the world, I am interested in nature writing as a way of the world's being in us, a way of our entering into and sharing the state of mind of a place.

The Lyric Stance

Nature writing, then, is ecologically imagined, landscape-leaning literature, mostly performed in prose. It tries to set aside the presumption of the primacy of humankind. Yet, it is deeply concerned with our fate, among the fates of all the places of earth and their other inhabitants. This means that, while it is oriented toward what is normally called the "natural world," while it engages with land and extends its compassion and imagination toward it, nature writing is concerned with the whole world, really. But it conceives of the world as a network of ecological connections and life stories, of bird and river and sky and mountain and humankind—their politics and poetry.

In nature writing, the land is the thing, is the whole, is the mind: we are a part of it, one of its ideas, one of its essential elements. Nature writing imagines the world this way, beginning, usually, with the author's particular encounter with it, within it.

Nature writing also concerns and tries to express the music that plays from place to man or woman. Nature writing is, itself, the music that plays back to the place—the response to the call of the land. And if the writer speaks of other matters, she speaks from within the land; and the voice she uses is that of her encounter, the music of her engagement with a place.

This literature does not so much attempt to write *about* nature—this place, this landscape—from one person's viewpoint, as to write one life-within-landscape from nature's viewpoint. And the life in question is the life usually of the writer, a listener within its sphere, lyrically disposed toward the place, a kind of everyman-poet. The writer's life, though, as expressed in a poem or an essay, stands not merely for itself; it stands for all of us. The writer is there as a witness. He or she stands for the human in all of us, and for how the world shapes and makes us over, time and again.

Nature writing is a literature of intimacy with the world. Intimacy with the world beyond our selves is what it practices and what it encourages in us. In his seminal essay "The Land Ethic" from *A Sand County Almanac* (1946), Aldo Leopold, if I may paraphrase him, asks, How can we save what we do not love, and how can we love what we do not know? This literature encourages intimate awareness of the earth where we are, so that by the poetry of such place-mindfulness we might save the world and find ourselves in it again, more fully human.

Nature writing, in most people's conception, happens in essays. But if I have described the work of nature writing accurately, it is hard to exclude other forms—particularly nature poetry—from the genre. Nor does there seem to be any reason, on the face of it, why we could not be talking about novels, too. I want to take a moment here to consider the real difference between poetry and prose and the more meaningful difference between lyric and narrative writing, in order to suggest that, despite the particular aptness of the essay for nature writing, it matters less what mode—fiction, nonfiction, or poetry— one chooses for the task of witnessing the world than how one goes about being in the world and speaking of it. What counts is whether one is there to discover the world and be moved by it (the lyric stance) or to invent it (the narrative stance).

First, a word on the lyric stance—and on prose and prosody. Then a short exploration of the essay, its lyric project, and its aptness for nature writing. Then I'll be ready to take you out among these writers, into their fields and forests, their deserts and mountains, across their meadows and along their shores.

Literature has long distinguished between the lyric and the narrative, as approaches to the creation of works of literary art and as writerly dispositions. Writers are inclined to experience the world and write of their experience in one mode or the other. A lyric writer understands their work as a kind of witness, as a response in words to a call they hear in a place or a moment. The work is intended to reverberate an encounter in the world. To that end, the lyric writer understands writing also as song rather than as tale. Language is music, for the lyricist, as much as it is an instrument of meaning. The narrative writer, by contrast, makes tales by imposing an order—a plot, the passage of time, a sequence of events—upon their experience. The work creates a world or describes one; it is not meant to be replete with one. In the narrative project, the words and sentences are there to carry the drama, to express the thought, and to get the story told. Their musicality is a small matter.

The writer of lyric disposition writes out of the heart of personal encounter with the world—not *about* other things (natural phenomena, lifeforms, and so on), as though they were objects of study, nor yet about herself as a watcher. She aims to capture the lifeworld of all that arises for her, this avid witness, in a moment, in a space. The lyric writer gives witness to the broken sequence of what SueEllen Campbell (following Roland Barthes) calls "figures":[2] those fragments of encounter, those steps within what seems also to be a dance, those momentary and, at the same time, meaningful "attitudes of the body"—in the wild, in love, in contemplation. The lyricist writes out of those figures; her writing belongs to that space.

In two elegant essays, "The Flexible Lyric" and "Ruthless Attention" (in Voigt 1999), Ellen Bryant Voigt, a poet, essayist, and literary critic, explores the lyric point of view, a stance oriented toward neither the self nor the other (place or lover or whatever) but engaged with what lies between. For the lyricist, significance lies in the world as it gave itself to the observer—the writer—at a certain moment, and it is *that* encountered world that must resound for the reader. One's own presence in the space and moment that one's poem or work of lyric prose concerns, writes Voigt, "becomes only another of the phenomena crowding around [the writer]. . . . One's relationship to one's

2. Campbell makes her book of essays, *Bringing the Mountain Home* (1996), out of such figures, known, she writes, "from the inside, with my bones, my muscles and nerves, my heart." She explains her idea of the "figure," which she takes from Roland Barthes's *A Lover's Discourse,* in her preface, pp. x–xi.

materials presumes that significance lies in the world, not in the poet's will to create it" (Voigt 1999, 178).

By contrast, the writer who adopts the narrative approach, making a story with beginning, middle, and end, orders what she sees; she invents or creates a world (her text). Significance lies within herself, and in her capacity to make something of what she sees. She will write sentences fit to carry her tale forward, but she will not make them fit for carrying the lifeworld of a particular encounter with the world to the reader. That is not her project.

Syntactical structures rule in narrative. In most narrative discourse, as Voigt puts it, words and phrases "perform as semaphore": they signify, in a more or less purely functional way; they are there to get the tale told, to let sense arise. They are there to say what a writer means the reader to understand; they are there to *signify* things, not to *sing*. In lyric discourse, by contrast (specifically in poems), "compression and song will freight the signifiers with additional, usually emotive, information. Compression and song, of course, are the characteristics most firmly assigned to the lyric, and they release a poem for 'excursions into particularity'" (Voigt 1999, 122, quoting Ransom 1984). Poems, along with lyric pieces of prose, do their work through what Voigt calls their texture, as well as by logic. That is, lyric relies on sound pattern, rhythm, compressed image, and tone to carry out its work. In addition, of course, it relies, like all writing, on grammatical, lexical, and semantic structures that allow the words to make sense and *mean* something. It sings, *and* it means—and the singing is not marginal. Lyric writing, when paraphrased (and, if we are not careful, when translated), loses that which makes it what it is: it is robbed of its music, its texture. The lyric sings and means, but *what* it means is the child of its music and form as much as it is of the signification of the words it sets to music. By contrast, the narrative tells and means— but meaning trumps telling; you might tell it differently and mean much the same thing.

If you wanted to write lyrically, you might write either a poem or a piece of prose. The difference between a poem and a lyric kind of prose, when made by a writer of lyric sensibility engaging with land, is so small as hardly to matter. But certain distinctions count, at least to the maker of the work. For poems not only look different from prose, they often come from a different place and so operate differently upon a reader-listener. Many poets think there is magic in poetry. Perhaps there is. As Edward Hirsch explains, the poem comes from air, depends upon voice, descends from song, is organized by music; it chants and enchants.[3]

So what's a poem, and what distinguishes a poem from a lyric piece of prose? Poems employ schemes and structural designs, such as patterns of rhyme, rhythm, and meter; and they break language into lines. The line orders a poem; grammar orders prose. Line breaks, even where they disarticulate a poem into word fragments of unequal length and divergent pulse, give a piece of writing beat. We read by that beat. And beat is the basic ordering, patterning device of music. So, poems are musically ordered. Prose, as I say, is grammatically ordered—by the sentence and its lore. But prose has rhythm too, and so it makes a kind of music, since it, too, is made of fragments of patterned sound, of phrases made of words made of syllables, some accented, some not (see Jourdain 1997, esp. 29–30; Voigt 2003). The prose sentence makes music as well as meaning. Its music, though, will always be looser and less regular, lacking the quality of meter that belongs to the poem, by virtue of those line breaks.

Some poetic forms observe strict rules about line length, line number, and metrical pattern—fourteen lines of iambic pentameter make a sonnet, for instance. Prose obeys no such formal rules. But some things we call poems—though they lack line breaks, or though they employ a pattern of lines so irregular as to more resemble, in their sound-effect, a piece of shapely prose—obey few rules of prosody. And yet we call them poems, if only because we find them in a book

---

3. See Edward Hirsch, *How to Read a Poem* (1999), 5: "I made it out of a mouthful of air," Yeats said of a poem; Hirsch quotes this and agrees. Every poem is made out of breath. The lyric poem exists in the register between speech and song.

of poetry. Some prose, though not broken into lines, sings to us in a musical voice that is highly rhythmic if not strictly metrical. And so the line between poetry and prose blurs. Ultimately, musical works of words, works of lyric quality, whether composed in lines or paragraphs, share more in common, prose with poem, than a work of lyric prose shares with another work of straightforward narrative prose—a scientific paper, say, or a novel like *The DaVinci Code*.

Poetry, says the poet and critic John Hollander (1981, 1), is largely a matter of trope, "figures of meaning such as metaphor and metonymy." Verse is a matter, he says, of "scheme or design." Poetry, on this measure, could include lyric prose, just as it could exclude mere versifying.

The distinction that counts, if we are to understand the kind of relationship a piece of writing has to the world, what it is expressive of and how it works upon a reader, may not be the one between poetry and prose but the one, for which Ellen Voigt argues in "The Flexible Lyric," between lyric and narrative modes of discourse (1999, 121ff.). Poetry may be every kind of lyric writing, verse or prose—works uttered through the first person (see Hirsch 1999, 15), attentive to figures, to moments and spaces, and voiced in that register between speech and song. Certainly it was such writing Confucius had in mind when he said that "poetry is the return to the right use of words, to the precise and magical relationship of words with music and the other intuitive rhythms of the universe" (Packard 1992, xv). Lyric writing, verse or prose, understands its source as lying beyond the writer's self. The lyric arrives as a suggestion, and is worked by the poet into an utterance "conformable to something *out there*"—whence it comes— "in the whole swarm of language and energy cycles and the great cosmic flow of things" (ibid., xv–xvi).

You can see how lyric writing, in verse or in prose, lends itself to the task of witnessing places, of catching the lyrics of places. Which is the point of all this. Most of the writers I study in these pages, most of those whose work I especially love, write prose of a lyric kind. Much of the prose in the nature writing tradition is of this kind, too. These

5

writers aren't just telling stories. They're trying to give us fragments of the world, remade in a mosaic whose pattern is somehow suggestive of the whole that would escape tidier narratives.

Cleaving to the Real

It has been traditional to think of nature writing as something performed in essays. So let me dwell for a moment on the nature of the essay and why it suits the work of nature writing so well: why, as nonfiction, it does the work of witness better than fiction; and why, as an essentially lyric form, it does it at least as well as poetry.

The essay cleaves to the real world. It reflects on the nature of what is actual. It speaks of a world—events, places, books, people—that a reader can find beyond the sentences. Both writer and reader understand that this is so. That is, in fact, the deal. If you write a book about a certain meadow and give me enough clues to its geography, I could go and find it and I could compare that place with the one in the book. As Lawrence Buell (1995, 91) puts it, nonfiction, particularly environmental nonfiction, "makes discourse accountable to the object-world."

Fiction, on the other hand (and at the risk, I know, of oversimplification), fabricates story and character out of the matter that life presents. The novel or short story tells the story of people and places taken from models in the actual realm, transfigured through the author's work of invention. It is, in this sense, an instrument of narrative. Its subject matter is manufactured. The understanding—the contract to this effect made between writer and reader—that the reader must not take the novel as a depiction of anything actual is what sets fiction apart from other genres of literature.

The novel does not witness what is; it creates what is not from what is. It attends to the world and turns it, on the page, into another world—sometimes, admittedly, a world very like the real one. It fabricates. It composes a narrative that doesn't so much depict reality as interpret it. Fiction heightens, it alters, it allegorizes and comments upon the real world. The novel gives us the picture of a world that lives only inside that story. The text is what counts, not the world to which it indirectly relates, of which it is, of course, born.

Take away the novel, and there would never have been such a place or time or story. Take away the essay, and the place and time and story remain.

The contract that arises, then, unspoken but understood, between author and reader differs fundamentally between fiction and non-fiction. Implicitly, the essayist invites the reader into a rendering of the actual world, a world of people and places they may meet and recognize beyond the text—though, without the help of the essay, which probes the mystery of those actual people and places, the reader may never know them so deeply. The essayist says, "I went here; I saw this. Or at least, this is how it seemed to me." Implicitly, the fiction writer invites the reader into an invented world. Fiction points to the world within—made by—the text, and only then, beyond it, to the sources it drew on and transfigured into fictive life, into a simulacrum of a world.

But I may be pushing an important, and perhaps obvious, distinction further than I should. Both essays and novels are works of literary production; both tell tales; both aim to engage through lyric and narrative devices, in different measure according to the writer's nature and disposition. All of it is writing. There is even an argument—which Annie Dillard makes, for instance, in *The Writing Life* (1989, 73)—that the novel chiefly "presents society"; it "aims to fasten down the spirit of its time, to make a heightened simulacrum of our recognizable world in order to present it shaped and analyzed." It mostly concerns the social world, as Dillard implies—the human realm. The novel, in its short history of a couple of hundred years, has always had that function, and that understanding of itself: as a social commentary, a mirror to society. And it accomplishes its purpose by distortion of some kind, quite deliberate, by exaggerating the actual in order to comment upon the state of (real) society, to diagnose its malaise. Dickens did this. So did Faulkner. Many novels, more and less literary, distill, abstract, and distort the social aspect of reality in order to comment upon it.

But this is not witness. Fiction does not plumb and resonate the mysteries of the real. "Metaphysics," Dillard calls that work, and it is done, she suggests, mostly by poetry and nonfiction (1989, 73–74).

I am emphasizing the fictive, fanciful, inventive element of novels not to suggest that novels do not have regard to the real world, but to make a case for the qualitatively different *relationship* that essay writing forges between a writer and the world and between the writer and the reader. The work that fiction does differs fundamentally from the work that nonfiction does. And within nonfiction, the essay is a particular case, because it is an artistic form that does essentially lyric work: it is uttered in the first person; it engages with vernacular moments, places, and times, and tries to elaborate their nature; its success depends not upon the tale so much as the telling. The essayist imagines and tries to render what is real—deeply, structurally, poetically, eternally real—in a moment, in a place, in a life.

An essayist, like a poet, tries to imagine how the real world really runs just here. That reality, particularly when one is dealing with the world beyond the human, is a complicated matter. None of us can ever hope to witness it—apprehend and write of it—without an imaginative leap beyond what we can observe; or, if you like, a leap *into* what we can observe. An essayist imagines reality somewhat as a geologist, for instance, or an archaeologist, or a physicist imagines it. These people, unlike novelists, are not working in the business of make-believe or fancy. Yet they are imagining things that lie inside and beyond what is observable—coherence or poetry or music; ancient, fragmentary, infinitesimal stories. To imagine is different than to invent—it is to form an image of something in one's mind, it is to intuit a whole from the parts, the pattern expressed by the particulars.

It is this discipline of imaginative engagement with the real, with "the essential prose of things" (to use Wendell Berry's deft phrase from "The Apple Tree" [1998, 5]), with the patterns at play in the actual world, that cuts the essay out so well to witness and to express in its sentences the genius of the place. In a review of Jim Galvin's book *The Meadow*, Franklin Burroughs suggested that as a genre the essay "offers the reader the simple authority of the eyewitness" (1994, 144). Thoreau, Burroughs notes, famously advocated a literature of fact in which each writer above all sets down an account of his actual life. Thoreau, in writing such an account himself, *Walden,* learned that the depiction of one's actual experiences on solid earth demands a kind of art, a music and an image-making—much as fiction does—and that the witnessed world is not so solid or actual a thing as he once imagined (ibid.). Still, no matter what artistry and fabrication writers need to render their subject truthfully, they are called upon to apprehend the actual and report on it well. The essay stands in a different relationship to the world of geology, biology, politics, and physics than the novel does. The essayist draws on, speaks of, points us back to, the uninvented world, the witnessed world beyond the page. This task sets the essay apart from the novel and tethers it to the world.

The essayist, though—at least the good one—speaks not *about* personal experience, but *from* it. The essayist relates engagement with the actual world. The essay is a lyric form, in this sense. It is predisposed to trust the world, particularly, but not only, that part of it the writer has encountered. It writes out of that encountered world, caught up in the figures of a singular and personal experience of the actual realm—it expresses *that.* The essayist does not write about himself, nor does he imagine he is making a creation that is independent of the ground from which it arose. He is witnessing a small part of reality. And for witness one must be both present, alert for what else is present, and detached—having the experience, involved in the figure, and reflecting upon it; one must be capable of encountering phenomena and noting one's encounter simultaneously.

The essay is a lyric engagement with the world. It listens. It participates in the actual.

The Middle Voice

So the essay is premised on the existence of a world—on a reality that lives independent of the imagination that looks into it, independent of the words that speak of it. The essay depends on a world and on an author: it stretches between them, author and solid earth, speaking of, made of, both of them. In his book *The Lie of the Land*, Paul Carter touches on "the middle voice" in literature (1996, 331). (In Greek grammar there was a voice between the active and the passive, in which the writing subject was not the agent of the action, nor was the sentence's subject the passive recipient of the action. The middle voice expressed the agency of the space between writer and place, subject and object.) English grammar these days uses only the active and the passive voices. Yet we still hear the middle voice. It is the voice we experience in essays and other literature, the voice of a "dance of words," the sound of "a poetic exchange" between the writing subject and the experienced place or event. The words seem to come not from one or the other but from between them, from the space the perceiver moves within, participates in by being there, by moving about and listening. The middle voice expresses the lyric experience of reality: this is what arose when I was there; this is how the place seemed to me; these things took place, and I was among them. It is the voice, I guess, of phenomenology, too. It is the voice one needs for reporting the lifeworld of encounter, of presence *with* the other, of figures, of experience-in-the-world.

The middle voice "dissolves the subject-object relation," Carter writes, "grounding each in the other, continuously redefining both in terms of each other, so that the two sides exist echoically or simultaneously" (ibid.). It is, as I say (though Carter does not), the lyric voice. In Carter's conception, the "I" or the author of a work in the middle voice is not a defined and finite identity, a resolved and finished self, not merely this man or woman moving within but keeping separate from what he or she observes. The middle-voiced writer is not separable from what she encounters—is not merely an agent of action, or even of observation. Nor is what she observes reducible to a lifeless object. Each affects and is affected by the other. And the voice we hear belongs to them both; the self of the piece of writing is a self composed of its many figures of participation with the place. The middle voice is the voice of reciprocity, of intersubjectivity.

The writer engaged in such a relation with a landscape, or any other subject matter, is a self living within that moment and space, in the process of continuous making and unmaking. That writing self is a mosaic of many selves touched by many parts of the other she engages with; and the words she writes are made not so much by her—or even by all those many bits of her—as by the relationship between herself and the other. This is the kind of self the essayist must be. This is, I mean, the kind of participation in a place, the kind of eco-logical reimagination of self and world, that the lyric writer must per-form. It is not far from the kind of thing the poststructuralist imag-ines the writer's engagement with the world to be, except that the essayist is readier than the poststructural theorist to believe in the continuing existence of the world when one's back is turned, when one's engagement with it ceases. This listening-becoming is the nature of the essayist's engagement with the real. And the middle voice, belonging to the ground between the essayist and the place he imag-ines in this way, is the voice his work speaks in. What it speaks of is the timbre and dynamic of the relationship that plays between the writer and what is not merely the writer—between, say, the writer and the land.

The lyric point of view is the middle voice—it speaks from within a writer's encounter with the other. It speaks of the space and time they share. It is the voice of the world of a moment's encounter between a listener and what the listener hears. It speaks for the many pieces of a place, for instance, that make themselves apparent to the (many pieces of their) witness; and it speaks of the witness in whom those pieces resonate. It is the music they make together.

The Essay and the Singing of the World

Perhaps what I am describing here, with the help of Carter's "middle voice" and Voigt's "lyric point of view," is not a genre—neither the exclusive terrain of the essay or lyric poem—but a stance, a way of imaginative being in the world. Because it inclines the man or woman who writes and imagines this way toward what is real, rather than toward fantasy and invention, it is the defining posture of the essayist, particularly one who turns to the world beyond the human, the nature of nature. The narrative stance is more natural in a writer of fiction. But you will find plenty of lyric novels. Equally, you can read plenty of essays in which very little lyric or middle voice is apparent. And among the essays of which that is true—discursive, narrative, expository essays—you will find many that might be called nature writing.

But essays—real essays, like those Burroughs had in mind, and Scott Russell Sanders, Montaigne, and I—are mostly lyric.[4] And when they are, they have this special role to play: witnessing the real world from within.

The essay is always personal, then, and always more than merely personal; it is intimate and detached at once. It speaks for this man or woman *and* this place; for all men and women and all places. It pays careful attention to the world, apprehending it more than merely visually, knowing that all it elaborates is how one or two of the many faces of the world seem, how they look and how they speak, to this one witness. The essay is a practice of attention, a wondering about the real, a dance with it, well made for nature writing.

4. See Scott Russell Sanders's important essay on the nature of the essay, "The Singular First Person" (1991), 187; and my own essay on the essay, "Nothing but the Truth" (1998). Montaigne, father of the modern essay, speaks of the art of the essay in "On Repentance" (1957, 610–20). Sanders (1991, 191) reminds us that, in *Nature*, Emerson, another master of the genre, encouraged writers to "fasten words again to visible things," thereby giving us both a good working definition of the essay and a reminder of the connection of words and voice to the things of the world, to which the essay cleaves.

2 *The Edge of the Trees*

BARRY LOPEZ

McKenzie River Valley, Oregon

The soul, he said, is composed
Of the external world.
There are men of the East, he said,
Who are the East.
There are men of a province
Who are that province . . .
There are men whose words
Are as natural sounds
Of their places
As the cackle of toucans
In the place of toucans.

—Wallace Stevens,
"Anecdote of Men by the Thousand"

We danced together on the bank. And the songs we
danced to were the river songs I remembered from
long ago. We danced until I could not understand
the words but only the sounds, and the sounds were
unmistakably the sound rain makes when it is getting
ready to come into a country.

—Barry Lopez, "Drought"

That one born in the forest, growing up
With canopies, must seek to secure coverings
For all of his theories. He blesses trees.
—Pattiann Rogers, "The Determinations of the Scene"

We have turned off the McKenzie Highway at the town of Blue River. White settlers found gold here once and mined it. Now Blue River is a logging town, lodged among tall conifers on the shelf of land where, back in another geological era, the river used to run. It stands near the place where today two rivers meet, where the Blue River comes down now out of the Cascade Range and enters the McKenzie, which flows east over its bed of stones—red chert, grey basalt, cream quartzite, black obsidian—to meet the Willamette forty miles away at Eugene. They used to float the logs of Douglas-fir along these rivers. Now their bodies are carried out by truck.

It's a Thursday in the fall of 2000. This truck—Barry Lopez's gray Toyota, Barry at the wheel—has carried us already past the Blue River Dam, its water level low after a dry summer, and up along a gravel road into the hills above the town. Barry drives slowly and distinguishes carefully among the trees—this Douglas-fir, that western hemlock with its trailing leader, that white pine, that red cedar—and understory—vine maple, dogwood, yew, salmonberry, and chinquapin. The day is mild, its note subdued, its light clear. I begin, under his gentle tutelage, to read the country.

Turning from the road, we pull up in a clearing among tall trees. There is another truck in the lot, a hunter's vehicle. But no one is about. Barry leads me to a lake that beavers have made, a flooded meadow encircled by conifers. We walk down toward the place where the beavers have dammed the stream. The water rests with a stillness that feels uneasy—contested. It is a holy and haunted place. The beavers have done their work well, for the body of the water, mostly hidden by the gray reeds and sedges that grow out of its shallows, spreads wide in this basin, this place where the headwaters of a creek once ran among grasses. Wolf Creek, it is called, though now the water belongs to beavers.

We stand at the lake's edge. The water has withdrawn from its flood tide at the edge of the trees, and the lake's margin is hard to find among the sedges. A boat lies decaying there, and we rest a boot each against its broken gunwale to look upon the lake. It has a handmade feel, this ruined vessel, now swamped by the water that holds against the dam the beavers have made of mud and cut poles. Barry tells me the boat has lain there as long as he can remember. It has become landscape.

He falls silent. His look is earnest, attentive, and there is sadness in it. The quality of his silence, it strikes me, is not unlike that of this still water itself. He listens like water, as though his life depended on it.

He turns after a minute or two, and we walk among broad stumps and standing trees, and he points up to a high gray monolith of basalt: the nose of Wolf Rock, raised and frozen, thus, in song. Pink and yellow lichens pattern its surface, Barry tells me, though I can't make out that fine decoration from here. He knows because he has seen it up close. Wolf Rock is a volcanic plug, rising six hundred and fifty feet above this terrace of flat ground. Barry climbed it when he was young, and once he fell. He shows me the scar on his wrist.

The meadow, now flooded by the beavers, is named, like the rock, for the wolves who once ran here. White settlers fast trapped beavers out of the range, and for a while wolves had the run of the meadow. But in fifty years or so the wolves had all been hunted out. This meadow—Wolf Prairie—was a killing ground. Its name recalls a massacred race. With the wolves gone and the trade in beaver pelts collapsed, the beavers returned to the Cascades in the twentieth century. They've made this meadow theirs now, as, no doubt, it was theirs, from time to time, in earlier days, before it was, briefly, the wolves' alone. But disquiet sleeps beneath the silent waters the beavers have gathered here; and disquiet troubles Barry's own silence, as he stands beside me looking up at the rock, as though he shared with the place a memory of terrible loss. For ten thousand summers until the white men came with guns, the Tsanchifin Kalapuya, another now-departed people, visited this meadow. They came for salmon and berries, for wolves and beavers and ceremony, and to stand, perhaps, as we do, stilled by this dreaming place, awed by the rock that sleeps above it. The dreams of the place are different now. They're flooded with sorrow.

The beavers are back, though. This is their flood. So all is not lost.

Barry tells me that he has learned only freshly from a Native American man he met on the coast that this site, to which he has been drawn again and again over the years, used to be known among the Tsanchifin as a place of particular power, a place as sacred, almost, as the Columbia River Gorge. "I have had animal encounters and witnessed celestial events at this place many, many times," Barry tells me. "It's always felt a powerful place to me. Even if you're uninitiated, as I am, I think you can feel the heartbeat here."

As we drive away, deeper into the forest, I look up through the open sunroof of the truck and see a halo of ice encircling the sun.

Barry drives on. I point out the halo, and he says nothing. Later, he tells me he saw another halo here once at a turning point in his life. Seeing it again today moved him, moved him to silence. But he is quiet, too, because he is tracking—he is reading the trail left by the tires of another vehicle, already long gone, on this dirt road. Its syntax is lost on me. My eyes are still trying to tell the conifers apart. "Those guys were hunting," he says, concluding this from their slow pace and meander and the way the tracks leave the road near a tree from which some pink flagging trails.

As we go on, I point to a shrubby tree, one of many of its kind I've noticed crowding a logged slope, its leaves the shape and color of an olive. I ask him what it is, and he cannot name it at once. He stops the truck and leaves it idling while he goes over to study its foliage. "See what it says about ceanothus in there," he says to me, pointing to one of the field guides in the door of the truck. I find *Ceanothus integerrimus*, deer brush. It seems to fit. "Strange how you can forget something like that," he says. "It's a plant I know well. The deer like it. But I can't have looked at it properly for a long time, and its name had slipped."

There is a story, "Homecoming," in Lopez's *Field Notes* about a man who lives right here, in the forested foothills of the western Cascades. The man in the story is a botanist, whose academic career takes him increasingly often and far from his home in these woods, and deeper into his narrow scientific specialization, until he finds himself one day humbled when walking the woods with his daughter: "he'd forgotten the names of half a dozen or more flowers that grew around his home."

In "Homecoming," the botanist feels ashamed by how far he has fallen away from his home and family. His wife reminds him how he used to know all the plants in the woods. "You knew by their shadows, how they dipped in the wind. You were *here* then. Now, you look around, it's not part of you anymore. Why should they remember you when you can't remember them?" It is a moral tale about intimacy, of course, about grounded attachment to the body and spirit of a place. It's a story from the very center of Barry Lopez's moral universe, in which the locus of mindful attention is not the capital, the forum, the global scholarly network, or the market; it is the home and the family, and it is that place where one feels particularly attached: the local community of biological forms and landforms *here*.

In the story, the botanist takes himself out into the forest dark and gives himself back to the plants—the purslane and wood sorrel, the hellebores and the western trilliums—and the place. So that when he returns to bed, he smells of the woods again, his wife tells him; so that he knows the flowers again, and they know him. The story gives poignancy to Barry's fleeting forgetfulness of this plant.[1] But Barry is not that botanist. Many causes, none of them narrow, call him away, but he always comes home; he is always *here*. Like the rest of us, only not nearly so often, he finds that words and names elude him. But the plants, I'm guessing, remember him well.

We drive on, and I follow our way on a contour map. When we join the highway again, he takes me into Belknap Springs. He speaks of the McKenzie boats, named for the river and made to negotiate its rapids and wild currents in the days before the dams. We head up

---

1. "And here's an embarrassment," Barry writes in the margin of a draft of this chapter. "A friend of mine is writing the definitive book on *Ceanothus*, and I have collected the plant here with him."

again into the folded and forested ranges, and I lose my orientation among the tall trees and the country's convolutions. But this is storied, loved, and intimately observed country for Lopez—it is his backwoods. Toward noon we are climbing a ridge above the Horse Creek drainage, headed for the wilderness.

"The steep riverine valley I live within," Lopez writes in "The Language of Animals," "on the west slopes of the Cascades in Oregon, has a particular human and natural history. Though I've been here for thirty years, I am able to convey almost none of it" (2003, 159). He goes on to speak of the occupation of the Tsanchifin Kalapuya people, a Penutian-speaking people, who traveled this valley to camps where the McKenzie meets the Willamette, near where Eugene lies today. He knows, he says, something of their story and has visited their old campsites with reverence.

> But I'm drawn more to the woods in which they're found. These landscapes are occupied, still, by the wild animals who were these people's companions. . . . When I travel in the McKenzie basin with visiting friends, my frame of mind is not that of the interpreter, of the cognoscente; I amble with an explorer's temperament. I am alert for the numinous event, for evidence of a world beyond the rational. Though it is presumptuous to say so, I seek a Tsanchifin grasp, the view of the indigene. And what draws me ahead is the possibility of revelation from other indigenes—the testimonies of wild animals. (ibid., 160)

Here I am now—a visiting friend—ambling and attentive in the valley of the McKenzie. I am with a man returning to ground he loves and knows pretty well. He's here to know it again, know it deeper, and to be known—not to show it off or show off, himself. There is something shy and humble about his passage into it with me. He is the husband long separated from his wife, returning now. At times, I feel I should look away.

Barry runs no commentary on what we pass. He notices everything and points out much to me, but he offers no interpretation of our encounters with trees and wild animals, the odd "numinous event." He names, now and then, a hill or drainage, a birdcall, a river-bend or meadow, and then he falls into almost Trappist silence. He leaves space for his valley to be for me what it will. He's witnessing. And that calls for silence, for which he has a gift. He has a gift for words, too, but they come later.

"When I walk in the woods or along the creeks," he writes in "The Language of Animals," "I'm looking for integration, not conversation. I want to be bound more deeply into the place, to be included, even if only as a witness, in events that animate the landscape" (ibid., 162).

Barry Lopez lives in a clapboard cottage within that river valley, forty miles upstream of Eugene, Oregon. He has lived in that house in that valley for thirty-five years, though he, like his botanist, has traveled far from it, and often. He came to Finn Rock in June 1970 with his wife Sandra. He had already published, then, one book (of reviews and stories), written while he was a senior at Notre Dame. He had spent a year or two traveling, writing in motel rooms. He had worked for a year in a publishing house in New York; fifteen months writing in Mishawaka, Indiana, in the home he made there with his young wife; and another eighteen months in Eugene, where he began but never finished his MFA.

After many years, Sandra has moved on, but Barry has stayed, and this is where most of his books have been written. He has apprenticed himself to these woods and this river and to all that they hold. "I have trained myself to listen to the river," says the narrator of his story "Drought." This is where, in this house in these woods, by this river, he wrote *Arctic Dreams;* and this is where, he tells me, up until his most recent book of stories, *Light Action in the Caribbean,* he has written every word of nearly every story and essay he's published. Many of the stories from his new book he wrote in New Mexico, and the wide light of that place, its spareness and lack of embellishment, inhabit them. But in all his other work, you can feel the nature of the McKenzie, this sterner, darker place: its dignified waters; its subdued light; its solemn conifers, austerely decorated in moss; the towering cottonwoods down on the riverbanks, the big-leaf maples, ash, and alder; the mink and black bear and beaver; blue heron and the other river birds; the salmon, swimming their cycle of eternal return; even the grief the place knows from the wounds of unabated forestry. The language all these articulate is the language he knows best. Its cadences are his own.

Beneath the rainforests and rivers, beneath this moist and elegant, gothic terrain, the Juan de Fuca plate slides inland and bears downward under the North American plate at half an inch a year. This landscape of almost archetypal stillness is in motion and under terrible strain. Within its mild and weathered body, huge and violent forces work, mostly in silence, mostly without expression at the surface, fashioning the future. They are there, inside the calm. They stir the volcanoes and hot springs of the Cascade Range. I wonder if this volcanic, hephaestian character is not also at work within Barry Lopez's brooding work, and within himself. When you are with him you feel a gatheredness, an imminence within his restraint—the same thing you feel in the country that is his home.

Barry's house sits on a shelf made by the McKenzie in an earlier age, before it found the bed it now runs on, down below the logging road, closer to the other side of this steep valley. Barry stands and points to the water's older course and explains how a river behaves through geologic time—much as, in "real time," a hose lying on the ground behaves under water pressure: it snakes. Once upon a time, the McKenzie snaked its way through here.

Lopez has written obliquely of his home place in the fables, the elegant myths, of *River Notes*. He has written about it sparingly in some of his essays—in "The Language of Animals"; in two essays in *Crossing Open Ground,* "Trying the Land" and "Children in the Woods"; in two of the essays gathered in *About This Life,* "The Whaleboat" and "Effleurage"; in a cycle of fifty-two small essays of his daily life here, on which he is working now; and in a couple of essays he gives me copies of, "A Natural Grief" and "The Near Woods." There is also a story published in *Orion* in summer 1996, called "Jedediah Speaks with the River," set just here on the McKenzie. So he has written of this country. But mostly he has written here of other landscapes, particularly the Arctic.

Barry once called himself a writer who travels. In *Arctic Dreams* he notes that a certain kind of traveler journeys to other places to deepen—by looking on and entering into an unfamiliar place, its different sets of living relationships, its different weathers and geological stories—his "sense of the worth of his own place, of the esteem in which he wishes to hold the landscape that originally shaped him" (1986, 279).

Barry has kept his home country, the cottage and the woods and the river, safe and secret, by and large. It is a refuge and a sanctuary. And it is the landscape that goes on shaping him. Here is the community of friends and familiar beings among whom he feels most himself. This is where he writes from. I see, in the days that follow, how deeply he knows this landscape and how many of its places move him when he meets them, as a meeting with a friend might move another man.

Though he lives today among these forests, Barry Holstun Lopez entered the world in January 1945 "east of the heights of New Rochelle in the watershed of New York's Mamaroneck River," as he recalls in "A Voice," the introduction to *About This Life* (1998, 3). The town of Mamaroneck, where Barry spent his first three years, lies in a bay of Long Island Sound, near the southernmost reach of that water. Until he turned three, Barry grew up with the sea, "that empty space above its surface," and the glare of the light. In the spring of 1948, with his mother and a new baby brother, he moved to California, to a house among farms in the San Fernando Valley. "For a long time," he writes in "A Voice," "I thought of California as the beginning, the place where my life took a distinctive shape, but something had already begun" (ibid.).

Barry's father had gone on ahead of them to California. The marriage ended two years later, but his mother stayed on with her sons. Although something had begun already in the light and water of the East Coast, this was the country of Barry Lopez's childhood, the light and landforms in which he remembers being young—the orchards and chicken ranches of the valley where he cycled, the Mojave Desert where his mother drove them, the Santa Monica Mountains where he hiked, Big Bear Lake and the beaches where they holidayed. In the light of this country, arid, transparent, "gin-clear," he learned to see landscape, and he concedes (in "Replacing Memory") that this experience may have affected, at the level of emotion, how he has come to see the world (1998, 208). Light flooded the spaces of his childhood.

And something terrible happened in that light, intruding upon that Edenic space. Lopez describes it in an essay published after my time with him, "A Scary Abundance of Water" (2002). He sends me a copy, with this comment: "It is the most autobiographical work I've ever written, and I think it puts into essay some of what I have been trying to say about landscape and the shaping of personality. And about landscape and healing. . . . This is about the San Fernando Valley in California and what happened to it and me while I was growing up there. You can't separate the memoir from the landscape."

What happened to the valley was that irrigation inundated it with people, altered it, and began to tame it with suburbs. As a boy he saw water efface—almost utterly—a place he loved. And yet he saw how the place, altered, and sometimes diminished, went on. It endured. In his essay, Barry speaks of how his experience of water, in the California of his youth and in his adulthood by the McKenzie, taught him that life and land persist no matter (almost) what, that places (and people) heal, after inundations; that there is an order of things to which water belongs, which "could never be lost, never destroyed." He writes: "In a dry, fault-block basin in the transverse ranges of Southern California, where the Gabrielino once lived well on 60 different kinds of plants and a hundred types of seed, another group of people built a world of well-watered fields. However they may have reasoned the water was theirs, they made an arid land bloom. . . . The water, it turned out, was ordinary life. The water was the *braceros,* working every day in the fields, making a curiously knowing nod to a young white boy passing on his bike. The water was the ordinary determination of everyday people to contain something deep in their lives" (2002, 31).

Water, which, in human hands and sometimes on its own, can be a force of destruction, can also heal. When Lopez returns to places he knew as farmland and finds them made over into suburbs, he realizes that, although they are not the half-wild places he loved, they are still vibrant locales and that all of them were sung up, in a sense, by the rivers that were tamed and the aquifers that were tapped and put to work upon the land. The water brought forth these places, and the water, though much put upon and shrunken, goes on. Water speaks of abundance. It allows, and it teaches, forgiveness.

What happened to the boy Barry Lopez was that "along with three other boys . . . , I had been sodomized repeatedly in the mid-'50s by an older man who ran a drying-out clinic for alcoholics on Riverside Drive in North Hollywood" (ibid., 32). And in the throes of his torture it was the light and the land, the knowledge that these things went on regardless, that kept him alive. Above all, what sustained hope in this child—overwhelmed, almost annihilated, by what had befallen him, as the valley he lived in had been almost annihilated by water and all that it brought in its train—was his knowledge of what water could do to land, its power to make arid valleys bloom. "And so," Lopez writes, "I understood as a boy I could do the same. I could address the thing in me that threatened to become a vast and spreading desert. I had only to discover the water to make it happen" (ibid.).

That remembered light, the consolation of water, the perseverance of land, have gone on saving him all of his life. How a place can transcend the horrors that occur within and to it is one thing, one critical thing, Barry learned in that California light, from that valley and its waters. But the wisdom that came to him as a boy about the endurance of landscapes oriented Barry Lopez not so much away from human society as toward the larger order that contains it. "The water, it turned out, was ordinary life," he concludes (ibid.). Water became his metaphor for the holiness and beauty of vernacular human lives, lived in connection, not always benevolent, with the land.

Barry has kept his silence about this event all of his life. His whole life has harbored and expressed this secret (in voice and mood but not, until now, in words), much as the calm Cascades go on holding and hinting at their tectonic secret. And now that he speaks of his abuse at last, he speaks with characteristic restraint and dignity, with courage but without hyperbole. We should not make more of it, nor less, than he does. It is one important event in his life, inseparable from his experience of place. But it is not everything; by it alone his life and works are not explained. Lodging the revelation of this abuse two-thirds of the way through his essay, a third of the way into a paragraph, Lopez tells us how integral, and yet how connected with everything else, that incident was. Take away the light and the water, the valley and the birds, the farms and the scent of eucalyptus, and the life of the man would not be what it has become. Take away the place, and he might not have survived his trauma. Take away the trauma, and he might not have discovered the life-sustaining secrets of the water; he might not have given himself over so deeply to the land. Barry Lopez's story of survival is as much a metaphor for the San Fernando Valley's transcendence of everything done to it, as the valley's story is a metaphor for Lopez's life. You can't abstract the memoir, that one human life, its troubles and joys, from the landscape.

And so when in 1956 his mother, now remarried, took the family and moved back east to an apartment on East Thirty-fifth Street in Manhattan, young Barry felt like a caged animal freed; and yet he also "missed California to the point of grief" (ibid.). Back east, Barry continued his schooling at a Jesuit prep school. The landscape of his adolescence, then, was New York City and places on Long Island and in New Jersey and Alabama where he vacationed or went to summer camp. In 1962, after a summertime trip to Europe after school's end, he began college at the University of Notre Dame in Indiana, intending to become an aeronautical engineer. Soon he switched to a degree in communication arts, in which he later graduated. During vacations, he traveled America widely by car, visiting nearly every state, working often on a friend's Wyoming ranch and spending time with a West Virginia farmer, Odey Cassell, whose storytelling gifts and sense of local geography helped school the writer Lopez would become. (He writes of Cassell, and of two other landscape elders, in his essay "Grown Men" in *Crossing Open Ground*.)

He thought of entering the priesthood for a time and traveled down to the Gethsemani seminary in Kentucky, drawn there by the presence of Thomas Merton and the intimation of a calling. But Lopez chose the world, not retreat. He decided, at first, that teaching would suit him, so he returned to Notre Dame to enroll in a master's program in education. Though he finished the program, he never taught. Writing called him instead.

Barry had been writing stories and reviews since his undergraduate days. A sense of vocation dawned on him at Notre Dame, though not the one his coursework proposed: he would travel and write the stories that places offered up to him. And so in 1967, he moved with his new wife, Sandra, to Oregon to begin an MFA in creative writing. But it was writing itself that he wanted, not a degree in it; he felt more and more urgently the need to learn what writing itself had to teach him. Without finishing this second master's degree, he left school to try his hand at the writing life—one he's lived out ever since.

The first book for which Barry is known, *Desert Notes: Reflections in the Eye of a Raven*, was published in 1976. It is a collection of short stories set in the Alvord Desert of southeastern Oregon. *Giving Birth to Thunder*, transcriptions of Native American stories, followed in 1977. *River Notes: The Dance of Herons* (1979) was the second book of a trilogy begun in *Desert Notes* and finished in *Field Notes: The Grace Notes of the Canyon Wren* (1994). In these books, which are cycles of stories, Lopez allows the world beyond the human to come alive in a remarkable way, so that the human lives that participate in the places are enchanted too. They draw, these stories, and they draw *upon*, the landscapes of the McKenzie River valley and the deserts of eastern

Oregon, the deserts of Australia, the streets of Manhattan—places he knows from staying home and from traveling afield.

Of Wolves and Men, a natural history of wolves based on his own travels and experiences and his wide reading in science, literature, and native wisdom, came out in 1978, became a bestseller, and won for Lopez the John Burroughs Medal. The literary scholar Sherman Paul has said that that book, though composed with the care one expects of Lopez, is the work of an apprentice, whereas *Arctic Dreams* (1986) is the work of a master. In *Arctic Dreams,* his second major work of nonfiction, Lopez's reflections on light and space, imagination and desire, landscape and its wisdom; his personal experiences of traveling widely, often with Native peoples, in the land; and his wide research among, his deep reflections upon, the literatures of science, exploration, art, and anthropology—all this is wrought by the alchemy of his imagination, his memory, and his reason into a work of astonishing lyricism and power. This book won for him the National Book Award and wide acclaim.

A selection of essays, *Crossing Open Ground,* appeared in 1988, and another, *About This Life,* in 1998. Since *Arctic Dreams,* Lopez's published work has mostly taken the shape of essays, a genre that suits his intimate, restrained voice, his gift for research, and his talent for story. It is a good form for a man so committed to telling the truth as he sees it; to speaking of where he goes and giving a fair account of what he learns there. In 1990, he published a novella-length fable, *Crow and Weasel,* a book that practices the disciplines of the storyteller, of which he writes in many places, most pointedly in "Landscape and Narrative" (1988, 61–71); and in it he explores many of his enduring concerns— friendship, community, quest for wisdom, care with language, attentiveness, the intelligence of places.

At the edge of a dark forest, Barry Lopez works away at enlightenment, in a house of attachments. Nothing anonymous ornaments his cottage. On its wooden walls hang paintings, drawings, and tapestries made by friends or by the people he has traveled among. He tells me the stories of their making—this rug, that print, that pot or pipe. And his telling wakes each object until the house is alive with them. Everything has a history. There are pots made by Richard Roland (he is Jack in "Effleurage"); masks made by Lillian Pitt, a Wasco woman; paintings by Rick Bartow, a Yurok man; paintings by Robin Eschner and by Alan Magee (one of which was the cover illustration for *Crossing Open Ground*); photographs by Robert Adams; sculpture by Tom Joyce; carvings made by an Ainu elder; furniture crafted by Kevin Sherwood; glasswork shaped by John Rose; pottery by the hand of Alyce Flitcraft. These are friends; these are objects with biographies. On the walls, too, are maps and charts of places Barry has been, photographs. We eat at a table made by a friend from a tree Barry felled, a slab he cut.

He lives among authentic things, made by hand with love, things whose histories twine around his own. He lives among stories, among gestures of love, embodiments of loved places. He lives in a place made light, thus, in the dark forest.

It is my first night at Finn Rock. After dinner, we sit in the front room, Barry in a rocking chair pulled up by the woodstove, I on the couch, its back to the windows that look down toward the river. And he says that the literature he attempts "concerns itself, finally, with the nature of reality, life as we live it. I am a writer who is deeply concerned with landscape—this one, others I know, and by extension all landscapes and our place within them, our relationships with them. People, interviewers and others, have wanted to call me a philosopher, a naturalist, an environmentalist, a theologian even. But I am none of those things. They are other people's ideas, too narrow ideas, of what I am. I am a writer."

Barry Lopez has grown impatient with the limits the term *nature writing* implies. Writing is what he does, and land is at the heart of it, not only because he loves the land, not only because he finds consolation and hope in it, but because that is where everything comes from and where, in the end, it returns to. *Nature writing,* he believes, focuses people's mind too much on the literal subject matter—animals, rivers, mountains, trees—and not enough on the reason he and others have turned to the natural world. He has said that natural history, geography, and anthropology are his ways of understanding the world: "These disciplines," he told the *Bloomsbury Review* in 1990, "are my metaphors." They let him approach—taking his readers with him—the question that most concerns him, that concerns all writers deep down: how to live right together on earth. Many other things than the natural order interest him, influence him, and find their way into his work, he says to me now: democracy, music ("some music is sacred," he throws in), poetry, theater, crafts. "But among the community of people working in those many ways toward the same ends," he says, "we [writers] are the only ones working with the literal."

Barry writes and speak like this—in epigrams. He does not wish to explain everything. By "the literal" he means, I think, that writers use *words* to make sense of the actual world—not that we are the only ones attempting facsimiles. (Indeed, facsimiles are the last things one ought to attempt to make of the living world with *words,* those signifying and music-making abstractions.) Writers make art out of language. With the names of things, these metaphors and their sounds, the writer tries to fathom the world, to tell stories about it, to wonder and sing. But before I have time to ask if I've got this right, he goes on. He talks in a river of aphorism. He tells me he feels he is writing in a tradition that is very old, much older, say, than the novel or the ecological narratives of our time, much older too than Thoreau or Gilbert White. Even their books were nothing new. Nature writing stands discrete, he says, from the solipsism of much mainstream literature of the present day. It is in this sense a literature of humility, of movement beyond the self. His work, he hopes, continues an older literary tradition, an ancient discourse about living honorably, ethically, justly, joyfully on this earth with all its beings, but particularly among ourselves. All the wisdom the earth's first peoples possess on these matters, he writes in *Arctic Dreams,* arises out of their intercourse with the land, their seeking a "congruent relationship with it," their wanting to "fit well into it" (1986, 297). The first peoples' dream of a "transcendent congruency" or "reverberation" with the earth—this, as he sees it, is the aspiration his writing shares with all storytellers since the beginning of time; and it is a congruency he seeks not just for himself, but for all his readers through his work. This, he thinks, is what storytellers have always wanted. And such a literature may matter now more than ever, for in our time people stand more out of harmony with the earth than ever. Intimacy with the land, which has been the source of the wisdom of all the ages, is a failing practice, a language falling into disuse.

Sitting by the fire, tending it, Barry Lopez says to me, "The aboriginal lifeway is the manifest form of our intercourse with landscape. In it you see embodied immediate awareness of the lore of the place, as it touches people and all things, and you find a practice of ritual that celebrates, remembers, articulates those truths." And that is the literature he attempts.

It is my second night at Finn Rock. We have spent the day driving and walking in the woods, along the ridges, and down in the drainages of Barry's native ground. Now cloud is building in the night sky. Rain is coming again to the Cascades. In the front room after dinner, Barry builds a fire in the stove, and he asks me what it is I want to know. And suddenly, it's hard to say. I want him to talk about how he enters into this and other landscapes, how he knows them, how they reveal themselves to him, how he writes them, what they teach him. But after the day in the field, out in the weather, I feel the emptiness, the impertinence, the abstraction of my questions. He has been sitting with a draft of the introductory chapters of this book. "There's a lot of work here," he remarks, then waits. Taking my cue, I ask him what he considers the defining practice of nature writing, or whatever this literature is to be called. I wonder aloud if he has ever thought of it as a phenomenological endeavor—and immediately wish I had thought of a better way to begin.

It strikes me now, on reflection, that my gathered thoughts on nature writing, my attempt to take its measure, my exploration of the preoccupations of its literary scholars, may have given off the odor to

him that night, after our day in his home country, of the tedious equations gathered into notebooks and delivered to the narrator of his
early story "The Bend." My draft chapters and the question I posed
were just like those arid formulations: abstractions from whose cold
grip the life of what it is that Barry does had fled, from which he, himself, had taken flight, like the mergansers in the story, in alarm.

Curtly, impatiently, he responds: "I don't care what nature writing
is. It is a term, often followed by some narrow definition, applied to a
group of writers and their craft from the outside. It implies a rubric
where there is none."

He pauses, checks the fire, and comes at the question his way. He
has, he says, always been attached to the idea of intimacy. "I've looked
for it, in the woods and everywhere." He explains that as a man and as
a writer he has wanted deep engagement, understanding, immediacy,
truthfulness with people and things. "And language," he adds, "is a
petition for intimacy with a reader. All good writing seeks that."

He didn't set out to be a nature writer, he tells me. He wasn't
looking for some deep communion with nature. He didn't even begin
as a nature lover. "I was drawn," he says, "to people and fields of study
engaged with the world beyond the self. So I was drawn to ethology,
nature observation, geography, archeology, anthropology; and to other
arts: music, painting, woodcarving." His own writing grew out of what
he began to learn from people who knew about such things, from his
reading, from his field work, from his wondering, thinking, and
reflecting. It grew out of a search for intimate awareness of truth, of
patterns that hold, in and between lives beyond one's own. A large part
of his orientation toward landscape, he explains, arose from his sense
of the consolation offered by and written into orders of light and
geology, into the patient histories of water and of those "other
nations," the animals, as Henry Beston phrased it in *The Outermost
House*. And he had, always, an explorer's instinct that who you are and
what you believe—what a human life means and how it might elegantly be led—will occur to you once you leave the shelter of the

familiar: this instinct guided him in his reading and traveling. All this led him outside the usual haunts of writers; it led him to the land.

In "A Voice," the autobiographical essay that opens *About This Life*, Lopez speaks a little more of the things that shaped him as a writer, among them the western light, the desert air, the orchards and creeks of his California childhood. In his junior year at the University of Notre Dame, a sense of a writer's calling grew on him. "I understood the urge to write," he says, "as a desire to describe what happened, what I saw, when I went outside"—though this was "regarded as peculiar territory by other nascent writers at the university" (1998, 10–11). He found his models for such writing, for weird and sometimes exquisitely beautiful storytelling, for evocations of the life of places and their people, mostly among poets and novelists—Gerard Manley Hopkins, William Faulkner, Willa Cather, Herman Melville.

He writes in "A Voice" of a teacher at the University of Oregon, Barre Toelken, who steered him toward anthropology. There he found other cultures that "approached questions of natural history and geography in the same way I preferred. They did not separate humanity and nature. They recognized the immanence of the divine in both. And they regarded landscape as a component as integral to the development of personality and social order as we take the Oedipus complex and codified law to be" (ibid., 11–12). Teachers like Toelken, and later indigenous guides, led the young writer to non-Western aboriginal cultures that believed what his own intuition told him: that places make us, school us, offer us the guidance we need for good lives (with "place" here understood not to exist separate from but to include the people who inhabit it).

"My passion is landscape and language, and those two are inseparable for me," Barry Lopez said in a conversation with E. O. Wilson, chaired by Ed Leuders before an audience in 1989. "That is where the focus of my life is. . . . Each of us," he said to Wilson—meaning the writers of literary natural history, like-minded artists, and, I think, scientists like Wilson—"is making a contribution to something that all of

us believe in, which is enlightenment, bringing light into this dark forest" (Leuders 1989, 33).

Moving on from my inept opening, which has nonetheless yielded a
rich conversation, Barry tells me he is also stirred by questions of spatial volume, leaning with wonder toward the nature of the spaces we
live in—how we shape them, how they shape us, how we stand in
relation to them, how we imagine them and make them home, how we
want to possess them, what we learn about what is real, what is beautiful, what is right, what is just, and what endures, from the spaces we
come to know. Others, such as the geographer Yi-Fu Tuan, have spoken of the process of making mere *spaces* into *places* by the way we
grow intimate with them (and what is invisible within them) through
story and true dwelling. The *space* Barry has in mind here is something
like the amplitude of a particular place, including its light and atmosphere and governing sensibility. Space is abstract, immaterial, and
voluminous distance. Place, on the other hand, or at least *a place*, a
locale, the land *here*, is the enfolded natural and cultural histories that
indigenous Australians have traditionally referred to (in English) as
country. It includes the local sky, geology, and the cultures of the local
peoples. Place is material, if elusive. And a place will possess, among
other things, a characteristic space or amplitude, by which we come to
know it. Its space is the way the light sits and the winds move, the way
sounds travel. Its space is the quality of the intervals between its many
pieces, between great horned owl and jackrabbit, between the notes of
the raven's song, right down to the vibrant voids between the atoms in
the grains of its sandstones or granites. Its space is, to anticipate James
Galvin, what holds a place's pieces apart. It is the tone of its millions
of interrelationships.

   These two terms—space and place—intergrade, I concede. But it
is worth holding them apart, too. Different meanings attend them.
What Barry is talking about is the ineffable, voluminous expanse that
overarches and in which the land, in a sense, bodies itself forth. Once,
he says, he had a letter from an architect who commented on the way

Lopez makes spatial volumes with his words, how Lopez's words do the work that he, the architect, performs with lines on paper and with metal and steel—articulating, enclosing, and characterizing space.

I nod that I understand. I have come to think over the last few years that the real work of the writer is the creation of spaces, gestured into life in the mind of the reader by the line and form of his sentences, by the patterns of sound as well as the suggestions that his sentences make. As an architect and builder enclose a space within the structure they imagine and construct, so too a writer encloses a space within the structure he composes with language. Into that space—which the writer patterns and animates with images, with ideas, with tones and scents and events—the writer draws the reader. This is the space in which the story occurs, where learning or revelation happens. A year later, as I sit at home with my notes of our meeting, it occurs to me that in a review of Barry's *About This Life*, in August 1998, I had written: "Something like faith infuses the spaces he makes with words." This thought, apparently, was on me earlier than I realized, and it's interesting that it arose for me about, and out of, the writing of Lopez himself.

"It was my love of the interplay of orders of space and volume that led me to the Arctic and the Sonoran desert and such places where space abounds," he comments this night in his front room. In his chapter "Migration" in *Arctic Dreams* he writes of a night he woke and slept and woke and slept again beneath the migration of snow geese: "I felt a calmness birds can bring to people; and, quieted, I sensed here the outlines of the oldest mysteries: the nature and extent of space, the fall of light from the heavens, the pooling of time in the present, as if it were water" (1986, 154). The space he lay in there was articulated by the wings and cries of birds, the ancient rhythms of flight through sky. He writes of a dynamic, auditory space; of a moment animated, quick with the rush of time through it. These are, I think, his abiding themes—space, time, consolation, mystery, intimacy with the life of the land.

Back home now, in my own cottage, sheltered from a stiff cold wind that's come in from the south, I have been rereading Lopez's writing, noticing the stress he places on space, on form. I sense now how important this notion has always been for him. I see how his passion for the world's spaces and shapes, their play and mystery, is the river that runs through all his writing. He knows that space, each place on earth, is a dynamic order, and he listens hard, he participates bodily, in order to sense something of its logic, its musical structure, knowing that in that music he will find what he needs to know. In the introduction to his first collection of fables, *Desert Notes,* his narrator says: "When I first came into the desert I was arrested by the space first, especially what hung in a layer just above the dust of the desert floor. The longer I regarded it the clearer it became that its proportion had limits, that it had an identity, like the air around a stone. I suspected that everything I'd come to find out was hidden inside that sheet of space" (1976, 8–9). Lopez seems to have intuited long ago that truths— the things one seeks to shape a life, to know the world, to find faith and hope, and even love—have physical form; they occupy space; they lie in the ground; they inhabit the relationships that compose a landscape.

Since my return to Australia I have reread *River Notes,* his marvelous second book of stories—enchanted, strange, utterly selfless inventions, emanations of a palpable intimacy that grows between a man and a place, in particular the river that runs down the valley he has lived in now for the greater part of his life. There, Lopez's narrator speaks less of space than of form: the shape things take. Truths lie like sediments in a river stone; wisdom is hidden in a sheet of space; knowledge is articulated by the way a river bends around a promontory and reads "the surface of the earth over which it flows" (1979, 133). I read these as metaphors for the same notion: what we need to know has a body. *Desert Notes* is a book of space and light; *River Notes* is a book of form and water. And these are stories, not disquisitions, that Lopez writes. They make a space within which realizations occur, truths are embodied and left to be discovered by readers. Meaning arises for the narrator from—indeed, meaning *is*—the shape of water, the form of stone, the space above a desert, the flow of song, the play of light, the voice of canyon wren, the odor of cottonwood buds carried downstream.

In the lovely story "Upriver," the narrator speaks of "moments of complete vulnerability in each of us to form"; he comments that the ground above the falls is "in some ways the most dangerous country, reverberating with hope"; he studies a book he finds, "written in a language I do not know . . . as though sensing a promise in the very form of the words and sentences and the feel of the chapter breaks of imminent revelation" (1979, 132).

Revelation always lies near for Lopez. Revelation is always imminent. We will not find it in the abstract. We will find it in the shape and body of things in the world—in the trillium, the halo, the valley's light, the forgotten *Ceanothus integerrimus*. We will find it in the ground. The ground, the place, *is* wisdom. Truth inhabits space; it takes particular form. We will only find it by engaging with the world, bodily and respectfully, by walking and listening in it, by moving with its rhythms. Intimacy with the mysteries patterned into things is what Barry Lopez seeks, and what we all, deep down, fall toward in each other, and in places we love.

Barry Lopez turns from the fire and asks me, "What is it about a landscape that makes it hopeful?" He doesn't mean me to answer. "I am struck," he says, "by the way a landscape can hold and give rise to hope." Hope, for him, is embedded and expressed in the natural history of a place, its evolution and persistence, the relationships at play within it, the continuance of life against all sorts of odds; it is particularly eloquent in the dignity of untrammeled places. It is the moral of the story of the salmon, their return home to spawn and die and give rise to new life; it is the lesson found in the survival of the stunted trees and the hibernating bears of the unforgiving Arctic; it is the meaning of the lives of indigenous people. Hope, like beauty and dignity, is immanent in land—that is, in the pattern of relationships within a place, where human agency has not severed too many of those connections and impoverished the place—perhaps even there. "I believe hope is substantial," he says. "It is not an affect. It is integral."

Where dignity holds, unbroken and celebrated, within a landscape, that landscape gives rise to hope. Where its dignity has been taken, no hope arises, and no healing can come of it to us, who have broken it, until we attempt its restoration. Where hope still lies, we may begin to fathom it, to loose it for our understanding, by giving ourselves to that landscape. And we may give the gift of that place to others best by turning what we find into a story, telling it plainly and in keeping with the order that holds in that hopeful terrain.

Trees are shifting in the night. Though no time seems to have passed, I sense, as they do, that it's growing late. But the attention of the whole place—dark sky, cloud, river, tree, and coming rain—seems concentrated on this man by the ebbing fire, who offers me an image of what he means when he speaks of the life and agency of spaces. It is an image, I believe, at the heart of the thinking he is turning into his next large book. "I have pictured Charles Darwin," he says, "at sea all that time on the *Beagle*, far from land, set in all that vast, round, black void, reading at the same time Lyell, cramped on a small vessel, on a massive sea, walking under the vault of the stars at night, unable to discern an edge of things. And it occurs to me that his experience in that space—traveling, walking at night on deck, thinking the thoughts that arose in his mind from his reading—gave rise to the idea that man has no special significance, looked at with the kind of detachment that's possible, the sense of proportion manifest in that vastness; that man is just one of the many parts of the whole." This devastating and revolutionary idea is the thought of the space, and of the man within the space. It occurred to Darwin out of that space, because of his smallness and vulnerability within it, because of the way he walked and thought within it.

"There are symmetries in the world, harmonies and proportions in the disposition of things in space," Barry says. "Today," he reminds me, "when we came across the ridge between the watershed of Horse

Creek and the East Fork of the South Fork of the McKenzie, you and I talked about the lie of that land, the symmetry and body of that country. I can't say just why, but that draws me, that moves me. And I have always felt I needed to write about it, its dignity, its suggestions for how to conduct a good life."

The world articulates, it dances out, what we need to know in space. The storyteller, too, is a shaper of space in which material truths may be discovered in musical structures and forms akin to those at work in a place. In *Arctic Dreams,* Lopez offers us a word from the Eskimos, *isumataq:* "a person who can create the atmosphere in which wisdom shows itself" (1986, 298). Such a person is the storyteller. The wisdom he allows his listeners, his readers, to divine—as a landscape may allow wisdom to arise too in the heart and body of a man or woman who approaches it with patience and respect—does not belong to the teller (nor to the place). It may be shared. It occurs within a space, dynamic and animate. It is a timeless—but not a spaceless—wisdom that the teller seeks and that she hopes, perhaps, will rise from her sentences. "It is understanding how to live a decent life, how to behave properly toward other people and toward the land" (ibid.).

The wind has risen outside. Among the trees, it sounds like falling rain. But it isn't raining yet. It's getting on for midnight. "So, I suppose I think about a lot of things," says Barry. "And I go out and encounter the world, and I write about what arises for me when I do that. I feel an obligation as a writer, if I get to go somewhere, to pay attention and come home with some kind of story that helps to clarify my sense of the dignity of the world. Apart from that, when I sit down at the type-writer, I do not have the remotest sense that I have to fulfill at that machine some particular mission, a piece of nature writing, say, or whatever else."

He does not write, he says, within the bounds of a definition. Any characterization of his, or any writer's, work should simply attempt to articulate its nature, not limit it or narrow it.

Later he says that he thinks literature—and all art—ought to contribute to the making of a society in which people might live rewarding, meaningful, joyful lives. "What makes a good life is the degree to which one can imagine love: for the people and the things, the places, among which one lives, the things right here now, not the things one might aspire to own or build. I am not one of those who believes we can build a better life. Heaven is right here in front of us."

Critics and commentators usually misunderstand writing altogether, Lopez says. "I have had interviews on radio and television where the anchor—and this is the same with some critics and academics—asks questions about what I intended to do, to say, to achieve in my writing, as though the writing is intentional or purposive. They think that you sit down to write down what it is that you think about something. Writing does not work like this at all. I sit and write, and in the writing I am simply present—with the thought, the place, the idea. It arrives."

He tells me how it was he wrote *Arctic Dreams*. "I spent time in the Arctic until I felt suffused in it. Then I came home, and I read and read, and piled up notes and books. I had the scheme of *Arctic Dreams* in my head eighteen months before I wrote it. I typed notes from my journals and from books and left them in ordered piles with flags marking passages I thought I would use. Then I sat and wrote the book over nine months, working in a three-week cycle. One week planning and rereading; the second week making piles of notes ready; the third week writing; the fourth week working in the woods or whatever, not touching the book."

In his understanding of writing, the writer's discipline lies in steeping oneself in landscape and subject, and then in making oneself present enough for the story to rise, for the words, like things one might find in a landscape, to present themselves. The writing, for Barry Lopez at least, happens out of that immersion—the first immersion in the place, and the final immersion in the complex space in which recollection and research, thought and imagination, are all enfolded. It is a kind of engagement of mind and body with the original place, gathered, held, and ordered in the country of the writer's mind—much as music is ordered on paper by its composer's choice of key, tempi, and so on—made perhaps simpler, but also more meaningful, by the play of thought and memory with the remembered particularities of place. The writing is a reflection on a place and thoughts that rise from it; it is also relationship enacted with, even within, that (recalled) space, the performance of a dance with it.

About now Barry notices the time. He damps the fire, says goodnight, and each of us goes to bed, he upstairs and I downstairs in the library, where sleep is slow in coming.

While I am with him, Barry Lopez touches again and again on the moral dimension, specifically the human element, of nature writing—the social justice it pursues. His writing has always been—and he wants me to understand this, I think—deeply moral, grounded in a humanist tradition. We humans must remember our duties to the land, to the local places we inhabit, to earth as a whole; we need to return to natural history to take some lessons in proportion, restraint, order, modesty, and beauty. But we are not in the woods or on the tundra or the sea ice for the wonder of the outdoor experience alone, or for our own redemption. We are there to find out what justice means and how we might promote it among our fellow men and women—and not only among them, but also among all forms of life in "the reticulated miracle called the ecosystem" in which we live (Nelson, Lopez, and Williams 2002, 33). That, above all, is the lesson we need to learn from the lore of the land; and as writers, we must try to pass it on—to tell stories in which the patterns of landscapes, the virtues of certain spaces on earth, run clear and authentic, and may perhaps teach us what we need to know to live well.

I find myself thinking about Joseph Carroll's (1995, 2002) idea that literature is a biological act, one of the things people have learned to do to survive. For Lopez, as for Carroll, literature is an engagement with the lived and living world, and it is a way men and women use to make sense of their environment. It is a seeking out of patterns in the larger world that may be useful for men and women to know about in order to live long and well.

Peter Fritzell, in *Nature Writing and America* (1990), notes that two quite different approaches to the natural world and mankind's role within it have shaped the literature of nature writing: Aristotle's *Historia Animalium* and Saint Augustine's *Confessions*. From Aristotle, nature writing takes the discipline of detached observation of the natural world; from Augustine, a personal mode of writing concerning itself, through autobiographical reflection, with metaphysics, spirituality, and ethics (Cooley 1994, 6). This observation is helpful. It notes the marriage of the spiritual and the scientific projects in this literature. And it touches on something important in the makeup of Barry Lopez and his writing.

Both these traditions run strong in Lopez's thought, but compared with many nature writers, and despite his dedication to the close observation of the world, the articulation of its forms, he is very much the Augustinian. He is concerned with the sacred, with finding the face of God in the world, with discovering how to lead a life that is in some sense exemplary, with learning how to shape a just and beautiful society. And he has learned to work through a reflective, confessional first-person voice, sometimes austere, always unstintingly honest. This is a voice and a mode he discovered between *Of Wolves and Men* and *Arctic Dreams*, whose defining structural approach, as Sherman Paul and Scott Slovic have noted, is to frame every chapter (and each essay) within an episode, expanding discontinuously, into a meditative journey, of personal encounter with the landscape (Paul 1992, 100; Slovic 1992, 155). Lopez models in his way of being present in a landscape the very *humilitas* (gentle, inquiring incorporation of the self within the sacred space of country) that he advocates. His way of being present is tough-minded but soft-hearted; it is priestly, monkish—Augustinian. Although it is the land we must witness, serve, and converse with, each of us must put ourselves inside a place in order for that witness to occur; we must let the land come to us. And what we seek is not a mastery of the names of things, but some meta-physical insight that will allow each of us to make a worthier human life and to shape, perhaps, a worthier human culture. Lopez goes as a seeker, not an expert; he goes to find and to return with useful wisdom. And he would have each of us go—indeed, live—that way.

Lopez is much more apparently a humanist—much gentler toward his fellow men and women, I mean—than, say, Ed Abbey. He is adamant that whatever it is we humans have to learn and practice—forgiveness, honesty, storytelling, metaphoric wisdom, stewardship, farsightedness—we will learn it and must then apply it in society, in community. We may find patterns for all these things in the land—in its dignity, in the beauty of its long and shifting patterns, its elegance—but we must practice and share them with each other. Our humanity is enlarged by leaving our mere humankindness aside to recover our place in the land. But in the end we must return to human society, to family and spouse and community, and get on with knowing each other well. He concludes in "The Language of Animals": "I believe I have come to whatever I understand by listening to companions and by trying to erase the lines that establish hierarchies of knowledge among them. My sense is that the divine knowledge we yearn for is social; it is not in the province of a genius any more than it is in the province of a particular culture. It lies within our definition of community" (2003, 166).

We are standing high above the Horse Creek drainage, looking inland over the Three Sisters wilderness area. The spine of the Cascade range, running north and south, rises in three places before us. The mountains are sleeping volcanoes, ten thousand feet tall. They are called Faith, Hope, and Charity—three embodied virtues. Beyond them, north, Barry Lopez points out Mount Washington, another old volcano, which rises seven thousand feet. All of these peaks stand, this mid-October day, under snow to their forested shoulders.

Barry Lopez stands some twenty feet apart from me. We're on a gravel road, built for logging, and the mountain falls from our feet to the river, rises like a wall at our backs. We breathe and say nothing for a time inside a calm air, the soft light of midday on us and all that we can see. The mood of the place, mine within it, is of autumn as it nears its end.

We hold our ground on a slope logged bare a generation ago. The forest about us is young and spare. It contains a few large, old trees left by the cutters because they were not straight enough for good lumber; some returning conifers—Douglas-fir and western hemlock; and some understory plants—salal, huckleberry, bracken fern, red alder. Below us, reaching to the Three Sisters and beyond, the country has never been logged. It stands as it shaped itself from this volcanic ground. It gives off an air of infinite patience. Some of the trees down there may be five or six centuries old. And within their canopies—depending on the soil and light, the slope of the ground, its orientation to the sun— will grow many of the nations of plants Barry has named as we drove along the Blue River and Deer Creek drainages, up near the headwaters of the McKenzie, on an intricate journey among the trees.

From above, my unaccustomed eye can pick out nothing but a dense canopy of fir. There will be Oregon white oak, sugar pine, bigleaf maple and red alder, Pacific yew and lowland hemlock, thriving in the shade; along the rivers and creeks, black cottonwood, vine maple, and red cedar; there will be the berries and heath plants of the middle story—rhododendron, salal, huckleberry, snowberry, dogwood, and, where it is drier, madrone; and beneath everything, sword and bracken fern. Among the tall trees will rise some firs now silver with death but not fallen, some ancient trees slowly losing their form like salmon coming home to spawn and die; and on the floor of the woods you'll find the bodies of dead trees, claimed by moss and birthing young trees out of their decaying bodies. These are things, slender particulars, Barry has helped me see within these woods. Once, we stopped before a washed-out culvert because his eye had picked out a roughskin newt bathing in the afternoon light on the road. In season, elk and deer will step among the ferns, black bear will graze the berries and the bear grass down on Quaking Aspen Swamp. Bobcat, coyote,

and mountain lion will hunt the smaller mammals—marmot, rac-
coon, red squirrel, and marten, and beaver too, if the cats can find him
in his water fastness. Rufous hummingbird will plumb spring flowers;
blue heron, the "river monk" (1988, 60), will priest the shallows; chi-
nook will return to the headwaters of creeks where they were born.
Today it is mostly birds we see and hear: the helmeted and sky-blue
Steller's jay, the riversong of the varied thrush, the flash of winter
wren.

   "It saddens me to think that we are looking here at the last tattered
flags of the primeval world," Barry says, given over to the elegiac note
the country below us strikes in this light. There is faith here, generosity, but little hope—although a little may be enough. I sense in this
man, again, a great depth of sorrow, of anguish at what has been done
to the earth, to its people, by its people. His countenance and posture
are composed, right now, in the manner of the narrator of his story
"Upriver": he stands in "dismay and acceptance." I read grief and complete surrender in his mien, his open awareness of this place. He is
searching for hope, for something to heal what seems the despair, the
woundedness, that is native to him and this besieged forest, this remnant of the wild.

   At this moment, a single raven flies over us, silently, wide black
wings extended, the feathers at the tips splayed like fingers. She comes
down out of the second-growth woods, passes high between us, and
carries on in a stately trajectory over the ancient forest. As she goes, she
lets out a soft cry. I look at him and say, "Raven." He nods.

That night it rained at Finn Rock.
   In "Upriver," Barry's narrator explains that at the headwaters of
the rivers,

> ravens are meditating, and it is from *them* that the river actually
> flows, for at night they break down and weep; the universal
> anguish of creatures, the wailing in desolation, the wrenching
> anger of betrayals—this seizes them and passes out of them and
> in that weeping the river takes its shape. . . . Any act of kindness

of which they hear, no matter how filled with trepidation, brings up a single tear, and it, too, runs down the black bills, splashes on small stones and is absorbed in the trickle. (1979, 129)

And that night I woke now and then, in the room where I lay among books, to the soft fall of rain on the house and on the big-leaf maple and the fallen pine needles outside. Grief, forgiveness, elegy—the work of raven? The weeping of the earth that sustains this country of rivers, its nations of trees and birds and fish and mammals? Moist air rolling in off the Pacific and lodging, as it does, against the flanks of the Cascades? Any of these metaphors would be a way of observing, poetically or more plainly, one of the other characteristic gestures of this place: its rain, its moisture, and everything that condition gives rise to, in a man, in his work, in the quality of his walking witness.

If you read Barry Lopez's writing, you will find the deepest sorrow. You will find expressions of grief, often of forgiveness, rarely of anger. The order he discerns and elaborates so calmly, so elegantly in the places where he goes; the images of hope he always finds, even on a beach strewn with dying whales: these counterpoint his sorrow, the grief that sounds, all of our grief, within his prose.

There is always light suspended in his tall forests. It is somber and still, that light, subdued and indirect, except in a clearing here or there. Some of the trees are ancient and the shadows pool darkly around them. Inside his forests, however, you discover that you can move easily, that the space is generous and suffused with kindness. You can hear the silence between each river note, between each footfall and cry of bird. His paragraphs, too, look dense, forbidding, at first. Yet the light in his paragraphs, as in the forests, is as archetypal as a dream. It holds densest to the feet of the trees and the line of the streams. It feels timeless, eternal, like memory.

His sentences themselves are nearly weightless, though the images they carry, the thoughts suspended in them, weigh heavily with us. He composes woods hung with gentle air, strung with rain, haunted by the kind of dense wisdom that congeals in old standing timber.

"I stood for a long time at the tip of Saint Lawrence Island," Lopez wrote in *Arctic Dreams,*

> regarding the ice, the distant dark leads of water. In the twilight and wind and the damp cold, memories of the day were like an aura around me, unresolved, a continuous perplexity pierced here and there by sharp rays of light—other memories, coherence. I thought of the layers of it—the dying walrus moving through the chill green water, through the individual minds of the hunters, the mind of an observer. Of the very idea of the walrus living on, even as I ate its flesh. Lines in books about the walrus; walrus-hide lines tied to harpoons, dragging walrus-skin boats over the sea. The curve and weight of a tusk in my mind, from a head as dense with bone as a boulder. Walrus-meat stew is waiting back at the house, hot now, while I stand in this cold, thickening wind. At the foot of Sevuokuk, Lapland longspurs build their nests in the walrus's abandoned crania.
>
> Glaucous gulls fly over. In the shore lead are phalaropes, with their twiglike legs. In the distance I can see flocks of oldsquaw against the sky, and a few cormorants. A patch of shadow that could be several thousand crested auklets—too far away to know. Out there are whales—I have seen six or eight gray whales as I walked this evening. And the ice, pale as the dove-colored sky. The wind raises the surface of the water. Wake of a seal in the shore lead, gone now. I bowed. I bowed to what knows no deliberating legislature or parliament, no religion, no competing theories of economics, an expression of allegiance with the mystery of life.
>
> I looked out over the Bering Sea and brought my hands folded to the breast of my parka and bowed from the waist deeply toward the north, that great strait filled with life, the ice and the water. I held the bow to the pale sulphur sky at the northern rim of the earth. I held the bow until my back ached, and my mind was emptied of its categories and designs, its plans and speculations. I bowed before the simple evidence of the moment in my

life in a tangible place on the earth that was beautiful. (1989, 413–14)

These paragraphs teem with the life of images, some lovely ("the ice, pale as the dove-colored sky," "wake of a seal in a shore lead," the stew brewing nearby), some mournful ("the dying walrus moving through the chill green water"), some hideous ("the walrus living on, even as I ate its flesh"), some marrying the pretty with the ugly, the hopeful with the grim ("Lapland longspurs build their nests in the walrus's abandoned crania," "a head as dense with bone as a boulder"). All these scenes and thoughts Lopez draws delicately and starkly, simply. And among these images, these sounds and odors of stunning immediacy, he places some equally delicate abstractions. The sounds these abstractions make are angular, sharp, stark, and stern like trees or dark leads of water: memories holding like an aura, "a continuous perplexity pierced here and there by sharp rays of light"; "no deliberating legislature or parliament, no religion, no competing theories of economics, an expression of allegiance with the mysteries of life." These consonant-rich words and the thoughts they express may be the floor and walls of the storied spaces he makes and fills with the rounder sounds, the smaller forms, of one place on earth. Those sounds and shapes move within the infrastructure of his ideas, beneath its canopies, among the limbs of elegant thoughts, tall as trees.

This passage looks with equanimity, though not without love, on life and death. This passage of writing, like any place on earth where life is lived, includes beginnings and endings, tones of grief and notes of happiness, happenings and images both pleasing and distressing, simplicity and complexity, mystery and contradiction.

In the country of this passage, as in many passages of Lopez's writing, I feel that I am led outside profane time, into archetypal time. I can't explain fully why this is so, just as I cannot explain it when it happens in certain physical places: it is the work of the light and sound of that terrain (or text), its amplitude and shape and history, the way the terrain is limned, the way it draws me in. It is the power of his lyric voice. I notice how, in these paragraphs and elsewhere in Barry Lopez's work, he moves without our noticing between the present and the past tense, suggesting the eternal truth of a moment, slowing time to the order of geologic or deep time. He shifts from the near at hand to the distant in his focus; from the particular to the universal; from the tangible to the abstract—and back. I am certain these are not the devices of an author anxious to have us feel the effect he intends. They are qualities of a moment and a place he allows to live in his mind, to coax thoughts there, marry with them and take shape as text through the keys of his typewriter in an upstairs room in a riverine valley.

Lopez's prose is washed with sorrow in the same manner the forests about his home are visited by rain. It is the weeping of the raven, which rises out of grief and forgiveness and thanks; and it is the weather that comes in off the ocean to the land as it always has, and without which the place would not be what it is and would house no hope at all. The raven apprehends the world through his sorrow. Lopez, like raven, sees it in a somber light—the light of the place of trees and rivers where he has grounded his affections all these years. He has no prejudice against darkness: the place is like that. He moves at ease deep into what might seem to others gloomy territory. He makes his way toward high ground where there is prospect, to the very headwaters, the source of the streams, to open ground. He persists toward the light.

The land he has chosen as home contours his writing.

In *Arctic Dreams*, and in the essay "Landscape and Narrative," written in 1984 while *Arctic Dreams* was shaping itself in his mind and on the tables of his upstairs study, Barry Lopez fashioned a credo, a theory of storytelling in which he articulates how landscape molds human mind and character, and how story serves land, speaks for places, and heals disembodied human lives. Characteristically, Lopez draws his thinking from his time among indigenous peoples, the Navajo and the Eskimo particularly. In many indigenous cultures, he observes, "the land is thought to exhibit a sacred order. . . . Each individual . . . undertakes to order his interior landscape according to the exterior landscape. To succeed in this means to achieve a balanced state of mental health" (1988, 67).

For the Navajo, one's individual nature is always prone to disarray. Story and ceremony help one order one's life according to the "obvious (scientific) and ineffable (artistic) orders of the local landscape" (ibid.). Lopez himself holds that "the exterior landscape is organized according to principles or laws or tendencies beyond human control. It is understood to contain an integrity that is beyond human analysis and unimpeachable" (ibid., 66). Ritual—performed in ceremony, dance, art, architecture, and story—within indigenous cultures serves to invoke and is itself "derived from the perceived natural order of the universe"; the purpose of the invocation is to "make the individual again a reflection of the myriad enduring relationships of the landscape" and, hence, whole (ibid., 67). The purpose of storytelling, then, for Lopez, is similar: "A story draws on relationships in the exterior landscape and projects them onto the interior landscape" of the listener or reader. "The purpose of storytelling is to achieve harmony between the two landscapes, to use all the elements of story—syntax, mood, figures of speech—in a harmonious way to reproduce the harmony of the land in the individual's interior. Inherent in story is the power to reorder a state of psychological confusion through contact with the pervasive truth of those relationships we call 'the land'" (ibid., 68).

Any story that is true will then contain elements of land, of a known country. What orders that country orders the telling; or at least, the telling reproduces the order of relations alive in a place. But the place's harmonies do not enter the story, or reach the reader, without the disciplines of good storytelling: humility and attentiveness to the order inherent in the landscape, the patterns at play in this place; transcendence of self; a good ear; and the gift for choosing words that are apt, in their own form, for the land they engage with.

Even in "Landscape and Narrative," an abstract piece, Lopez holds true to the storyteller's art, beginning in a place, the Brooks Range, Alaska, in a setting where grounded stories of wolverine and other wild animals are being told. He is a man present in landscape, observing the order of things on the ground. Look at all his work, and you will find the ideas set out in "Landscape and Story" enacted over and again. His words are full of weather, hydrology, the flight of birds, the eloquent tracks of animals, the work and words of men and women, the anguish of wolves, the grief of streams, the sound of shifting basalt river stones, somewhere—and they seem to be both sound and also elusive, as places are, as the land is. From these elegantly limned relationships in the land he allows ideas to rise like fish to the surface of his mind; and he allows an intuited poetic order of place to tincture and illuminate the spaces made by the tender forms of his sentences, just like dawn on the land.

We need story, then, to reconcile us with land, in order to make ourselves and our societies authentic and enduring, as the land is. And we—all of us—need to come into intimacy with land, for there lies the lore of right relations, of beauty and justice. "The land is like poetry," Barry Lopez writes in *Arctic Dreams* (1986, 274), and we cannot do without a literature that attends to country, seeking its coherence, its embodied wisdom, and mediating between the land and us. Such writing discerns and reenacts the essential relationships that make a place what it is. And to write it, we're going to need a language lively enough to acknowledge, to explore and express our local places, a prose open to and therefore patterned by the local order of things. It falls to writers to find, to fashion, and articulate such a language— to reanimate the world for, and *in,* us all.

Lopez's emphasis on the almost sacerdotal role of the storyteller, who provides that necessary mediation between the land and its people, gives rise in me to a momentary concern. It may seem to follow that the land (and the wisdom within it, its immanent truths, its poetry) remains a closed book to people who do not have the gift for apprehension of the storyteller or the help of the *isumataq.* But his own body of work banishes that worry, for he tells us over and again that the earth is open to all of us, directly. The necessary work of the storyteller, of a literature of place, does not stop the rest of us from practicing ecological imagination all on our own. We may not all return with stories, but we can return to the land—and it to us. What counts is not who you are—priest or parishioner—but how you approach the rest of creation, the quality of the relationship you essay with the living world. What counts is how you come: as a pilgrim or an improver, to learn or to manipulate, to surrender or to possess.

Lopez holds that our minds and characters are shaped by places. In "Landscape and Narrative," he writes of an "interior landscape," "a kind of projection within a person of a part of the exterior landscape." This landscape comprises a set of relations, "the speculations, intuitions, and formal ideas we refer to as 'mind,'" whose

> shape and character . . . in a person's thinking, I believe, are deeply influenced by where on this earth one goes, what one touches, the patterns one observes in nature—the intricate history of one's life in the land, even a life in the city, where wind, the chirp of birds, the line of a falling leaf, are known. These thoughts are arranged, further, according to the thread of one's moral, intellectual, and spiritual development. The interior landscape responds to the character and subtlety of an exterior landscape; the shape of the individual is affected by land as it is by genes. (1988, 65)

So, as Lawrence Buell glosses this passage, "the contours of human subjectivity, as he [Lopez] sees it, are molded by the configurations of the landscapes with which a person has been deeply associated. Subjectivity is not a mere function of landscape; but it is regulated somewhat by landscape, and as far as Lopez is concerned landscape is the most interesting variable" (1995, 94).

It is clear from Barry Lopez's life's work, his way of being present in the land, as well as from these elegantly argued paragraphs of his, that he understands a man or a woman's life and work as arising from his or her natural history—not just that, of course, for cultural belief, genetic disposition, education and other things count in making us who we are. Natural history—which might even be understood to include such matters—gives rise to character and to the art, the stories, the characteristic syntax a man or woman may make. Merely *having* a natural history will not be enough, however, to open the genius of the place to each of us. An act of attention, of imagination, of spiritual engagement, of what Scott Slovic (following Lopez himself) calls awareness (1992, ch. 6), is required of each of us: the kind of surrender to land that Lopez depicts in the stories of *River Notes* and practices himself in *Arctic Dreams*.

I have seen this man give himself to a place with deep attention and vulnerability, respectfully and patiently. What seems to count is how we choose to be present in the land, how deeply and subtly we look. There is a practice of place, of ecological imagination, that each of us who wants to learn the land will need to work at, to live out.

In *Arctic Dreams* Lopez draws on the writing of the geographer Yi-Fu Tuan and concludes that "it is precisely what is *invisible* in the land . . . that makes what is merely empty space to one person a *place* to another" (1986, 278). Tuan is speaking of the way we find meaning in places through stories and memories of our own and our people's attachment to places; he is emphasizing the capacity of culture to bring meaning to space and make it "place." Lopez attributes more power than Yi-Fu Tuan to the land itself, one feels, than to memory and culture—how land enters dreams and stories; and how then those dreams recalled and stories shared, allow the place itself (in its authenticity, not as some cultural production) to arise, to become *visible* for others local to the place (and even others not native to the place, if these stories are well told). In other words, Tuan seems by *invisible* to mean stories notionally embedded in places and retold in song and ceremony, whereas Lopez means by *invisible* that coherent, ineffable identity expressed in the particularities and recalled in memories of places. While acknowledging the way that places to which peoples are attached are rich with cultural association, Lopez emphasizes the meaning-making power of landscape itself. There is an invisible order at work in a place. That is what gets remembered, reproduced, and celebrated in ceremony—and story. Barry's story-tellers discern that invisible order and enact it in narrative. What is called for—to discern this invisible landscape—is intimacy, imagination, a sloughing off of layers of self-reference, so that the being of the place might enter one, and one might enter the being, the poem, of the place.

Lopez knows this practice will elude most of us, particularly in these times when "no one remembers how to live anymore," as Blue Heron says in "Drought" (1979, 99); in these secular days, which disparage, marginalize, and fetishize, in advertising and nostalgic romances, the very idea of deep, poetic engagement with place. But a few of us, Blue Heron observes, have the gift, and perhaps others may learn from them. "For some people," Lopez writes in *Arctic Dreams,* "what they are is not finished at the skin, but continues with the reach of the senses out into the land" (1986, 279).

This is true, I think, of Barry Lopez.

But *none* of us is finished at the skin, according to ecology. Place and person intergrade, interpenetrate. Neil Evernden, in his influential 1978 essay "Beyond Ecology," quotes Paul Shepard as saying that the epidermis is "ecologically like a pond surface or a forest soil, not a shell so much as a delicate interpenetration" (Evernden 1996, 93). The skin of the perceiving self is like that too. The intermingling of person and place is to be understood, writes Evernden, as an aesthetic process, whereby place influences the perceiving self and the perceiving self helps compose place. Place and self are not distinct, not disjunct. Nothing in an ecology is discrete or entire—nothing except the place they compose, and even that coalesces with its neighbors. The writer who reaches out through sense and imagination to the place, Lopez is suggesting, opens the pores of the skin of the self that much wider to the place being witnessed.

Land affects us all, more than it is conventionally acknowledged. But land affects some people more than others—those like Lopez who give themselves to it out of love, out of an instinctive feeling that it is the land itself that holds, embodied in particular places, the answers. He reaches out to it with every sense; he is not complete at his boot-toes and fingers, and you will not have met him, seen his edges, until you have ranged with him up the rivers and ridges and into the trees, where he has set his life down.

In his essay "The American Geographies" in *About This Life,* Barry Lopez speaks of "local geniuses" of the American landscape, ordinary men and women steeped in their home places, "in whom geography thrives . . . for whom the land is alive." What distinguishes these locals is not so much the impeccability of their knowledge of names and details, but "the respect they bear these places they love. . . . Their knowledge is intimate rather than encyclopedic, human but not necessarily scholarly" (1998, 134, 138, 139–40). America, he says, "teems with such people"—as does Australia. The problem is that the commercial and political cultures of these places purvey faux national geographies, for reasons to do with markets, constituencies, and economic agendas, and the local geographies get missed. In fact, says, Lopez, the very enterprise of "discovering where one lives is finally disdained" (ibid., 137).

If this is so, what we need is a literature that celebrates that enterprise of becoming intimate with place, that finds and talks with those local geniuses, that lets the country and its wisdoms speak to all of us, that models a way of living close to land. Without it, the process of alienation from land is doomed to continue, and even those people—and perhaps that is all of us—in whom the ancient hunger of the mind for "concordance with that mysterious entity, the earth" persists (Lopez 1986, 278), will not recall the ways and words in which that journey of belonging is accomplished. We need stories that reenact geographies; and we need locals in whom geography lives, people not finished at the skin.

While I am with him—I think it is the first night—Barry plays some music on the compact disk player that sits on the floor. He has spoken of music a lot. He favors a spare and elegiac music, nothing lush or hard of edge, but melodic: sacred music, plainsong, Bach's cello suites, Keith Jarrett's jazz piano, Jan Gabarek's baleful saxophone, Arvo Pärt's works of despair and wonder. The music that moves him, I notice, comes clear and clean out of silence. It makes no compromise; it disdains fashion. It is superficially simple and repetitive, yet it contains complex chords, seems to carry an uncompromising light. It suggests intense thought and expresses the deepest feeling—often in a form like prayer, like worship.

He tells me, while Pärt's "Cantus in Memory of Benjamin Britten" plays, how Pärt, the Estonian composer, and his wife once came to Oregon. He, Lopez, went to meet them at the house they had rented on the coast. "Pärt's English is limited," he says, "so his wife had to translate for us. I told them how once I had returned to Ellesmere Island—where Adolphus Greely's party foundered in 1884, where the young Edward Israel died, where now an archeological dig was, to good end, dismantling an old Eskimo village. I told them how I had stood and grown overwhelmed at the hopelessness of ever finding words to speak of everything that had been lost in that place—those men's hopes, the way of life of the indigenous people who came before them. Sometime later I heard that piece of Pärt's for the first time, and I sat and wept. This piece of music says everything I felt in that place, but could not find words for. This is what I told Arvo Pärt."

Lopez is awake to how music can *adéquate* country—a space, a landscape, how one felt there. That phenomenon—the lifeworld of one's encounter with country, the music of what one discerned within the ineffable order that is a place—is just what he wants his words to articulate. Music can *be* just like what being in a place was. But so can a work of words. The musical order of the work or words, like that of a piece of music, can sometimes cohere or harmonize, he believes, with the order of a place on earth. Indeed, it may be above all the music of a place, its structure, its aesthetic—not only its soundscape, but the defining quality of the pattern of relationships at play there, between rock and tree and river, bird and animal and insect, soil and weather and human history—that a nature writer (or any writer, in Lopez's conception) is trying to divine; it may be that which sometimes finds its way into his or her prose, out of the silence (as Pärt has put it, speaking of the process of composing music), and carries to the reader in the music of the work.

For one's writing to sound out, even to sound *like*, the way a place felt, and how one felt, how one was changed, within it: this, for Barry Lopez, is to have written well. To know that even one reader felt about his writing as Lopez himself felt about Pärt's music—that would be to have succeeded beyond one's hopes, and to have served both land and reader well.

This musical impressionistic capacity of literature is what the critics Sherman Paul and Laurence Buell had in mind when they employed the poet Francis Ponge's word *adéquation* (Buell 1995, 86). At the heart of his exposition of what he calls a "nonfictionalist" reading of ecological literature, Buell argues that it is through those elements of a piece of writing that are, in a sense, most personal and least literal—through its voice and music, and what he calls its "stylization"—that a text can allow the reader an experience of the place very like the writer's encounter with it, of which she speaks in her work. A text might not only give evidence of but also *embody* something of the nature of its native place, by having a kindred sound, shape, quality, gesture—a "gestalt," as Buell puts it, that might impress the reader in much the same way that the place impressed the writer. To explain what he means, Buell uses Ponge's word *adéquation,* which was first taken up by Sherman Paul in his book *For Love of the World.* Paul defines the notion this way: *adéquation* is "a literary equivalent that respects the thing and lets it stand forth. *Adéquation* is not to be confused with *correspondence:* It is not a symbolic mode but an activity in words that is literally comparable to the thing itself" (Paul 1992, 19).

John Burroughs was talking about the same thing when, long before ecocriticism had a name, he spoke of how Walt Whitman's writing offered a "spiritual auracular analogy" of the land it spoke from. The poet managed, Burroughs was suggesting, to make his work sound like the spirit of the place from which he wrote (Burroughs in Mazel 2001, 36–37).

In *Arctic Dreams,* Lopez challenges what may yet remain the conventional idea among anthropologists, literary theorists, linguists, and postmodern theorists—that language is an entirely cultural artifact, a device we humans use to order the land and give meaning to it. Here is Lopez's response to that orthodoxy:

> I think there are possibly two things wrong with this thought. First, the landscape is not inert; and it is precisely because it is alive that it eventually contradicts the imposition of a reality that does not derive from it. Second, language is not something man imposes on the land. It evolves in his conversation with the land—in testing the sea ice with the toe of a *kamik,* in the eating of a wild berry, in repairing a sled by the light of a seal-oil lamp. A long-lived inquiry produces a discriminating language. The very order of the language, the ecology of its sounds and thoughts, derives from the mind's intercourse with the landscape. (1986, 277–78)

Lopez is speaking here of indigenous languages, which have evolved out of people's long relationship with their country. David Abram explores these ideas compellingly and in great depth in *The Spell of the Sensuous* (1996). It seems clear that not just words but whole language systems evolved out of particular places and people's intimate engagement with them; suggested themselves to people intimate with the ways of places by landform, weather pattern, wind and river sound. Sound out indigenous languages, like that of the Gundungurra where I live, the Wardandi of the Margaret River, the Hopi of America's Southwest, and you hear patterns of sound, cadences, that differ as the places differ; and you will hear the pitch and meter of those places in the words. Indigenous languages then arise out of intimacy between a people and a place. Words among them are still the daughters of earth (as Johnson thought was the case even for English in 1755); sentences are still the children of rivers;

paragraphs and stories the offspring of entire watersheds. Humankind learned language, it seems, from the run of rivers and the voice of wind, learned grammar from the logic of the land and the seasons. Though we write now in text abstracted from the living earth, still perhaps our words sound, if we let them, with what the wind and plateau have to say.

I wonder if we can extend the idea that place shapes prose from the context of the phonetic language systems of first peoples to the text of an individual writer, these days, a man or woman working with, say, English, the colonizing tongue, in country to which that tongue is not indigenous. Is it possible that a writer's relationship with a place, such as Barry Lopez describes in the passage I quoted, may order his language, shape the music of his text, influence "the ecology of its sounds," the nature of his syntax, and the structure and form of his work, so that we might find the work expressive of the country? Certainly a work that's heedless of the order at work in a place, that does not listen to it first, will give rise to no true sense of that place. It will ring false to it; the country will not live in it. In my introduction, I alluded to the failure of the Australian literature of place to express Australian geographies in this way, to speak as they speak, by listening to them. If it is possible to write without an ear for place and express next to nothing of its nature in one's sentences, is it, in contrast, possible, by listening, to let one's country shape one's syntax?

I can hear—and have tried to show—how "the ecology of sounds and thoughts" within Lopez's writing resembles the country he writes within, the landscape he has long conversed with. I sense how his "mind's intercourse with the landscape" has shaped a prose that is consonant with the ecology of that place. I have seen him lyrically disposed within his landscape, laying himself open to it and its rhythms. It is not only the landscapes of his childhood, his explorations, and his chosen home that have ordered his life, the country of his mind and writing, of course. But it would seem strange and inadequate to offer an explanation of the prose of a writer like Lopez—a man so unfinished at the skin, so awake to the ineffable order alive in the land—

that did not take account of his natural history, that did not look for correlations between his language's aesthetic and that of the land.

I find in Lopez's prose the timbre of two places in particular: the Arctic, the place he has written about most, and the McKenzie Valley, the place in which he has shaped most of his sentences. Like the Arctic, his best prose has an austere yet tender form, like reaches of shifting sea-ice singing, hauntingly, with yearning and grief as the dark sea moves beneath it; like the endless tundra decorated sparely with ground-hugging, windswept trees; like the "blue-black vault of the winter sky, a cold beauty alive with scintillating stars." He makes spaces with his sentences, he sounds and patterns them around you. But those spaces, though stark and stern, are not arid. Within them he places a delicately observed gesture (riffle of stream, trajectory of bird), expression (gaze of seal, howl of wolf, tatter of human conversation), or image (of cruelty or forgiveness), and so gives those spaces life.

And then, like the valley he lives in, the order of his language is dense and dark, temperate, elusive, washed by grief, draped with mist like a benediction, a gesture of forgiveness; it is angular, well rooted in good soil, so that it stands true; it reaches high to heaven like a Douglas-fir. It is stern, a little unbending, simple in form, from the outside, like a forest, but with a complex interior landscape; also like a forest, it is clustered and intertwined, sustained by sturdy structures (image and thought), harboring under a dark canopy soft and delicate forms (the hanging moss, the flowers and vines of the forest floor, the berries and the bears that eat them, the owls); it holds caves in which are hidden "certain mysteries"; it grabs at your passing feet, your racing mind, like vine maple and insists you slow to a more contemplative pace; it houses "that river monk, blue heron, meditating behind the lightning strike of his beak in a downwater pool" ("Trying the Land," 1988, 60); it runs with the rivers he has learned to listen to, on the beds of which he notices a rock loosen, turn, and settle again— rivers that have their source in the tears of raven, rivers whose running "is the weeping of the earth for what is lost" (1979, 66).

Notes of river, notes of desert, notes of ice, of tundra, of sand, of sea; notes of the forest's edge: these sound in the song of his prose. They sound also in his speaking voice, in his stillness and animation, his sternness and vulnerability, his kindness.

He is wolverine, its resilience and fierce intensity; he is crow, its lofty and ancient wisdom, its restless curiosity; he is blue heron, its meditative posture; he is McKenzie River, its lean and languid passage; he is beach, its conversation of shifting tide and steadfast shore; he is Douglas-fir, its rootedness in earth, its reach and talent for standing still. Imagine standing among animals in a sudden clearing in a forest, into which light falls, through which perhaps a shallow stream runs; imagine Wolf Prairie—to read a Lopez paragraph is to be in such a place.

> On the far side of the Thomsen . . . herds of muskoxen graze below a range of hills in clusters of three or four. In groups of ten and twelve. I sketch the arrangements in my notebook. Most remarkable to me, and clear even at a distance of two or three miles because of the contrast between their spirited, bucking gambols and the placid ambling of the others, is the number of calves. Among forty-nine animals, I count twelve calves. The mind doesn't easily register the sustenance of the sedge meadows, not against the broad testimony of the barren hills and eroded plateaus. It balks at the evidence of fecundity, and romping calves. The muskoxen on the far side of the river graze, nevertheless, on sweet coltsfoot, on mountain sorrel, lousewort, and pendant grass, on water sedge. The sun gleams on them. On the melt ponds. The indifferent sky towers. There is something of the original creation here. (*Arctic Dreams*, 1986, 44)

The formal note of "the mind doesn't easily register" sounds beside the personal note of "I count" and "I sketch." Diction and syntax combine conversation ("in groups of ten or twelve"; "among forty-nine animals, I count twelve calves"), science ("the mind doesn't easily register the sustenance of the sedge meadows"), and sermon ("broad testimony of the barren hills"; "there is something of the original creation here"). Some of these words are plain and familiar, others are antique or almost fussy in their precision *(gambols, fecundity, creation, testimony, pendant, sustenance)*. There is that decorative quality I was referring to, like the moss-draped trees, in the two long, complex sentences, in which a simple observation is elaborated and made ornate by the attachment of a precise description of the calves' movements and by the biblical reference to the hills and plateaus. The author's care for sound is betrayed by the syntax of the sentence that begins "The muskoxen on the far side of the river graze": no straight list of plants, instead a carefully phrased list—two percussive *ons*, two plants without that preposition, and then its repetition, to round out the sentence and sustain its rhythm. The dense and angular music of those three long sentences (none of which is as long as it seems), is given snap and irregular beat, the smoothness is unraveled, by the short sentences and sentence fragments strewn among them: "In groups of ten and twelve"; "The sun gleams on them. On the melt ponds. The indifferent sky towers." Sometimes the movement is limpid and gentle; sometimes it jolts us.

Here as elsewhere, Barry Lopez's writing employs blocks of patterned sound of differing lengths; it creates long musical phrases and short ones; sometimes it sustains a rhythm, sometimes subverts it. And what is their effect? All this stopping and starting? The slow, easy flow of surprising words and references, and then its abrupt dislocation (a parenthetic clause, some jarring punctuation, a sentence fragment); this admixture of familiar short words with less familiar longer ones; this blending of different tempi and tones; this combination of dense, complex structures and short, sunny, simple clauses—all this resembles a landscape of dense forest, of river and meadow. And it slows one down—slows time itself. The tempo of the writing is a largo. It stills you. It seems to put you inside mythic time. But there is lightness here too, a delicacy of tone. We are at the edge of the trees, out of the stern woods, standing in a sudden ecstatic moment.

If we are, it is because of his writing's music, made under the influence of places he loves. As Lopez was in those places, so those places are in his writing, and we, his readers, are then in those places too.

Lopez's writing at its best achieves a congruence of a musical nature with the place it concerns. His writing is a dance with the place it considers, a dance, also, with the place in which it is composed, and it moves to rhythms that we sense pattern those places. His best writing has a way, now and then, of getting places moving. Notably this is so in the landscapes of *Arctic Dreams*, where Lopez manages to write the frozen landscape into life, to render its dynamic space real, and then to dance with it. The book we read shapes itself between his own syntactical gestures of sacred dance and the world he animates around him. This happens in his early fiction, too, as Paul has noted (1992, 82), set in deserts and rivers of his close acquaintance; and it happens in many of the essays gathered in *Crossing Open Ground* and *About This Life*. Lopez's early stories, wrote Paul, are "essentially oral and performative. Their slow dance . . . is as much a sacred gesture as the dance of the herons in which the narrator participates" (ibid.).

In *Arctic Dreams*, thought Paul, Lopez returned in nonfiction to that earlier performative writing: "in surging prose, Lopez gives us an entire *ecos* in motion over geologic time, an intricate dance to the rhythms of life in all the spaces of the Arctic world" (ibid., 105). Each chapter takes its readers with him into the landscape—into the sky migrations of birds, into the cold deeps with whale and narwhal, across the tundra, over the ice pack with polar bear—and immerses us in those worlds recreated in the movement of his words. This is nature writing as a performance of, and with, a place; it is the kind of ecological apprehension and musical engagement with landscape that Paul Carter had in mind (see the introduction). It is *adéquation* in a dance of words.

Dance? Well, if not always a dance, Lopez's writing is at least a grave and shapely walk in the company of country. He moves in places; and because he moves, the places seem to move about him. I noted earlier how Lopez developed a characteristic technique in the essays collected in *Crossing Open Ground* and perfected in *Arctic Dreams*—he moves his narrator (that is, himself in a mode of careful contemplation) through the landscape, on foot mostly, or by truck, raft, boat, or aircraft, and he elaborates places out of that mobile observation. His landscapes seem alive and shifting, as any landscape is to an observer who does not stand still in it but walks or drives or rides or swims through it. Such a relationship with a place brings to light the truth that places are indeed never still; they are composed of sets of constantly shifting relationships, including the one between the moving witness and the landforms and lifeforms of that terrain. Places are dynamic, right down to the level of geology and atoms—everything is on the move, and those many movements, or vibrations, make a kind of complex rhythm of energies, a set of lifeforms at dance with each other, in dissonant and consonant patterns. Lopez's writing makes his places feel alive because he keeps his point of engagement with them mobile. This is one way in which he manages to set the "*ecos in motion*," as Paul puts it. It is an example of the kind of artistic relationship with places that Paul Carter advocates, in which the artist's work elaborates his or her dynamic relationships with a dynamic space, moving through it, not just standing and looking at it.

"This is an old business," writes Lopez near the start of his circumambulatory chapter "The Country of the Mind" in *Arctic Dreams,* "walking slowly over the land with an appreciation of its immediacy to the senses and in anticipation of what lies hidden in it" (1986, 254). And how do the rhythms of his body as he walks, of the country in motion about, and with him—how do they find their way into his syntax? Partly, I suspect, it is through the body's memory, the cells' recollection, of the syntax, as it were, of the occasion, of his being-then-in-that-place—which it recalls later, inside, in the act of writing it down. For the writing, itself, is a walk, not discontinuous with the first; it engages—not the feet but the fingers—in a walk across keys, stepping and dancing to make words and patterns of sounds. And on this second walk, the body might be imagined as reprising the rhythm of the first moving encounter, or making one of many possible variations upon it.

"I wonder what you might say the place of fiction is in all this?" Barry Lopez asks me, meaning in what I call nature writing, the literature of place. He asks, I suppose, because we have already spoken of the special role that falls to nonfiction, to the essayist; because in this house, by this water, he fashioned his early works of fiction and has fashioned many stories since; because he believes that storytelling, narrative—regardless of whether we call it fiction or nonfiction—performs the central work of knowledge-making and healing in our world;[2] because he has been moved and shaped, I am sure he would say, by some works of fiction (Charles Frazier's *Cold Mountain,* Cormac McCarthy's "Border" trilogy, Melville's *Moby-Dick,* the stories of Borges, for instance); and because, I guess, he has spent the last year or so at work on a collection of stories, an advance copy of which he has just put in my hands. I sense he feels I am overlooking the possibilities of fiction.

I answer that fiction by its nature seems to me to make more difficult the project of intimacy (between author and land, and author and reader) he has spoken of, but that in the right hands it may transcend that problem. Later, flying across America to attend a gathering of nature writers (including Barry himself), I read his new book, and I find in it such wonderful parables as "The Letters of Heaven," "The Mappist," and "Emory Bear Hands' Birds." And when we meet again at Harvard, I tell him I have begun to soften my thesis about fiction. It, too, may catch the land's wild music sometimes.

Back home, I have read again most of his stories. Most of those in his first two books are, I now see, exercises in emplacement. They are grounded fables, and they are works of astonishing ecological imagination. They stand, though, almost alone in Western literature in that way—they are things of their own kind, myths really, prayers to places, studies in the kind of humane and spiritual geography Lopez discovered in his early anthropological studies. In *River Notes,* Lopez wrote a book about the endeavor to enter into the being of a place—the

2. In "Landscape and Narrative," Lopez writes: "I am convinced . . . that these observations [about the capacity of narrative to achieve harmony between inner and outer landscapes] can be applied to the kind of prose we call nonfiction as well as to traditional narrative forms such as the novel and the short story, and to some poems" (1988, 68).

river, its bend, its life and history. This is a book of short myths of his own tender making, allegories, meditations: beautiful things, innocent as dreams, and as oracular in their storied way as fables. It is a better answer than any he gave me in conversation, perhaps, to the question "What is the nature of the nature writer's encounter with the land?"

In "The Bend," his narrator wishes to understand the life of the river at one of its bends, to know the heart and body, the gathered wisdom of that place. At first he engages science, hiring hydrologists and others to observe and measure the river. But he gains nothing but loneliness and illness from that interrogation. The detached, determined, secular inquirer falls ill from his attempts to plumb the place with equations. His obsession with the place holds fast, though, and he grows depressed. He takes to his bed, and in time all his notebooks turn to stone, grown thick with moss. Water starts to fall from them in the corner of his room, and he wakes to the sound of mergansers exploding into flight from them. After that, he rises and goes to the river and surrenders to it, sits by it and wonders and listens. In that posture of regard, that attitude of respectful observance, he finds the place revealed to him. The river makes itself known to him; he and it become one. He takes the measure of the water, finally, by abandoning measurement and engaging with it imaginatively.

The more he knows the place that way, its wildness, the less he stays merely himself. "For myself," he writes, "each day more of me slips away. Absorbed in seeing how the water comes through the bend, just so, I am myself, sliding off" (1979, 88). The story ends with his imagining that now, sitting thus with the river, he must look to a hawk in the air inseparably a part of that place, "like salmon or a flower" (ibid., 90). Rereading this story, I feel the arrogance, the lack of suppleness of my opinions about the limits of fiction. I wonder whether the problem lies less with its form than with its modern practice, for it has fallen out of touch with the wider world. I think, too, how far his stories are from mainstream fiction—not only in the amount of place that inhabits them but in his instinct and talent for ecological imagination. He writes fiction as though land mattered. His fiction is nature writing, too, part of the ancient discourse that hopes to embed us again in the wisdom of the land.

After our day out in the Cascades, I went down to the river below his house and sat on a seat Barry has set on the bank among red cedar and cottonwood and maple. I watched the river and took notes of the day; and as I sat, a bird I didn't know came skimming onto the water, stayed awhile on the moving stream, turning bottom stones with its bill, and later exploded into flight and left me. Back at the house, I described the bird and asked after its name. "That," he said, "was merganser."

Lopez wrote "The Bend" when he was twenty-seven, sitting out in front of his house. Having sat in what may have been the same spot and seen mergansers fly, I feel as though I've entered briefly into the life of that story and into its narrator's effort to lose himself in, and to, a place. I learned from sitting by a river and noticing a merganser's coming and going, and then from going away myself and reading a story Lopez wrote where I had sat, what it means to give yourself to a place as a storyteller must. This experience, quite unscripted, enacted the answer to the questions I still had in my pocket about why and how a writer goes to a river, or any place, and listens. The writer must not measure a place, but surrender to its rhythms, its river songs, sung in merganser and current and turning stone and drifting leaf and salmon. And that, I think, is how he would want it to be, how he would want me and all of us to learn: from the river itself, a little while in its company.

Months, not the many years that coursed by in the story, have passed. I look at my notes. They have not grown moss yet. These thoughts arise from somewhere among them like the merganser from the water, and the pattern of that experience, some meaning it held, now, only now, comes clear. "I hope your notes come together well," Barry Lopez wrote to me on my return home. Well, they come together chaotically, wildly; and yet they find a certain order, not altogether out of keeping with the order of my time with him, as though I have no part in organizing them at all.

Barry Lopez comes from a childhood of clear light and spare ground; he lives now in a place of subdued light and densely forested slopes. Between his past and his continuing present lie the reaches of the Arctic desert. His mind and his prose are touched by all of them, by the landscape he walks and writes in and by remembered lands and light where his life took shape. His writing, you would say, is austere and clear—it is a lighted forest. It is dense: it draws you in and holds you; it offers you more and more, the more you stay and look. Like a forest, there is great delicacy, as of lichen and moss and berry, within an apparently simple, somber form. The landscapes of his life play in his prose. In the lands he has loved as in his prose lie similar paradoxes.

Lopez is a man of sorrows seeking hope, believing in it and finding it despite everything. He finds light in the dark forest. He is a man with a gift for solitude and silence who feels deeply the virtue of community and intimacy. Each tree in a forest stands apart, full of its long unique history and its own intricate interior landscape; but a forest is defined by interconnection, by the touching and collaboration of trees and understory, of bird and fruit.

Lopez is a man apart, a man given to deep quietness, close and dignified. But he is also a man of fluid eloquence. There is in him the quality of the tall, standing trees, the low light—and also of the running streams, shaped, colored, and filtered by the trees through which they run, these chords, these cords, that bind the country, as he has called them.

He is a scholarly man mistrustful of scholarly abstractions; a storyteller of deep and careful learning. "Unlike the scholars," he says to me, "I am not interested in proving my theory; I trust the words and the sound of the thoughts on the paper. I am interested in the shapeliness of the ideas."

His is not an arid scholarship, but a grounded wisdom. It grows—

it grows strong and tall, anchored by deep roots—from ferment and shadow on a forest floor, reaching for light.

These paradoxes within him and his prose are the paradoxes of the forest, too. And they are the discords between the landscapes he has lived within, traveled in, and loved: sandy desert, Arctic tundra, temperate coastal forest.

The place he has chosen to live and write within is a space densely filled, elaborately articulated, richly inhabited, crowded with a dignified and gracious wildness. The invisible landscape articulated by the woods he walks is immanent within his thought and writing. The countries of his memory, of his home here, of his mind and of his prose, share some patterns and lore.

Sitting on Barry's couch, my back to the window and the river, I read from a book of Pattiann Rogers's poems, which Barry has pulled from his shelf and offered to me while he cooks. I come across this:

> By the twist of leaves
> In a forest of poplars, I understand how light is fractioned
> And born again in the aspects of your words.
> I listen like an eddy in deep water turning easily
> From one existence to another.
> ("Seduced by Ear Alone," in *Firekeeper*, 1994, 24)

Why do I read it first in the space of his house this poem that says what I have been trying to fathom?

"And then, of course, there is the great John Fowles," Barry Lopez says to me. And in this way, after dinner on a Wednesday evening in October, he introduces me, in his tidy cottage among wild trees, to a small book that helps me grasp Lopez's elusive nature, the protectiveness he shows toward his art, toward his perambulatory practice of attention, toward his husbandry of the wild everywhere.

In 1979 Fowles, an English novelist known for books such as *The French Lieutenant's Woman* and *The Magus*, wrote a book-length essay,

The Tree. "The first trees I knew well," that book begins, "were the apples and pears in the garden of my childhood home" (1979, 3). *The Tree* grows into a tough meditation on the nature of wildness, on the need for a poetic engagement with the rest of creation, the need for a transcendence of scientific method in our dealings with nature, and the need to rediscover in ourselves the green man or woman at the heart of ordinary experience, without whom we cannot hope to know nature anyway. Though his father cultivated orchard trees and espaliers in London's outer suburbs, Fowles writes, "I must confess that my own love is far more of trees, more exactly of the complex internal landscapes they form when left to themselves" (ibid., 25). He means that he loves best the wild woods and the rich communities of other plants and animals, left to get on with the business of being and creating in mutual dependence, free from human interference.

The wild woods embody an untamed, elusive, constantly creating, essentially purposeless, utterly immediate quality, writes Fowles—one that lives in us too but one we have learned to distrust. Just as ordinary experience is complex and wild and cannot be captured by sociologists, psychologists, and biologists, so all of nature—including the forest—is wild. Only when we learn to trust the wild in ourselves can we know the wild in the rest of creation, in the woods or any place. Fowles writes:

> Our fallacy lies in supposing that the limiting nature of scientific method corresponds to the nature of ordinary experience. Ordinary experience, from waking second to second, is in fact highly synthetic (in the sense of combinative or constructive), and made up of a complexity of strands, past memories and present perceptions, times and places, private and public history, hopelessly beyond science's powers to analyse. It is quintessentially "wild," in the sense my father disliked so much: unphilosophical, irrational, uncontrollable, incalculable. In fact it corresponds very closely . . . with wild nature. (ibid., 36–37)

We might understand our capacity—increasingly deeply buried or sublimated these days, says Fowles—for complex and immediate apprehension of the world, and of each other, as the wild or green man (or woman) within us, of which many mythologies speak: the man in the trees. But to know nature, to live poetically, to know oneself deeply, Fowles discovered, is not to abandon intellectual engagement with it. "Achieving a relationship with nature," Fowles writes, "is both a science and an art, beyond mere knowledge or mere feeling alone" (ibid., 39). It does not lie in meditation, escape, or the quest for self-improvement. It seems to lie in a knowing, discerning, yet unmanipulative state of being present. That, writes Fowles, is the state of nature and the state of artistic creativity in men and women.

But we must not imagine that we will ever render such a state of presence, of immediate apprehension, of wildness, in words, he continues. To attempt to capture nature in a book is to try to "capture the uncapturable" (ibid., 33). He makes these remarks within a critique of the way systematic, analytical scientific method has become the dominant way of knowing, and indeed of writing about, nature. Then he goes on to elaborate what he sees as another epistemology—a wild way of knowing, the way of the artist. A certain way—that reductive, scientific way—of approaching and reporting the experience of nature will, it is true, fail to express the nature of nature itself, and the true nature of a wild engagement with it. The experience of presence in a place exists only in that moment; when we sit to write of it, it is gone—this also is true. And equally it is true that the piece of work that responds to a place is not itself the place, is different from it, is its own thing.

But Fowles's own work, and that of Lopez and others, contradicts him on this point: the wild may be written, if not "captured." It is not beyond words or art, though it is beyond science, with its genetic parsings and Linnaean systems. What counts is the degree to which the creation of the words—and the experience of the place that comes before it—happens in that state of being Fowles calls wild. It is possible—as Barry Lopez's writing shows—that a wild encounter rendered wildly may produce a work of art in which the way the artist felt, and the way the place felt, are truthfully contained, are alive. Sometimes a reader may encounter a piece of writing in much the same way the artist encountered the wood, and it may affect him or her in a way at least analogous to the way the place affected the writer. Just how that happens may not be fully understood—it is necessarily mysterious, like all artistic and natural processes, writes Fowles; but it does happen. It has happened for me, I believe, many times, reading Lopez and the other writers here.

What Fowles may be warning us against is the temptation, as writers, to attempt anything other than a truthful expression of what we are moved to write of a place—of anything, for that matter. Just be present in the woods; then be present in the prose. Wild writing, true art, must never be purposive: it must intend nothing other than the truthfulness of its own process of creation. It must simply be, just as the wild green chaos of the trees simply is.

Often in person, often too as the narrator of *Arctic Dreams,* and strikingly in the "I" of *River Notes,* Lopez is the man in the trees, the green man, the wild wisdom of the earth embodied. In *River Notes* his narrator is strange, does odd things—or so they seem unless you imagine him as the green man. He is in nature, utterly; he is part of it, sinking into sand, dreaming he is salmon. His "I" is like Whitman's "I" in *Leaves of Grass:* not just all men (and women), but that part of all men and women that remembers the earth from which we all rose. He is writing and speaking, on many occasions, from inside the *ecos; he is* nature, writing. What is strange and unmanageable in his writing is not him, the narrator, but the wild itself. For the aesthetic of Lopez's writing is not conventional, its order not merely human. It will not be known and named. It includes chaos, for without that nothing new is made, life itself may not proceed.

At the point of creativity, when he is most the green man, the man in the woods, it *is,* I suspect, those woods, the land, its genius and amplitude, that shape his art, because the disjunction between him and them is bridged. His writing, if you like, is the ground between the

interior and exterior landscapes he lives in; it is the song of their reconciliation, a dream he shares with the place.

When I read Fowles's book a month after my visit with Lopez—in the
Library of Congress, and then (the last twenty photocopied pages) on
a plane flying from Washington, D.C., to Denver—I discovered the
same prickly resistance to academic inquiry into the writer's relationship with nature that I met in Lopez. For both of them, literary analysis of their work is part of that conventional, reductive, classifying
enterprise epitomized by the scientific method (ibid., 31–32). I have a
sense now that both men, Lopez and Fowles, are at pains to shield a
mystery—the act of creativity, the encounter with the wild—from an
inquiry framed too narrowly, that interrogates in arid and inadequate
language, that is premised on the idea that everything can be understood best only when it is seen in isolation from its context. Fowles
reminds us that the wild green man "possesses the characteristic of
elusiveness, a power of 'melting' into the trees" (ibid., 38). You may,
these two men seem to be saying, come to know me and my works
only in the wildness and chaos of the woods (physical and psychological) where I live. You may not abstract the wild green man from his
trees and still know his nature. It seems to me that, like the green
man, Lopez retreated that night, faced with my inquiry and its academic sound, from the edge of the woods, where we were in his house,
to the woods' dark green, obscure heart. Where I found him most truly
was within the trees themselves, the birthplace of his words.

It strikes me now, too, that a forest, such as the one Lopez lives on
the edge of, keeps the wild—the ferment at its feet, the complex web
of biotic relationships within it, its secret life, its hidden landscape—
canopied and walled off from all but the initiated, the well-guided
searcher. The mystery and darkness and danger of the forest deter
and defeat the inquirer not prepared to set down his literary and
scientific presumptions. This quality of the woods also imbued the
words with which he met my interrogation of his art, and it imbues his

written prose, for it too is like a forest, in this way—in it one finds a guarded, stern (if also elegant and courteous), indirect, and elaborate articulation of the thoughts, the deep, deep thoughts and emotions, he knows.

Fowles's rich, small book takes me to another secret at the heart of Lopez's thought. We go to the woods and wild places, we cultivate reciprocity with them, we practice love and humility in those parts of the world men have not made or manipulated, not only for the sake of those places and their integrity, but for our own human sake. The wilderness is as necessary to our spiritual health as a species as dreams are to our mental health. How we treat the forests is how we treat ourselves and all our fellow men and women. "There is a spiritual corollary to the way we are currently deforesting and denaturing our planet," writes Fowles. "In the end what we must most defoliate and deprive is ourselves" (ibid., 78–79).

Lopez writes in a similar vein that what we learn when we "pay attention to what occurs in a land not touched by human schemes, where an original order prevails," is what integrity looks like (1986, 405). All the relationships at work in untrammeled places are innately dignified, not always good or beautiful, but ordered authentically. For this reason we need them, and we need to respect them. We need then to cultivate such integrity in our own lives, to make relationships with our fellow men and women marked by the same "impeccable integrity" and to extend that dignity to all living things. All writing and all living, in Barry Lopez's natural philosophy, as in Fowles's, should pursue this "oldest dream of mankind": a just and dignified order among all living things on earth (ibid.).

As we drive in Barry Lopez's truck (I am recalling now the day of my arrival) up the McKenzie River valley out of Eugene toward home, we pass field after field of neat orchards beside the road, south, by the river. It is afternoon in late autumn, and the light is thinning. In my memory now, the orchards run in dark, orderly geometries, away from the road. The ground at the trees' feet is trim with grass, gray with the onset of evening, and most of the leaves have fallen. Some of the trees I have never seen before. They are filberts, he tells me, when I ask. They grow them for the nuts. He says no more.

Later, at his house, he hands gives me a copy of his new book of stories, *Light Action in the Caribbean,* one of the advances sent to him by the publishers. The book will not be out for another two weeks. I am touched by the gesture. That night, while he prepares our meal, I sit on the sofa and I read the first story, "Remembering Orchards." It is about a man, a printer, who lives up a river valley in western Oregon and passes filbert orchards each day on his journey to and from the town. Just lately he has experienced two moments of mundane epiphany as he drives past them, and those moments, in which, in a certain light, he apprehended the wildness, the chaos, the beauty of these herded trees for the first time, have led him to a belated understanding of his stepfather, a man who tended orchards in California.

The narrator confesses that, as a boy, he viewed his stepfather's orchards as "penal colonies" and could only see in his stepfather's work an obsession with order. He understands, suddenly, and long after his stepfather has died, that he missed altogether the meaning of the man's work and his relationship with, his affection for, the trees. "What I saw as productive order he saw as a vivid surface of exquisite tension" (2000, 4). What his stepfather had responded to most deeply was not the system but the chaos beneath. "The trees were like sparrows frozen in flight, their single identities overshadowed by the insistent precision of the whole. Internal heresy—errant limbs, minor inconsistencies in spacing or height—was masked by stillness" (ibid., 5).

The coincidence of my noticing the orchards and then, later, my sitting here and reading this story struck me only afterward. No one planned all this. I am sure Barry Lopez intended nothing so obvious as to make plain to me the passion within his steady craft, the chaos and wildness within the order of his courteous lines. But life sometimes delivers small surprises, mundane in themselves, in a meaningful cluster, which weighs with us and seems to hold significance, which asks us to stop and discern a story embedded in it. And I feel the weight of significance even more because his story quotes Robinson Jeffers, cautioning us not to miss the depths that make a life beautiful because of its apparent calm now; and because the narrator, when he experiences his first epiphany, has just been typesetting the *Maximus Poems* of Charles Olson—two men whose poetic project has been compared with Lopez's own (by Sherman Paul [1992, 101]). That shared project is this: to show that ego will not lead us to the truth, which lies deep in native ground, and the things that grow from it. It strikes me, too, that "Remembering Orchards" is an oblique homage to Fowles's *The Tree*, an essay on the love of wildness that grew from the memory of a father's orchard.

Thinking, months later, about my sitting there, reading "Remembering Orchards" under those circumstances, I am led to reflect that the story that runs through a man's life and work may not surrender itself easily; that appearances can deceive; that the world itself—a play of light among trees, the landing of merganser—can sometimes offer up, unbidden, the answer to our questions (mine, for instance, about Lopez, his work, its nature and its process), an answer more useful and meaningful than any that might be given under interrogation. And so, on reflection, I think I see in these small events a storyline that speaks a caution against simple-minded inquiry—against subjecting something so elusive as the nature of a man's art, the nature of a whole literature, to narrow intellection. If Barry Lopez was anxious that I might grasp too narrowly, using conventional terms of analysis, that I might abstract and diminish the craft of men and women like himself, who enter into the living world and bring forth words—he was right to be anxious. Many have done that. Each of us is given to haste.

But his place, and his stories of it, tell me that all the elegant work of his hands is not an ordering of the wild but an act of love for it, an affectionate partnership, a courtly dance with the mysteries we live among. If there is an art that practices selflessness and ecological imagination, that reawakens us to the life of the land, and the land to us, that shows us how we might, through love and attention, restore ourselves, in imagination, to the dignified, unmanipulated order of life into which we were born, it is the art of Lopez's prose. As the wild lives among the filbert orchards, as the yet unbroken watershed of the McKenzie sustains and finds orderly expression in those trees, so the wild breathes in the words of Barry Lopez and moves in the rigor and beauty of his life.

3 The Long Coastline

PETER MATTHIESSEN

Sagaponack, New York

The tides are in our veins, we still mirror the stars, life
is your child, but there is in me
Older and harder than life and more impartial, the eye
that watched before there was an ocean . . .
Mother, though my song's measure is like your surf-
beat's ancient rhythm I never learned it of you.
Before there was any water there were tides of fire, both
our tones flow from the older fountain.

Robinson Jeffers, "Continent's End"

The restlessness of shorebirds, their kinship with distance
and swift seasons, the wistful signal of their voices down
the long coastlines of the world make them, for me, the
most affecting of wild creatures.

Peter Matthiessen, The Wind Birds

"It's too late for nature writing," Peter Matthiessen said at a conference
in New York in September 2001. We have lived to see days, he went on,
when corporate thinking and consumer behavior rule most of the
world; and there is no room in their logic for nature. "You have to be
an activist-ranter now, and a pain in the butt."[1]

1. Speech to first U.S. Resurgence Conference, quoted in Suzi Gablik, "Morning
Glory," *Resurgence*, no. 210 (Jan./Feb. 2002), 60.

At about that time, Matthiessen was bringing to an end a book he had been working on for a decade, *The Birds of Heaven,* a study of the world's cranes (the stately birds of the genus *Grus*). It is a lyric and stringent celebration of these heavenly birds; it is also a well-argued defense of wildness in the world. It is, in other words, a piece of nature writing, and a good one. When I read his New York remarks, a year or more had already passed since I had visited Matthiessen and seen his cranes manuscript on the screen of his computer. His words made me reconsider everything I am concerned with in this study; made me stop and think twice about the value of a literature of place, about the place of my own writing, and about the worth of his. Is it too late for *The Birds of Heaven?* Is it too late for nature writing?

If it is too late for *The Birds of Heaven,* I suspect it is too late for all of us. For this is beautiful writing—hopeful, stirring, honest, wise. We will always need such literature. We need it for the same reasons we need the cranes themselves: to remind us of the beauty we may lose, in life and in literature, if we cannot take the time to care for what counts.

Matthiessen is often called a nature writer, and has always spurned the label. What he rejects is a kind of writing we have all properly lost patience with: pastoral, romantic nature appreciation without bite. But nature writing was never merely that, not when it was any good. And Matthiessen's writing—whatever we call it—has always been good. Including his nine novels, the book of cranes is his thirtieth book. At its best, as in a few passages of the new book, his prose is painstakingly made, musical, rich with detail, precise. Its characteristic note is heartbreak laced with anger, recollected in quietness. He condemns atrocities and he witnesses miracles; he goads us to attention and calls us to action. Good nature writing does that. That's why we need it.

"Who cares about cranes?" a neighbor asked Matthiessen on his return to Sagaponack in late summer 1992 from research in Siberia. *The Birds of Heaven*—the entire body of his work, really—is his answer. If we cannot care for cranes—beautiful in themselves, holy in the imagination of men and women, travelers of the earth, gifted singers, inhabitants of marvelous geographies—then we are lost. "If one has truly understood a crane," Matthiessen writes, "one has understood every-thing." If that still needs to be said—and I suspect it always will—it is not too late for nature writing. It is, I think, why Matthiessen bothers to go on writing, instead of confining himself to "activist-ranting," something he also does well, something he was doing (no doubt ele-gantly) at the Resurgence conference that September. There is a future for Peter Matthiessen, there is a future for nature writing, as long as there is a tenuous future for the cranes and long coastlines of the world, as long as we care for the wildness and austere beauty they express.

"Sons and daughters of Thoreau abound in contemporary American writing, if we can believe the reviewers," wrote Edward Abbey, one of the literary progeny, himself (1979, xx). One of those he had in mind was Peter Matthiessen, whom he dubbed "the Thoreau of Africa, South America, the Himalaya, and the wide, wild sea" (as opposed to Edward Hoagland, "the Thoreau of Central Park and also Vermont"; Wendell Berry, "Thoreau of Kentucky"; and Annie Dillard, "Thoreau of Vir-ginia," whom Abbey believed to be the "true heir"). Of Matthiessen, Abbey went on: "I cannot forgive him for writing *The Snow Leopard, Far Tortuga,* and *At Play in the Fields of the Lord,* that strange, green, haunting, and lovely novel" (ibid., xx–xxi).

Today, anyway, a dull gray Thursday late in October 2000, I take to the open road to find Matthiessen, Thoreau of the South Fork. I come to him out of Harvard, where I've been at a gathering of nature writers, poets and essayists and ranters, an assembly of other Thoreaus (Bill Kittredge, Laurie Kutchins, Barry Lopez, Bill McKibben, Richard Nelson, Carolyn Servid, Pattiann Rogers, Annick Smith, and Terry Tempest Williams, among them); and I come to Peter Matthiessen out of Concord, a week after I stood in that com-pany, in weather as hushed as this, at Walden Pond, the source of this literature for which, Matthiessen tells us, it is now too late.

I find, after much circling about, route 95 out of Boston, and I point my hired car southwest toward New London, Connecticut. Then the car and I take the ferry from New London to Orient Point on the

North Fork of Long Island and on, via two more short ferry crossings, to Sagaponack, on the South Fork, where Peter Matthiessen lives. Matthiessen has had to put up with a reputation as a kind of Thoreau-on-the-Road since he drove west with a box of field guides from his home on Long Island in the late 1950s and returned with that requiem to a wilderness lost, *Wildlife in America,* which was published in 1959. He has been traveling all the years since, far afield from Long Island, indeed all around the world; and, since 1960, he has been returning here, to a house set back from the ocean shore at Sagaponack, to write what he finds in the high and low, the deep and far places of the world. In the same house behind hedges where I find him, Peter Matthiessen has for forty years been turning his travels in the wild places into prose—into novels and an array of more and less literary nonfiction—of deep feeling and lyric power. "He is," wrote a reviewer once in the *New York Times Book Review,* "our greatest modern nature writer in the lyric tradition."

"Our greatest modern nature writer," who thinks that nature writing has had its day, has let me drop by for a couple of hours' conversation and a bit of lunch. I know he can hardly spare the time, working as he is to finish his book of cranes against a pressing deadline and the approach of his own winter migration.

His Thoreauvian reputation dismays Matthiessen, McKay Jenkins writes in the introduction to *The Peter Matthiessen Reader* (1999, xii), and of course it is a trite commentary on an unequaled literary achievement, a body of work that speaks of deep independence of mind, determined literary ambition, and the service of a cause much larger than anything so merely personal as a reputation. The cause I have in mind is the defense he has made so eloquently, beginning with *Wildlife in America,* of wildness and authenticity, wisdom and honor in the world of men and women and the wider world of all beings. But Matthiessen is an emphatically outdoors writer, a wanderer, and a fearless prophet—so the label sticks. His writing, too, is Thoreauvian (though it bears other comparisons and draws on other sources) in a stringency and integrity, in its experimentation, its muscular lyricism, and in its eloquent rage at the diminution of life, of wilderness and wonder, being wrought by unrestrained commerce all over the world.

But he is, above all, his own man; not Thoreau's, nor anybody's, heir—though, ironically, it is in this way more than any other that he may be seen, in life and in literature, as a modern Thoreau. His deepest commitment, like Thoreau's, may be to personal integrity, self-determination, and the authentic life—for himself, for each of us, for places and animals and marginal cultures.

I am not going to meet Peter Matthiessen, though, because he may be Thoreau's heir. I am going because his writing stirred me before I found the writing of many who have come after him. It helped me find my subject matter; it helped me recognize my cause; and it encouraged me to find a voice, if I could, that was as honest and strong. Like Abbey, I found Matthiessen's writing strange, haunting, and grand.

I am going because his work and life have, to some degree, inspired the writing of some of the other writers in this book. Early in his career, Barry Lopez took himself to Sagaponack to visit Matthiessen. He recalls that visit and pays homage to Matthiessen in his essay "A Voice" in *About This Life*. Matthiessen remembers it too, and speaks of it when I am with him. Terry Tempest Williams, when I visit her in late November, acknowledges Matthiessen's influence and her admiration for his work. In her essay "A Patriot's Journal" in *An Unspoken Hunger,* she goes to hear him speak against the war in Iraq, in early January 1991 at the American Museum of Natural History in New York. That night, Matthiessen told a crowd that the part of the American mind that wants war is the same part that can't abide wilderness. Apt words still—another American war against Iraq drags on as I write. In her essay, Williams (1994, 108) quotes some of Matthiessen's words—a gentle, powerful rant: "'It's about an empathetic intelligence,' he said. 'Issues of peace and issues of the environment are rooted in a sacredness of life.'" Both war and the human assault upon the wild offend and disdain, he said, the sanctity of life. The lives of all beings warrant awe and wonder—not shock and awe. Williams's tone, describing this speech, is reverential. She depicts the two men that Matthiessen is: the naturalist-writer and the peace warrior.

Peter Matthiessen's work has also changed, I think, the tide and current, the tone, of nature writing. Matthiessen, now approaching his middle seventies, began writing in the late 1950s. So he stands on the divide between an older era of the literature of nature and a new one, which runs through till the present moment. Something new—a sensibility more overtly political, more concerned with indigenous and traditional wisdom, less formal in its diction, a temperament more modern—began in the field with *Wildlife in America.* And it changed the genre. Although his work carries echoes of older writers, it also stands apart from them. It seems to me to stand at the beginning of the literature we think of as of our own time because it speaks in a modern voice about the concerns—loss of diversity, degradation of habitat, decline of indigenous human cultures, retreat of wildness, the ecological and human costs of rampant global capitalism—that preoccupy us now. His writing seems to make a transition from old-style literary naturalism to an edgier, politically engaged, spiritually charged nature writing. This has happened partly, I guess, because he has written so long, from the 1940s right up to the present day. But there is more to it than that. He modeled for a postwar generation a prose that danced with the *ecos,* to use Sherman Paul's term, and yet did so in the literary vernacular of a new era, in sentences as cool and lyrical as anyone else's from the Beat generation. He is the archetype of the engaged writer of the ecological age.

His life and work allude to older forms and yet belong with and seem to inspire newer ones.[2] He marks the passage between, on the one

2. You could say the same perhaps of John Hay, but he is not so much a modern in his style as Matthiessen. John Haines, a man close in age to Matthiessen, writes a prose and a poetry of powerful, elegant modernity, yet his life has been more hermetic, less forceful in its symbolism than Matthiessen's. Wendell Berry, another writer of Matthiessen's vintage, has inspired the writing of many younger writers, but his work belongs less clearly than Matthiessen's to the modern era. It is

side, John Burroughs, Mary Austin, Henry Beston, Joseph Woods Krutch, Rachel Carson, and Aldo Leopold, whose work, though beautiful and eternal, now sounds out the music of a former time; and, on the other, Edward Abbey (who shares Matthiessen's birth year of 1927 but whose influential writing began to appear later than Matthiessen's), Annie Dillard, Barry Lopez, Terry Tempest Williams, Richard Nelson, Linda Hogan, Bill Kittredge—and all the other Thoreaus of the baby boom. His prose, like the shore, belongs to two realms. His body of work is a littoral zone, where the literature of place has remade, and keeps remaking, itself.

The sustained accomplishment of his writing, his rare literary voice, his undying commitment to social and environmental causes, the vigor of his fieldwork, and the rigor of his research: all this has helped, over fifty years, to keep the genre of nature writing alive—even, to some extent, sexy—and its standards high. But all along, Matthiessen has been reluctant to call himself a nature writer. "There can be something self-indulgent about nature writing," he told me over the phone the first time we spoke. And self-indulgence sits high on his list of personal and literary vices.

The range of his work—novels, travel and place essays, nature studies, two books on Native American issues, a book on Zen Buddhism, and books in defense of endangered tigers and of the fishermen of Long Island—clearly extends beyond "nature writing." But he loves the wild places and the lives of animals, and all of his books are alive with them. He is a writer who takes the natural world as seriously as he takes anything. Read his prose—fiction and nonfiction—and you will know the nature of some places on earth, their people, their other lifeforms, their vulnerabilities and pulses. This is what one would like all nature writing to be. A reader wants—in nature writing, and some of us would like it in everything we read—to get a feel for the world

---

unapologetically old-fashioned, and admirable enough for that. Its voice is prophetic and nostalgic. Matthiessen may not be alone on this threshold, then. And yet he stands apart.

to which the words allude. And we do in Matthiessen's books. Not only that: we hear his own heart's beat; we encounter his mind's fierce engagement with the world.

He is a writer, then—among other things, a nature writer, shy (like Lopez) of the name. But he is a writer who has very often put his craft to the service of those that cannot speak—disenfranchised peoples, threatened places, and endangered wild animals. Matthiessen has wandered pretty much from the start, going far beyond the civilized world to which he was born, to find the wild places, and himself within them; to find the voiceless people and to find his voice among them. Peter Matthiessen came into the world in New York City on May 22, 1927, the second of three children of Elizabeth Carey and Erard A. Matthiessen, a Manhattan architect, who became a director of the Nature Conservancy. Peter Matthiessen learned to walk on Madison Avenue and Sixty-fifth Street. He went to school at St. Bernard's in Manhattan, and later to Yale and the Sorbonne. But he inherited more than good manners and good looks, and he carried from a privileged childhood more than a good education. He learned at home an orientation to the wild, and he got from his father, perhaps, the gene for serving the world, for conserving the land, and for speaking out. He began writing early, at school and seriously at college, and found that it suited him; but before he found his calling as a writer he had discovered the natural world. On childhood vacations at Fisher's Island in the mouth of Long Island Sound, down in the Florida Everglades, and on the family property in Pennsylvania, he entered the world of the snakes and the birds and the fish. And he has never really left. If he had not become a writer, the only other thing he would like to have been is a marine biologist, like his brother. He would like to have known intimately the life of the sea and the character of the long shorelines of the world.

Nearing one o'clock, after an hour's passage across the sound, I find a phone booth at Orient Point and tell Matthiessen I am close. He gives me detailed directions to his place, but I find it hard to get them all down: the wind blows my page about, and I have to keep feeding coins into the phone, cradling the handset against my shoulder. My road lies east to Greenport, then south to Shelter Island on a small punt; from Shelter Island on another ferry to the South Fork, and on across dry land to North Haven, Noyack, and Sagg Road to somewhere close to Sagaponack. I lose my way at the point where my notes petered out, and I double back to a gas station outside Sag Harbor, where I am sure they'll know who Peter Matthiessen is and where he lives. But they don't. They've never heard of him. And why should they have? They run a gas station, not a bookshop. Matthiessen has only lived nearby for forty years. And he's not someone famous like a movie star, a politician, or a basketball player. He's just America's greatest nature writer in the lyrical tradition, a reluctant literary hero. Clearly it is much too late for nature writing, here. Or too soon. But the guy knows where Sagaponack is, at least, and he sets me on a course across fields of potatoes toward it. And quarter of an hour later, I find the lane where Peter Matthiessen lives in a house behind a privet hedge.

The book by which most people know Peter Matthiessen—*The Snow Leopard*—unfolds high in the Himalaya, deep inland and far from the sea. There, on his pilgrimage for hope, his search for the fabled, the actual, snow leopard, Matthiessen finds some ammonite fossils that speak of a time when these highlands lay deep in a restless sea. Many of his other books also rise from firm earth (much of it, like most of the earth, also once under water)—*The Tree Where Man Was Born, In the Spirit of Crazy Horse*, and *African Silences* among them. But the sea, the "wide wild sea" and other kinds of moving water, are rarely far away in his writing. Many of his books, most of his journeys, his life's work and passions, walk the shores, swim the rivers, negotiate the estuaries and the swamps of the world. Some of his books are spawned like striped bass upriver, or they are born and raised in the tideline, along one of the sandy reaches, the unquiet beaches, where land and ocean give themselves up to each other. Water—river and ocean— runs strongly through his body of work: *At Play in the Fields of the*

Lord, On the River Styx, The Cloud Forest, Under the Mountain Wall, Blue Meridian, Far Tortuga, Men's Lives, The Wind Birds, the Mister Watson trilogy, *Nine-Headed Dragon River,* and even his latest book, *The Birds of Heaven.*

Matthiessen's first nonfiction book, *Wildlife in America,* though it tells the natural history of wildlife across all of North America and its sad decline, begins with a longboat putting out to sea from an Icelandic shore, to take the lives of the last great auks: "In early June of 1844, a longboat crewed by fourteen men hove to off the skerry called Eldey, a stark, volcanic mass rising out of the gray wastes of the North Atlantic some ten miles west of Cape Reykjanes, Iceland. On the islets of these uneasy seas, the forebears of the boatmen had always hunted the swarming seabirds as a food, but on this day they were seeking, for collectors, the eggs and skins of the garefowl or great auk" (1959, 19).

The shore, more than any other terrain, is the distinctive territory of Peter Matthiessen's writing. Even when he isn't writing *about* the beach, when he isn't evoking that meeting ground of water and earth—that edge where he has lived and written many long years—the tidal zone sounds in his words and in the ideas he shapes with them. The marriage of the soft and hard, the steady and the restless, that which holds us here and that which speaks of elsewhere—those moods and ideas, those qualities of a place—the shore—pattern much of his writing.

For the character of the shoreline—land's edge, sea's end, place of ending and beginning, of wreck and launch—is the geography of Matthiessen's prose; it supplies his prose's meter, its ebb and flow, its elegiac weather. He is steeped in the life of this shoreline from his years fishing in a dory off the Sagaponack beach, his long years since surfcasting and beach-walking, studying the lives of the shorebirds, researching the social and natural history of the South Fork fishermen. It shouldn't surprise us, then, if his prose sounds like the shore. Its note is like the sighing of the sea wind, like the sound of waves falling and receding.

That tone plays through this passage, for instance, from *The Tree*

Where Man Was Born, a book set in the deserts of Sudan, far from the sea but made of sand and haunted by birds:

> Night had fallen by the time the truck had cleared the city, and a spray of stars froze on a blue-black sky. The vague track wandered south into a soft emptiness of cooling sand, haired over thinly, here and there, by bitter thorns of drought. In the headlight's jogging beam danced ghostly gerbils, hopping and fluttering on tiptoe, like stricken birds. And farther onward, close to midnight, where the sands relented, came the birds of night— the African owl, and nightjars, and pale Senegal stone curlews whirling straight up into the dark like souls departing. (1972, 2)

That timbre sounds again in the lines that open his novel *Killing Mister Watson,* a book set, this time, on the shore:

> Sea birds are aloft again, a tattered few. The white terns look dirtied in the somber light and they fly stiffly, feeling out an element they no longer trust. Unable to locate the storm-lost minnows, they wander the thick waters with sad muted cries, hunting signs and seamarks that might return them to the order of the world. (1990, 3)

What we hear, in both cases, is Matthiessen's voice; and it is the sound of the shore, an element he trusts, a place of his long acquaintance; it is the music of the meeting of his mind and the winds at the ocean's edge. What we hear is the tonal character, I imagine, of their conversation, the sea and this man. It is wise, sad, quiet with grief, alive with the knowledge that life and death are two parts of one thing, in constant ebb and flow. This is the sound of the wisdom of the shoreline. Peter Matthiessen's writing, at its best, holds steady like the beach, but it is strung with intimations of distance and depth, just as the beach is with kelp and the bodies of mussels; it is visited, in the sound of crashing surf or the voices and motions of migratory shorebirds (plovers, turnstones, sandpipers, oystercatchers), by the songs and rumors of far places and times long ago. It speaks always of a deep repose and always of longing and long journeys. His prose expresses the same tension the beach does—that his life does—between what holds and what is never still, and it surrenders this paradoxical truth: the things that seem eternal to us—the ways of men, the bodies of continents, the mountains—will always, in the long run, fade or fail, while the things that seem impermanent and elusive—the tides, the migratory patterns of the birds, the changeful winds, ancient truths—will most likely endure and prevail. The duality of the shoreline, the meeting and accommodation of contrary worlds, warring worlds, neither of which is what it seems—this duality lives in Matthiessen and his work; this is the tension that quickens his writing and his being. He is a man who practices meditation and a man who argues without mercy or stint for wild things, for noble, dying cultures, for dignified ways of life that are edging toward extinction because of how the first world wants to live.

He is a man who rages against the complacent realms of established power, while he pursues stillness in his own life. He rants, and he intones peace; his sentences, his sometimes dense paragraphs, go on and on, in ebb and in flood, in doubt or wonder or conviction, in relentless pursuit of some far or forgotten shore, and then surrender something sublime, and rest—and move on again to continue their questing. As the shoreline marries the dour and the delicate, the violent and the pretty, the recurring and the fleeting, the masculine and the feminine, the yin and the yang, so does Peter Matthiessen's prose. It is composed in a cottage on a fish-shaped island anchored just off the coast of American's industrial northeast. And on the long coastline near the house, the eternal drama of wave and beach, and the ancient—and faltering—engagement of men with the sea, continue daily. Like the wind birds, Matthiessen flies from this shore every year to distant places; but here, every year, he returns. His tales are often of elsewhere, but his voice on paper belongs to the shore, just as the voices of plover and sandpiper, curlew and godwit belong to it, though they carry within them the music of the far places and the distances they've traveled. For to belong to the shore is to belong both here and elsewhere at once.

Matthiessen's prose, though grand and sonorous, is not showy. It does not flash or sparkle. It makes a restrained and deep-voiced music, like cello and oboe. In *The Wind Birds*, he writes this passage about the tones and gestures of some of the shorebirds, and it strikes me, as I read it again, how aptly it describes his own writing:

> The pervasive monotones of bare terrains, encouraging cryptic markings, have made the wind birds rather subdued in plumage, and such bright color as they have is usually found in leg and bill; even the avocet, American oystercatcher and ruddy turnstone are more striking in pattern than in hue. But inevitably, a thing well suited to its surroundings—a snowflake, a sailing ship or a spoon—acquires a true beauty of refinement: the soft dove-brown of the buff-breasted sandpiper, the sun color of the golden plover, the warm leaf tones of the woodcock are essences of earth and grass, of cloud shadow and the swift seasons. (1973, 42–43)

The beauty of Matthiessen's best writing, too, lies in its refinement, and its characteristic tones might well be described as "essences of earth and grass, of cloud shadow and the swift seasons," its colors as "soft dove-brown" and "warm leaf tones" warmed fleetingly by sun. Through it all runs a "pervasive monotone" of bare terrain, like a didgeridu—or again, the cello. And every bowing, every phrase, is made with restraint. Plainsong, wind song, the cry of bird carried on the breeze, wave beat—this is how his prose, at its lyric best, sounds. When, after lunch, we are walking in the fields behind the shore, Matthiessen tells me he can no longer find the place where the lyric prose of *The Snow Leopard* came from. He says this calmly, in that very voice I have just tried to name in his writing. If what he says is true, we could forgive him after thirty odd books and five or six master-pieces. I think it is true that none of his recent writing achieves the perfection of pitch, the elegance and rightness of rhythm of *The Snow Leopard*, *The Tree Where Man Was Born*, and of his best novels. Perhaps the old music is nearly spent. But this passage from *The Birds of Heaven* suggests that it has not gone out of him utterly. This writing may not be as lean and plangent as his best paragraphs from the seventies, but it is in the same register, and it carries, I think, his signature: restrained celebration, hard-headed mysticism, elegy, all articulated in long, undulant sentences, their syntax demanding, yet original and carefully enacted:

> On a rare clear morning—the first day of summer 1992—flying across the Bering Strait from the Yukon delta toward the Diomede Islands and the Chukotskiy Peninsula of Siberia, I imagine the gray sun-silvered strait as seen from on high by a migrating crane, more particularly, by the golden eye of the Crane from the East, as the lesser sandhill crane of North America is known to traditional peoples on its westernmost breeding ground in Siberia. The sandhill crane commonly travels a mile above the earth and can soar higher, to at least twenty thousand feet. . . .
>
> That cranes may journey at such altitudes, disappearing from the sight of earthbound mortals, may account for their near-sacred place in the earliest legends of the world as messengers and harbingers of highest heaven. . . . Every land where they appear has tales and myths about the cranes, which since ancient times have represented longevity and good fortune, harmony and fidelity. . . .
>
> . . . The cranes are the greatest of the flying birds and, to my mind, the most stirring, not less so because the horn notes of their voices, like clarion calls out of the farthest skies, summon our attention to our own swift passage on this precious earth. Perhaps more than any other living creatures, they evoke the retreating wilderness, the vanishing horizons of clean water, earth, and air upon which their species—and ours, too, though we learn it very late—must ultimately depend for survival. (2001, 3–4)

It is two o'clock when, late for lunch, I knock on Matthiessen's door. The skull of a whale, six feet across and silvered by sea and salt air, sits on the verandah—it is the one he hauled from the sand at low tide under the moon in December 1984, down here at Sagaponack, as he was finishing *Men's Lives*. Matthiessen lives on six acres in a clapboard house, three hundred years old. Within the privet borders, along with the house, are an old stables, converted now to serve as a meditation hall, and a small cottage, restored in the 1970s, where Matthiessen writes.

Matthiessen greets me kindly at the door and invites me in. He wears old blue jeans, an old black pullover. His face is deeply lined. His hair is coarse and well on its way to white, and it looks like it has the weather in it. Today's, specifically. His eyes look gentle and steady, gray but full of light. At seventy-three, he carries himself like a man of thirty. Though I am feeling awed by him, it is not because of how he behaves; he seems simply interested to meet me, anxious to show me hospitality. He takes my coat and hangs it on a peg. The floor of the house is made of large flagstones, and the walls are made of timber. The ceilings spread white and low: it is a house built when men and women were shorter, and it seems hardly to hold him. Its spaces are long, its shapes lean. It is both austere and comfortable, full of books and papers, like a hermit's cell grown too large. The tones of this house he has lived in over forty years and lovingly restored from its original ruin are gray and white and brown, colors of the earth, essences of the beach and sea and sky. Nothing flashy; the beauty of refinement.

His wife is upstairs working. "Maria couldn't wait for lunch," he says in apology. "She's in the middle of things." He leads me into the kitchen at the back of the house and joins me in a bowl of soup—tomato and cauliflower, sharp and tasty. He cuts rye bread and toasts it. He hands it to me on an ironstone plate and comes and sits opposite me at the long wooden table. He talks easily, lightly, without affectation, and asks me as much—about my writing and the place where I live, about my wife—as I ask him. We mention his British publisher, Christopher McLehose at Harvill, whom we both know. "He is a very good editor," says Matthiessen, then corrects himself: "I should say *publisher*—he's a man of letters and a good businessman." He takes care with his words, even in lunchtime conversation. When I remark that one thing that distinguishes McLehose is that he makes a point at

Harvill of employing brilliant editors, he adds, "And very pretty, too." Which is true.

"Do you want to take a walk?" he asks when he sees I have finished my soup and toast. He suggests we walk down to the beach to feel the wind. The day has grown colder, and the wind is up. He makes sure I have a hat, that my boots are sturdy and my coat warm; he rugs up himself, calls to Maria, and we leave the house.

In the mid-1950s, before he settled here, Matthiessen lived in a small cottage on Fireplace Road, near the Springs, a little to the northeast of Sagaponack. He lived there with his wife and young family after having spent a few years in Paris. He worked three summers as a commercial fisherman on haul-seine crews off the beach of the South Fork, and he captained a charter fishing boat in the sound and the ocean. In the cold months he wrote and hunted on shore. When that marriage came to an end around 1956, Matthiessen moved out of the Springs cottage and set off to research *Wildlife in America*. "For the next four years," he writes in *Men's Lives*, "I was traveling to remote corners of the Americas, from Alaska and the Yukon to Tierra del Fuego, and I rarely visited the South Fork" (1986, 153). It was on his return to the South Fork after the publication of that book that Matthiessen found the house where I find him.

Wildlife in America, his first nonfiction narrative, came after two novels, well reviewed but unremunerative. *Wildlife*, a chronicle of extinctions, a tale of declining diversity, a ballad of poisoned wilderness, met with wide acclaim. It got read. It opened some eyes to the ruin civilization had visited on American wildlife. And it made him some money. He paid thirty thousand dollars for this property, he tells me. Now a single acre here goes for one hundred thousand dollars.

His house sits in a pocket of the South Fork still called Smith Corner. Matthiessen's acres and all the land in the vicinity were originally owned by Richard ("Bull") Smith, who settled here after his exile from Southampton for sins that included the illegal felling of trees for profit. As we walk, Matthiessen points out the original family home of

Richard Smith, which stayed in the Smith family until the present generation, when his descendants caved in to soaring prices and sold it off. It was Smith, I guess, and those who followed him to the flat lands of good soil between Wainscott Pond and nearby Bridgehampton to the north, who opened the country up thoroughly for farming; who cleared the scrub-oak moraine—denuded it in places that had been farmed and kept lightly timbered for generations by the Montauks, its indigenous inhabitants. Smith and the settlers planted wheat, and then, when the American Midwest cornered that market, they moved into potatoes, corn, strawberries, cabbage, and other crops. Potatoes have dominated since the beginning of the twentieth century. Sagaponack takes its name, as does nearby Acabonack, from the Montauk word for an edible tuber (the ground nut, *Apios tuberosa*), which they cultivated and gathered in both places (Matthiessen 1986, 154n.1). The Montauk, long before the coming of Smith and the others, "dressed" these fields for cultivation with tons of menhaden, a local fish. The sea and the land here have been informed by one another since time began.

On the lane, Matthiessen talks me through the natural history of the ground at our feet, ground he loves, whose wounds he feels. *Men's Lives* (1986, 157ff.) includes a short description of the overfarming, the remorseless development of the lands about Sagaponack, the impoverishment of the ground and wetlands, the decimation of the fish and bird life through the fifties and sixties. It is a dismal and familiar tale: pesticides and fertilizers leach into earth and creeks, pollute the water table, slow the fish and thin the crabs and kill the birds who feed on them. The spawning grounds of marine animals, the nesting grounds of seabirds, are lost when wetlands are filled and oil spilled. Small local farms fail against huge agribusinesses on the mainland, and then surrender to the influx of city folk.

The decline of the fisheries and the loss of livelihood of the proud baymen who worked them is, of course, the story that book narrates. The tale and the telling are pure Matthiessen: a mournful, precise, heartbroken recital of the waning magic of the world—the dying out of humane skills and good, hard work, of customs that cannot withstand what is called "progress."

Men's Lives was fashioned from long interviews with members of the old fishing families, from Matthiessen's usual careful research in libraries, and from his own memories of fishing in dories from the shore of Long Island in the fifties. It reads as an accomplished piece of social history and recollection, sewn together with lyric threads. It is a quilt of memoir, advocacy, evocation, oral history, and journalism. And the seams show. While not in the first rank of his work, it remains a fine book, a more literary thing than the two Indian books *(In the Spirit of Crazy Horse* and *Indian Country),* for instance, or the book on the tigers of the east. Like them, *Men's Lives* is a book written more to serve a cause than as a piece of literature. He has worked at its prose, I think, more carefully than in some of his other pieces of functional nonfiction; he has crafted it with more love as a piece of art, perhaps because the country he describes is his homeland, and the people whose livelihoods he defends are his friends and neighbors. But still, compared to his fiction or *The Snow Leopard,* it is—as he himself has conceded about much of his nonfiction—"a utilitarian object," not a work of art (Matthiessen 1999b, xxii).

Matthiessen once told an interviewer, Kay Bonetti, speaking about his "political" nonfiction, including *Men's Lives,* that although he did not regret writing those books, "I don't have any illusions about [their] literary quality. . . . They are not as good as *The Snow Leopard,* or *The Tree Where Man Was Born.* They're not. And I could have made them good. But I couldn't make them good from a literary point of view and accomplish my purposes of social justice. It's very difficult to do" (quoted ibid., xxv–xxvi). He sells their virtues short. They are better books than he implies, and *Men's Lives* is the best among them.

It is interesting that he dichotomizes and feels a conflict between the kind of writing you do for social justice (nonfiction, in his case) and the kind you do for its own sake. Clearly his best writing, including some of his nonfiction, pulls off both: it is art *and* argument. But in his mind, fiction is for art, and nonfiction is for causes (including the making of a livelihood). Fiction is literature, labored over, fastidiously crafted, emergent and mysterious. Nonfiction, for him, is functional, no matter how well made. It is, as he puts it, a cabinet; it is for holding things. Only in fiction (and, Matthiessen adds, in the literary nonfiction he wrote in the seventies) does he work, as he puts it, "like a sculptor," polishing and polishing (ibid., xxii).

When I first spoke to him by phone in early 1999, Matthiessen firmly distinguished between his fiction and his nonfiction. "I only wrote nonfiction to pay my way," he said dismissively. The distinction matters to him. He wishes to be known as a writer; and it seems to him that the true work of the writer is fiction; that fiction is the only true literature. Though I may think this view is false, though I might argue that not only is some nonfiction literary, but it is in fact, in lyric mode, more akin to poetry than most novels are; and though I might hold up two at least of Matthiessen's nonfictions as evidence, these are my views, not his, and I keep them to myself. There may be some regret— certainly there is some feeling—lurking inside his disparagement of nonfiction. For his works of nonfiction outnumber his novels by nineteen to nine (though nine novels alone in a lifetime would satisfy most writers). He has spent, you see, most of his working time making cabinets when he would rather have been sculpting. This is a source of tension for him, I gather. It is a paradox that frustrates him, a polarity that defines him.

When Matthiessen, in 1956, took to the road to see what was left of America's wildlife, he did it not just because it mattered to him, but because he thought it might make him some money. And he was right: *Wildlife in America* sold in large numbers. It also touched the lives of many readers, becoming almost as influential as Rachel Carson's *Silent Spring*, which appeared a couple of years later. Then, through the 1960s, to buy himself time to write novels (*At Play in the Fields of the Lord* and *Far Tortuga*), he traveled widely at the expense of magazines, mostly the *New Yorker*, turning out for them fine travel essays, which found second lives as books—*The Cloud Forest, Under the Mountain*

Wall, Sal Si Puedes, Blue Meridian. In this period, he also wrote *The Shorebirds of North America*—another book that was published first as a set of essays for the *New Yorker.* Compared to the books that were about to follow, *Shorebirds,* along with the travel books of the sixties, feels like fine journalism heightened by a few poetic moments.

And then came the seventies, when he found that lyric vein and mined from it two extraordinary works of nonfiction—surely works of art, transcendent cabinets. *The Tree Where Man Was Born* (1972) was short-listed for the National Book Award, and *The Snow Leopard* (1978) won it. (His most writerly novel, *Far Tortuga,* belongs to this decade too.) He worked on these lyric essays as hard, finished them as carefully, as his fiction. And in the two decades that followed, though he traveled far and wrote many things, including the two Indian books, one of which wound him up in lengthy and costly court pro-ceedings, the work that claimed most of his artistic attention was his fiction trilogy, *Killing Mister Watson* (1990), *Lost Man's River* (1997), and *Bone By Bone* (1999a), books set in—and wonderfully evocative of—the Florida Everglades.

Although Matthiessen's fiction is very fine, and clearly more care-fully composed, more literary in ambition, than most of his non-fiction, still, there is much of his nonfiction that is manifestly written with an ear for the rightness of its music as well as an eye for the accu-racy of its content. We may read the best of it as the work of a writer—as literature. It is less finished, but it is not unfinished. Read through the selections McKay Jenkins has made from Matthiessen's nonfiction in *The Peter Matthiessen Reader* (1999b)—open it at any page and choose a paragraph at random—and you will find nuanced, lean, musical prose. And his nonfiction has one advantage over his fiction: his first-person presence, his voice. Even where he has dashed it off, his nonfiction speaks straight and true out of Matthiessen's immediate perception of the places and people he stands with, out of his acute awareness of the texture and character of things, out of his intimate participation in the world. And it speaks in his voice. It has the tim-bre of his own response, with body and mind, to the places he engaged with. In his fiction, despite its deep resonance and fineness, I find myself missing the intimacy of his nonfiction—missing him, in fact: his own voice, patterned by the place he writes in and loves.

For Matthiessen is above all a witness. His is a lyric rather than a narrative sensibility. He writes out of his own experience, not merely about it. He notices and gives expression to the world. He writes out of an engagement with a world he knows to be animate. He is not a fabricator of stories—at least not chiefly. In his travels, he is avid for the details that articulate and the structures that compose the place in which he moves, and in composition he takes care over the musical structuring of phrase and sentence, paragraph and section, so that his writing expresses some of the very structure of the world he witnesses. His gift for structure and detail is more profound, I think, than his gift for story making. His best works of fiction—*Far Tortuga* and *Killing Mister Watson*—are masterworks of structure and voice and color, not of plot. They are more like poems than conventional novels; they are symphonic, piecing together as they do fragments of story and shards of perspective to compose a whole work, cutting and pasting pieces of melody, as it were, to make dynamic, complex, though unified pieces of prose. They are lyric works, in the same way that his best nonfiction is also lyric, the product of "an avid resolve to turn over every rock" in self and place (Voigt 1999, 178).

But in Matthiessen's best nonfiction, this lyric sensibility is more purely and powerfully present. And therein lies the deep satisfaction of those works. It is *himself* and the sound of the world he has witnessed that one shares. It is the lyric of Matthiessen's own engagement with the world. The voice of his conversation with the way things were just there, just then.

Damaged and diminished though it is, Long Island's ocean shore is Peter Matthiessen's home. I can hear his pride and delight in this place as he recalls it for me. The place has a longer history than its fifty years of decline at the hands of progress, and he tells some of it as we walk under a white sky.

A full eighteen inches of loam covers the island, he explains. The glacier that shaped the whole of the northeast of America pushed all this good black soil here and left it behind, when it receded. Think what a paradise this must have seemed, he says, to all those settlers from Kent. All this deep black soil and good trees. Along with oaks and elms and alders, white pines covered the island when the white men and their families came. They took all the pines, all the old growth, for shipping. Their wood is straight and tall and supple—perfect for ships' masts. The pines will return, Matthiessen says, if they are allowed to, but they are nearly all gone now.

Just past Richard Smith's house, still among the trees of the lane, I pause, my eye caught by a gathering of headstones in the winter grass. "Oh," says Peter, "that's our cemetery. Deborah's over there." He points to a stone, the whitest, near the back. The way he puts this, without fuss or sentiment, brings to mind the way he first speaks of her death in the prologue to *The Snow Leopard*. At the end of a series of dense paragraphs describing his preparations in Kathmandu for an expedition with George Schaller to the Crystal Mountain, Matthiessen mentions a bazaar where, a dozen years before, he bought a bronze Buddha for his new wife. And then he writes one last sentence, like the final, restrained but heartbreaking stanza of a long poem: "My wife and I were to become students of Zen Buddhism, and the green bronze Buddha from Kathmandu was the one I chose for a small altar in Deborah's room in the New York hospital where she died last year of cancer, in the winter."

This revelation and the line of space that follows it explain the tone of foreboding that hangs over the closely packed paragraphs that open the book. This sentence says what cannot be said. This sentence lets us peer with him for a moment into the well of his grief. It launches the pilgrimage that follows. Yet Deborah's death is so quietly noted in this sentence, as though it were just another detail in his preparations for departure—as Peter's gesture toward the headstone now is just another detail he wishes me to know about the geography of Smith Corner.

". . . In the winter." The first time I read that phrase, with the comma that precedes it like a sob—I wept. Plainspeaking sometimes captures the thing itself and delivers it to a reader pure and true and full of that moment's native emotion. Matthiessen has the gift of such speech. Like the poet, he is able to make the vernacular strange and substantial again.

I stop a moment. There lies Deborah Love Matthiessen, the woman he first met in Paris in 1950 and then met again in 1960, on the beach where we are headed; whom he married in 1963; and with whom he lived a tortured and beautiful life in this place—for a while.

We walk on down Bridge Lane, toward the sound of the ocean. We climb the shoulder of the dunes. A cold onshore breeze, laced with salt and sand, hits me and takes the breath out of me. We walk down a path onto the beach. The Atlantic rolls in against the shore under the wind, its sets flat and uneven. Up the beach, five or six fishermen have cast their lines into the surf at a point where herring gulls dive after a school of fish.

The shoreline runs away into the afternoon. It is lean and long, a beach without a curve. I am used to the yellow crescents of Australia's southeast coast and the white ones of the west. He has seen those beaches too. Australia has some great stretches of sand, he says. But what is remarkable here, on his home beach, is the reach and linearity of it. The beach stretches in a dead straight line all the way from Montauk Point to Saltaire and Long Beach—almost to Manhattan. In reality, he goes on, this is an extension of the beach at Cape Cod; this is part of one long reach of sand, breached long since, made discontinuous by the endless insistence of the sea. This is part of what was once—and, being composed of sand, it was only ever a temporary arrangement between land and sea—an almost interminable shoreline. I see the long coastline—this vestigial one and that which preceded it—disappearing into the northeast. I can see how the form of this beach, its provenance, its lifestory, still astonish him quietly. This remnant of a once even longer line—an argument with the sea never quite won, a resistance to its advances never quite achieved—is vital to him. Its improbability; its persistence. He looks up and down its length as if for the first time, and I look with him—at the long shore of his home, its white sand gray in this low light, its dunes grassed and wind-blown. This shore is elemental and austere, in the way of all beaches, only in this case pushed to an extreme of liminality and sustained like a chord.

He shows me where he found the skull of the finback whale in the tideline, a story he tells in the preface of *Men's Lives.* The battered skull itself, his finding it and hauling it home, what he makes of it in prose—these are all pure Matthiessen. The finback is the second largest living thing, after the blue whale, that has ever lived on earth. What Matthiessen found in the winter evening, washed by the ocean, sinking into the sand, was the wreck of a wild and beautiful lifeform, an almost enchanted thing. What he found was the ruin of something—something like the natural world he knew as a boy, or the commercial fishery he worked along this coastline as a man—something once so large and flush with life that its death was unimaginable. Yet here it was washed up, hollowed out, upon the shore. The skull stands in Matthiessen's book and in his mind for the fate of all wildness on earth, the doom that befell the old days and hangs over us all. "The world is losing its grit and taste," he says to me. When we return from the beach, Peter shows me the skull on his verandah. He stands grimly inside the whale's gape while I take a photograph. Neither of them smiles.

But the whale's skull stands not only as a gritty epitaph for wildness. Its appearance to him, a gift of the sea, and his hard work to haul it home—these speak also of the cycle of birth and death and rebirth that is the natural world. He fishes something profoundly dead from the sea and makes of it an elegiac song of life, of resistance, and continuity.

> On December 4, 1984, finishing the first draft of these journals,
> I walked down to the ocean for a breath of air. The day was cold,
> with a northwest wind shivering the rainwater where ice was

broken in the puddles. Rising and falling in flight along the dunes, a flock of gulls picked up the last ambient light from the red embers in the west. The silent birds, undulating on the wind, shone bone white against massed somber grays, low over the ocean; the cloud bank looked ominous, like waiting winter.

From the beach landing, in this moody sky and twilight, I saw something awash in the white foam, perhaps a quarter-mile down to the eastward. The low heavy thing, curved round upon itself, did not look like driftwood; I thought at first that it must be a human body. Uneasily, I walked east a little way, then hurried ahead; the thing was not driftwood, not a body, but a great clean skull of a finback whale, dark bronze with sea water and minerals. The beautiful form, crouched like some ancient armored creature in the wash, seemed to await me. No one else was on the beach, which was clean of tracks. There was only the last cold fire of dusk, the white birds fleeing toward the darkness, the frosty foam whirling around the skull, seeking to regather it into the deeps. . . .

. . . Fearing that an onshore wind or storm might bury it forever, I went down at dead low tide that night, under the moon, and dug the skull clear and worked it up out of its pit, using truck and chain. Nearly six feet across, the skull was water-logged and heavy, five hundred pounds or better. Not until one in the morning—spending more time digging out my truck than freeing the bone—did I hitch it high enough onto the beach to feel confident that the tide already coming in would not rebury it. By morning there was onshore wind, with a chop already making up from the southwest, but the whale skull was still waiting at the water's edge. Bud Topping came down with his tractor and we took it home. When Milt Miller, who was raised by old whalers, had a look at it a few weeks later, he said it was the biggest skull he ever saw. (1986, xv–xvi)

In this passage, notice the large gestures of place (the cloud bank, the "waiting winter"), the delicate strokes (gulls' flight, the wind in the ice, "frosty foam"), the still and slow and hushed (the skull itself, the dunes, the "silent birds," the moon), the moving (the tides, the wind, his digging to free the skull, his departure and his return under the moon), the nostalgic ("the last ambient light from the red embers in the west"), the spacious and weather-worn ("massed somber grays," "dark bronze with sea water and minerals"). Here is a shore passage awash with the shore.

Set against this the start of Matthiessen's novel *Killing Mister Watson* from which I quoted above. The novel's opening is more thoroughly worked for sound and effect perhaps, but not much more than the preface of *Men's Lives. Killing Mister Watson*'s beginning is rich with sea smell and shore mood, bird habit and tide note. Its light—that was a much more humid, southerly shore—is antique, gray, and somber, and the air broods. The novel begins in the wake of a hurricane, and the tone of the passage, the nature of the space it creates, is not merely austere, in Matthiessen's usual way, but outright bleak, as befits the moment; its sounds are hushed, "muted." Listen to the cadence and melody, the resonance of phrase and vowel ("brown spume and matted salt grass"; "on the bay shores and down the coastal rivers, a far gray sun"), in this passage, the second paragraph of the book:

> In the hurricane's wake, the labyrinthine coast where the Everglades deltas meet the Gulf of Mexico lies broken, stunned, flattened to mud by the wild tread of God. Day after day, a gray and brooding wind nags at the mangroves, hurrying the unruly tides that hunt through the broken islands and twist far back into the creeks, leaving behind brown spume and matted salt grass, driftwood. On the bay shores and down the coastal rivers, a far gray sun picks up dead glints from windrows of rotted mullet, heaped a foot high. (1990, 3)

And into this scene, this patterned shoreline singing silently, comes (by foot and by water) human life. To the shoreline come two people to pick among what the sea has strewn there, to read what the ocean has told the land:

> A figure in mud-fringed calico, calling a child, stoops to retrieve a Bible, then wipes wet grime from the Good Book with pale

dulled fingers. She straightens, turning slowly, staring toward the south. From the wall of mangroves far off down the bay, the drum of the boat engine comes and goes, then comes again, a little louder.

"Oh, Lord," she whispers, half-aloud. "Oh no, please no, sweet Jesus." (ibid., 3–4)

We, too, are picking among the things the sea has left upon a shore. On the beach at Sagaponack, under a cold, low afternoon sky, shorebirds busy themselves along a line of mussels washed up, still clinging to each other, from the outer banks. Left by the past days' high tides, the mussels run a ragged line up and down the beach. Matthiessen tells me they've had storms here the last couple of days. I remember that it snowed two days ago in Cambridge. Winter is coming behind these storm fronts, which brought snow to Harvard Yard and mussels to the beach at Sagaponack. The storms were wilder, he says, out to sea than here inshore. The big seas have loosed the mollusks from the reefs and carried them to land, where they make a good feast for the gulls. These are herring gulls, he tells me, most of them juveniles, mottled brown all over, a few gray and white adults among them. They work the line of mussels and bicker.

Between the mussels and the lapping sea, scuttling back and forth ("like windup toys," says Matthiessen), run some Pacific golden plovers, in their last days before winter takes them south. They make way for us. "You have those too, of course," Matthiessen reminds me. And we do have them on our Australian shores, these astonishing, humble travelers of the world. I have seen them on a white sand beach in southeastern Tasmania in early May, thinking, I guess, about heading north again. It is even possible these are the same birds. Their soft, musical, two-syllable calls join our voices on the beach and the repeated outbreath of the sea.

As I write this, I sit in a cottage by another coastline, at Camden Head on the northeast coast of New South Wales. This was once the house of the pilot and his family. From here at the mouth of the

Camden Haven River, the pilot helped ships negotiate the passage from river to sea, taking timber from the mountains behind Laurieton down the coast to market; and he helped ships find the river's mouth, carrying in supplies to the town and surrounding community. I am just here to write. The sound of the surf from Washhouse Beach is loud in the house, and the air smells of salt and high summer. There are plovers here with me too this brilliant January day. The same sweet voices, the same scuttling, endearing forms accompanied me on a morning walk today along the shore. Encountering them brought Matthiessen to mind, and his affection for these modest shorebirds with their gift for distance.

"The black-bellied and golden plovers," writes Matthiessen in *The Wind Birds*, "are birds of Sagaponack . . . but . . . I have seen golden plover on Alaskan tundra and in the cane fields of Hawaii, and heard the black-belly's wild call on wind-bright seacoast afternoons from Yucatan to the Great Barrier Reef" (1973, 22). And here they are, farther down the Australian east coast on a January morning in the sun. These small birds can travel, in their two annual migrations, two thousand miles without putting down. They know wide sweeps of the world and how to thread their course from coastline to far coastline. When we see them on a beach, feeding and making ready for breeding or migration, "we stand there heedless of an extraordinary accomplishment," writes Matthiessen in *The Wind Birds*. For they are humble in every way, and nothing in their form or manner advertises their talent for travel or their acquaintance with great stretches of ocean and shore. And yet they belong to coastlines in two hemispheres, and they belong to vast distances in between. "One has only to consider," Matthiessen writes in *The Wind Birds*, "the life force packed tight into that puff of feathers to lay the mind wide open to the mysteries—the order of things, the why and the beginning'" (1973, 22–23).

To hear the universal in the particular, to be drawn by the bird at one's feet to the original, deep silence from which all life and sound come—this is a recurring idea, a motif, and a technique (of witness) in all Matthiessen's writing. It is the practice he follows, the cadence of observation-contemplation-reflection he travels again and again through his most interior, his most questing book, *The Snow Leopard*. It is a habit of mind, a discipline, a lyric orientation in which the shoreline can school one daily—because of the coexistence there of the local and the foreign, the here and there, the transitory and the perpetual, and because of the quiet eloquence that attends beaches and all wide-open, marginal places.

That embodied idea—distance and mystery incarnate—is almost the defining aesthetic, the characteristic note and gesture, of the shore. And that same note, I think, sounds in all Matthiessen's best writing. Often enough he strikes it by reference, as in the *Wind Birds* passage above, to "the mysteries"; or in tropes (synecdoches) where the mountain or the bird, utterly itself, stands as an archetype, an expression of the universe of which that landform or that lifeform and the observer himself are all a part.

Divinity is immanent within particular moments, in *The Snow Leopard* especially, and within the lives of man or woman, bird or river, alive within that moment. Each thing is an embodied mystery. The snow leopard, which Matthiessen never sees, stands as a metaphor for the fleeting beauty of all life and the elusiveness, and magic, of whatever one seeks. The wolves he observes at a distance in *The Snow Leopard*, hunting blue sheep in the snow, leap from the page with both immediacy and mythic presence. "In the frozen air," he writes at the end of a stunning description of this episode, "the whole mountain is taut; the silence rings. The sheeps' flanks quake, and the wolves are panting; otherwise, all is still, as if the arrangement of pale shapes held the world together. Then I breathe, and the mountain breathes, setting the world in motion again" (1978, 184). The animals live and breathe in the actual world; and they inhabit, they sing up, an archetypal world, outside time. What rings out in the silence is an enactment of a sacrament, almost, of life and death. And a quality of holiness rings out of the silence between Matthiessen's limpid words and phrases. We hear eternity in the wingbeat of a great black eagle high in the mountains just short of Dolpo: "What can it be hunting, this heroic bird, in bitter white waste, at the edge of darkness?" (ibid., 167). That is as rhythmic a sentence as you will find outside a poem. And it ends in the kind of synecdoche I mentioned before: "the edge of darkness"—meaning the actual fading of light, but also the kind of darkness that Matthiessen is exploring, the kind of hell that every such quest must circle and descend into, hunting for truth, the kind that Dante had in mind.

Holiness and mystery convey themselves to us in the way Matthiessen sets small details within a wide landscape; the way he extends space—silent or ringing—around the lives he observes. Like this:

> Gray river road, gray sky. From rock to torrent rock flits a pied wagtail.
>
> Wayfarers: a delicate woman bears a hamper of small silver fishes, and another bends low beneath a basket of rocks that puts my own light pack to shame; her rocks will be hammered to gravel by other women of Pokhara, in the labor of the myriad brown hands that will surface a new road south to India.
>
> Through a shaft of sun moves a band of Magar women, scarlet-shawled; they wear heavy brass ornaments in the left nostril. In the new sun, a red-combed rooster clambers quickly to the roof matting of a roadside hut, and fitfully a little girl starts singing. The light irradiates white peaks of Annapurna marching down the sky, in the great rampart that spreads east and west for eighteen hundred miles, the Himalaya—the *alaya* (abode or home) of *hima* (snow). (ibid., 23)

> Disputing the path is a great copper-colored grasshopper, gleaming like amber in the sun; so large is it, and so magical its shimmer, that I wonder if this grasshopper is not some old *naljorpa*, advanced in the art of taking other forms. But before such a "perfected one" can reveal himself, the grasshopper springs carelessly over the precipice, to start a new life hundreds of feet below. I choose to take this as a sign that I must entrust myself to life, and thanking the grasshopper, I step out smartly on my way. (ibid., 125)

> The nights at Shey are rigid, under rigid stars; the fall of a wolf pad on the frozen path might be heard up and down the canyon.

But a hard wind comes before the dawn to rattle the tent canvas, and this morning it is clear again, and colder. At daybreak, the White River, just below, is sheathed in ice, with scarcely a murmur from the stream beneath. (ibid., 194)

These are spare and melodic passages, in which the particular is rendered in pure, cold words and phrases, reminiscent (in that last paragraph particularly) of haiku, explored deftly for its suggestions of more universal meaning, and then surrendered.

Another lesson the shoreline teaches, over and again, is that nothing endures except the deep logic and pattern of things. The shore and the coming and going of the birds upon it show that what belongs to a place does not necessarily stay there. Nothing stays forever; things come and go. No one must expect a place to stay the same—it is not the same from moment to moment, let alone from year to year. To hold its integrity it must yield to the pattern of tide and season and weather—to the way of things. Love what the place in the moment expresses, and let it go. The shore may teach you this. The birds come and go and come and go. The waves are never absent, and they never stay. The beach teaches nonattachment, an idea that was at the heart of Matthiessen's writing even before he found, in Buddhism, a way of speaking of it.

If that idea—that change is the changeless way of things—can be said to have a shape and music—an incarnation—it is that of the shore and its birds. True presence on earth, some knowledge of the Way, and, finally, contentment come from living wide open to the moment-by-moment unfolding of life wherever one stands, without demanding that the moment hold: this idea finds expression often in Matthiessen's prose; but its aesthetic—tenderness in a minor key—sounds in his writing everywhere. His best writing is austere, yet rich and textured, replete with light and lives that vanish as soon as they appear. The idea of nonattachment, embodied and articulated by the long coastlines and their itinerant citizens, encourages a spare, unsentimental prose such as Matthiessen's—deeply felt, calmly expressed; delivered clean of comment; released.

. . . At daybreak, two great ravens come, their long toes scratching on the prayer-walls.

The sun refracts from the white glaze of the mountains, chills the air. Old Sonam, who lives alone in the hamlet up the hill, was on the mountain before day, gathering the summer's dung to dry and store as cooking fuel; what I took for lumpish matter straightens on the sky as the sun rises, setting her gaunt silhouette afire. (1978, 183)

We find here the perfect expression of Matthiessen's lyric sensibility. Ruthlessly attentive (to use Voigt's [1999] phrase) to the arrangement of forms and shapes in the world, he edits his prose to echo in the arrangement of forms and sounds in his sentences the way things organize themselves just here on earth.

In *The Snow Leopard*, Matthiessen discovers and elaborates—out of his experience in the Himalaya and out of the Buddhist thinking he does there—a way of being, a kind of spiritual philosophy, which is also a writing practice. (It is an idea that runs through much nature writing, of course, not just Matthiessen's, though his expression of it is powerfully his own.) It is not only possible but necessary—for one's sanity and to live rightly in the world—to be, from time to time at least, at one with the rest of creation; to transcend a narrow conception of oneself severed from the larger order of things; to identify with the actual, changeful, and eternal earth. "The secret of the mountains is that the mountains simply exist, as I do myself," he writes (1978, 195). "The mountains have no 'meaning,' they *are* meaning; the mountains *are*" (ibid., 195–96). "An instinct comes to open outward by letting all life in, just as a flower fills with sun" (ibid., 195). "I grow into these mountains like a moss. . . . I am returned into myself" (ibid., 212–13). He discovers in the mountains how to reimagine self more generously, to imagine himself and, indeed, the place about him ecologically. "There is a mountain opposite," he writes, "but this 'I' is opposite nothing, opposed to nothing" (ibid., 212). To live in this way demands a discipline of deep mindfulness. To live well is to open yourself to the world, to stay utterly present in body and mind, acutely aware of the life of things. Other lifeforms, Matthiessen notices, such as the wolves and the lammergeier, simply find themselves at the center of things; they "have no need for any secret of true being" (ibid., 227–28). To find oneself alive, a body inhabiting a particular space and time: This is a thing to be aspired to. This is to know a place and oneself. This is to *be*.

To be in the world, and to open oneself to it as though it were continuous with one's own life, the man or woman must learn to attend to the things-in-themselves (to use the phenomenologists' language). When Matthiessen pulls this off, as he occasionally does in *The Snow Leopard,* the world rings with life. "It is wonderful," he writes of the blue sheep, "how the presence of this creature draws the whole landscape to a point, from the glint of light on the old horns of a sheep to the ring of a pebble on the frozen ground" (ibid., 226), in a sentence that demonstrates not just how detail enlivens a landscape, but how noticing it and transcribing it thus animates also the text that arises from that encounter. Place and text here seem almost inseparable and also akin. Matthiessen's sentence has the same clarifying power as the hillside and its sheep. Such passages draw thought—the writer's and the reader's—to a point, as meditation and acute awareness within a landscape do. Such sentences express and also awaken in a reader pure presence—just as though the prose were that hillside and those wolves and sheep, and we their witness. This and some of the other passages I have in mind are, of course, *about* such a practice of attention. But they are also, in themselves, such an observance; and they are able to manifest deep wakeful calm in a reader:

> Often I scan the caves and ledges on the far side of Black River in the hope of leopard; I am alert for fossils, wolves, and birds. Sometimes I observe the sky and mountains, and sometimes I sit in meditation, doing my best to empty out my mind, to attain that state in which everything is "at rest, free, and immortal. . . . You never enjoy the world aright, till the Sea itself flows in your veins, till you are clothed with the heavens, and crowned with the

stars: and perceive yourself to be the sole heir of the whole world, and more than so, because men are in it who are every one sole heirs as well as you." (ibid., 194)

The quoted text, by seventeenth-century British metaphysical poet Thomas Traherne, encapsulates the state of ecological imagination, of avid awareness of one's place in the land and its place in you. Matthiessen then continues, describing his meditation on Somdo mountain above Shey:

> Now the mountains all around me take on life; the Crystal Mountain moves. Soon there comes the murmur of the torrent, from far away below under the ice: it seems impossible that I can hear this sound. Even in windlessness, the sound of rivers comes and goes and falls and rises, like the wind itself. . . . The sun is round. I ring with life, and the mountains ring, and when I can hear it, there is a ringing that we share. I understand this, not in my mind but in my heart, knowing how meaningless it is to try to capture what cannot be expressed, knowing that mere words will remain when I read it all again, another day. (ibid., 194–96)

But they are not *mere* words he puts on the page. They contain the music of that moment, and of the dancing mountains and the dance he shared with them.

Among other things, this practice of attention to the world makes Matthiessen a remarkable observer. Every book of his, fiction and nonfiction, swarms with detail—abounds with the name and nature of tree and rock and bird and animal; of scat and geology; of local hairstyles and local weather; of the work of hands and the cadence of human speech; of the architecture and beliefs and habits of native people; of the diet and customs of rare animals. The detail, as McKay Jenkins observes, makes us trust him as a guide (1999, xiv).

But it is detail of a particular quality. Lifeforms and landscapes are sounded out by his words—are sung—and take shape clearly in a reader's mind, surrounded also by a kind of mythic aura. "His scrupulous attention to the sensuous world," writes McKay Jenkins, "is one of his defining traits; the capacity to notice the particular and infer the universal is for him a poetic as well as a spiritual practice" (ibid., xvi). The best writers, like the Zen masters, know that God is in the details, that local texture brings life and music to the poem or the piece of prose. They know, too, that when one pays close enough attention to the lives going on around one and intuits something of the nature of the intervals and relationships at play between them, a sort of divinity may attach to the rendering one makes of that piece of the living world. And so it is sometimes in Matthiessen.

Matthiessen's practice of noticing in such lively detail lends his writing, most notably in the best of his nonfiction, an extraordinary immediacy, as though it were a set of field notes composed on the spot and barely touched, as perfect as the moments they relate. In fact, the journal entries he composes in the field get worked and worried over, drafted into more finished sentences and paragraphs, tried, altered, sounded out, altered again, and polished and made good over a long period—some years in the case of *The Snow Leopard*—in the writing house at Sagaponack. All his hard work goes toward making them sound as though they were immediate utterances arising out of the very moments they describe. And so, sometimes, they seem. This makes them, of course, shore creations as much as they are field notes, having been pondered and crafted so long in that nourishing terrain of his home.

But let me dwell for just a moment on this process of composition, and the paradox at the heart of it: that the more you work, in a certain way, at a piece of writing, the more it may sound like it has not been worked on at all—the more, in other words, it may sound like a natural, almost involuntary, expression of the moment of first encounter it describes. In an essay on the musicality of the poetry of Wordsworth and Yeats, Seamus Heaney speaks of "the testings and hesitations of the workshop, the approaches towards utterance." He has in mind the poet engaged in the hard work of musical composition, in response to the promptings of an original inspiration, a haunting—often something as slight as a single line or phrase.[3] If we take what Heaney calls the *donné*—by which he means "the given line, the phrase or cadence which haunts the ear and the eager part of the mind" (1980, 61)—and substitute a moment of original encounter with a place (which is sometimes also accompanied by a phrase one might scratch quickly into a notebook or determine not to forget), and if you will let me imagine a writer like Matthiessen at work on a piece of lyric prose such as *The Snow Leopard* as though he were a poet, or near enough: then we can put to work Heaney's metaphor of the poet's musical workshop to throw light on the relationship that plays between the encountered place, the words that arise from it, and the lyric essayist's rendering of them—place and phrase—into prose. Only if Matthiessen works, like the poet in Seamus Heaney's workshop, trying each phrase and sentence against the quality of the moment his journal tried to capture, against the cadence of his original experience, may his prose ring true to that moment; only then may the place and what he shared with it make themselves heard in his writing.

The craft of composition, seen this way, becomes a continuation of the dance or song or "ringing" of connection Matthiessen notes between himself and the mountain, between himself and the eagle. I imagine the place *continuing,* in this way, in its witness Matthiessen, here by his home shore, in his working and reworking of phrases. *That* is the dance, or the song; *that* is the rhythmic engagement the writer continues with the place: the pattern of his searching for the right words and rhythms, of his abandoning false notes, of his finding an apt mode of utterance for what transpired in that landscape.

3. Heaney is referring specifically to the poet's work, including matters particular to poetry such as lineation and rhyme. But his essay "The Makings of a Music" (1980, 61) is an exploration of the workshop processes by which a writer moves from first inspiration to finished work, attentive to the integrity and "pitch" of his or her original inspiration and notes. And since Matthiessen is a writer of lyric prose, careful about such matters as a poet is, perhaps I may be allowed to borrow Heaney's thought to cast some light on Matthiessen's work. I will have more to say about all this in my conclusion.

Through the rhythm of the making of the work, in other words, and the rhythm and shape of the work itself, the place—how it moved and how it moved the writer—may reach and stir a reader, phrase after rhythmic phrase.

The mountain or the blue sheep or whatever will only seem to be articulated in the writer's prose, the nature of the place itself will reach the reader as though it were singing itself directly to her, only if the writer works hard to shape an original utterance, apt for what it engages with. Only if his shaping harks to the music that was there then, and only if the writer tunes all his phrases to the pitch, and shapes them to the rhythm, of the original instance of avid attention will his telling belong to and perpetuate that moment in that place. All this work of revision takes place somewhere, of course. In Peter Matthiessen's case most of it takes place here near the shore. It takes place in an environment that has housed and nurtured him since he was a boy and through most of his now long writing years. The South Fork surrounds the work; it sustains and inspires the worker. It sounds out home for him. Even while he holds onto the original moment and hammers away at his prose, so that its forms and rhythms work in the same way, the rhythms of this homeplace goes on around him. It is here, in the hours and months, sometimes the long years, of the labor of typing and retyping drafts, which become pieces of finished prose— it is here, in this *work of writing* that the shore gets in. In Barry Lopez, it would be the forest and the river. In Peter Matthiessen, the process of writing seems to work, to advance and recede, in a meter not unlike the sea and the birds up and down a long coastline. It is the meter of the man, the meter of his workmanship, the meter of his finished lines. And the more it is present, the truer his writing rings with the life of a place far away—just as the cry of the shorebirds and the fall of the waves at Sagaponack ring true to where they've been and how they got here.

Matthiessen worries in *The Snow Leopard*, shortly before he must leave the mountain, that his staring about, "trying to etch into this journal the sense of Shey that is so precious," is but a misguided attempt to make permanent something that must be abandoned to itself; it is "to miss the point" and doomed, therefore, to failure. There is more of Shey "in a single sheep hair," he writes, "than in all these notes" (1978, 227). In fact, his note-taking and the writing that will follow are part of a practice of attention, an attempt not to capture the experience but to sing it once in the writing, and to let it ring again at every reading. Once written, a text of this kind cannot be properly understood as an object of silent signs set on paper. It lives for readers every time they sound its words in their mind and inhabit the space those sounds make. Both place and text live again at every reading, each of them separate but related and musically attuned. This is how a work may *adéquate* a place. The work starts as a response to a place; it continues in the crafting of an utterance; and it goes on and on each time it is read, each time it is sounded out, sung, and inhabited, in the reading of it. It continues, and the place continues in it; it is not, nor is the place, a fixed and permanent thing.

Matthiessen has written of his prose—the kind he takes trouble over—as an attempt to give the reader "the thing itself." Of his book *Far Tortuga*, for example, he said: "I wanted this novel to be absolutely spare . . . I wanted the thing itself, as is said in Zen" (Jenkins 1999, xxii). I guess he meant that he wanted to catch the immediacy of particular moments, of the place and the people, the boats, "the spareness of sailors" and their lives. To me he says on the beach that he is proud of that book. But it is a book, he comments, that writers loved and readers hated. His gray eyes laugh and his stern mouth shifts to let out a deep chuckle.

If a book is to manage such a spare singing of the thing itself, it will need grace and the disciplines of the poetic workshop. In the case of *Far Tortuga*, according to Matthiessen, it was a matter of shedding the kind of metaphor and elaboration with which his previous novel, *At Play in the Fields of the Lord*, was rich. Then too, perhaps every attempt to write the thing itself is destined to be another failure, to paraphrase T. S. Eliot, for each of our attempts will fall a little short of

the clean music (in which the thing sings) we strive for. But perhaps
the perfection of the pitch of the final work is not what matters. For
it is the striving that counts—the effort, the discipline, the essaying.
(This, I think, is one of the morals of *The Snow Leopard:* the creature
itself may elude you, but you will find it, you will know it, by jour-
neying in its country. For everything that relates to it—its prey, the
rivers it drinks from, the terrain it negotiates, the weather it has to survive, the tracks it leaves, its scat—speaks of it; and your seeking it in
mind and place and on paper speaks of it too.) A work may seem, as
sometimes Matthiessen's writing seems, to ring with the original place.
I think a reader discerns in the near-perfection of the words—in the
seeking but not quite finding—that the writer has employed just about
all the craft and care he is capable of, all his courage and power, in
order to articulate in sound and sign the truth of the world he encountered. The *striving* sings the thing itself—the thing the writer seeks to
recall truly and articulate without affectation. The striving is part of
the dance, of the ringing. Perhaps it is most of the dance.

Matthiessen began to pursue Zen Buddhism with Deborah Love in
1971. He writes about his journey in *The Snow Leopard* and, in greater
depth, in *Nine-Headed Dragon River*. In 1990 he was ordained a Zen
priest.

   After we have left the beach and made our way back through the
cleared fields to his place, Matthiessen shows me the cottage he has
turned into a prayer hall. Here he prays, meditates, and teaches. It is a
space of austere tranquillity. He does not speak to me about his practice; he looks nothing like a priest, nothing like the robed and
inscrutable monks he found waiting in his driveway one year on his
return from long travels, an episode he describes at the start of *Dragon
River*. As the plovers do not show off their migratory calling in their
plumage and posture, neither does Matthiessen want to clothe himself in his faith. He has said that "if people come along and want to talk
about Zen, that is wonderful, but I don't want to brandish it. It's just
a quiet little practice, not a religion . . . just a way of seeing the

world . . . and I find myself very comfortable with it" (Jenkins 1999, xxvii). And so he seems. But I have not come here to talk about Zen, and so we just touch on it. He shows me the meditation room. I take off my shoes to enter; I feel the stillness of the space. Then I pull my boots back on, and we leave. He takes me to the cottage where he writes.

But, writing up these notes, I began to think a little harder about the place of his Buddhist faith in his life, how it squares with his temperament, with his activism and his writing. In *The Snow Leopard*, Matthiessen confesses to a "distemper" that has run through his life, a feeling of being lost, exiled from home, severed from a realm of meaning and truth, unsure who he is. He recounts an episode on board a naval vessel in a Pacific storm in 1945 when "I lost my sense of self, the heartbeat I heard was the heart of the world, I breathed with the mighty risings and declines of earth" (1978, 48). The experience was not frightening but exalting, a reconnection with the heart of things that he yearned for ever after and sought to find again partly through the use of drugs. In the end, all his seeking, all his wandering in search of meaning, leads him to the realization, dawning in the Himalaya in 1974, that there is no abstract place or order of meaning. There is just this moment and this; this mountain; this wave; this shore; this plover; this man, now. Each of these is holy and part of the universe of holy things. " 'All the way to Heaven is Heaven,' St. Catherine [of Siena] said, and that is the very breath of Zen" (ibid., 63–64). The mountain does not have meaning; it *is* meaning.

It strikes me that Buddhism, this "way of seeing the world," fits well a man so gifted at paying attention, so oriented to discover the unity of things, so committed to speaking the truth. It fits the still man, the man with a gift for silence, the man wary of abstraction, the man who loves the grit and grace of things-in-themselves. But it also soothes the impatient man, the man of haste and anger. That complex man and his struggle for equanimity we see in *The Snow Leopard*, and I suspect we are shown his anguish and disquiet—the clash between the tough and the saintly Matthiessen—in his novels: in

Mister Watson, in Lewis Merrieweather Moon in *At Play in the Fields of the Lord*. Had things turned out differently, he writes in *Dragon River*, he might have found himself a Native American rubric; but he found Zen, and it works.

Zen suits the kind of writer he is; it suits the man he is. It suits his lyric disposition. It fits well an ethic and aesthetic that seem native to this man, and it matches the lore articulated by the shoreline where he makes his home—the impermanence of material things, the cyclical nature of reality, the interconnection of life and death. But how do we reconcile with its quiet wisdom of acceptance the other Peter Matthiessen—the man of causes, the outspoken and uncompromising critic of global capitalism and other modern evils, the defender of the rights of young Native Americans: the pain-in-the-butt ranter, the warrior?

Somewhere he has written that although Buddhism speaks of acceptance and understanding, it does not entail surrender. It has room in it, in Matthiessen's understanding anyway, for engagement; for passionate opposition, in words and actions, to ideas and institutions that threaten the lives and dignity of humans and other beings— particularly disempowered beings. It allows protest and action against injustice and on behalf of the sacredness of life. In this sense, too, Zen suits Matthiessen, the passionate and sometimes fierce conservationist, the outspoken advocate of social justice. This has been clear since *Wildlife in America* and *Sal Si Puedes; Tigers in the Snow* continues his work for threatened animal species, and *Men's Lives* argues fiercely against powerful lobby groups (industrial fishing interests and sporting fishermen) on behalf of the commercial fishermen of Long Island.

His strongest political protest came in *In the Spirit of Crazy Horse* (1983), a book prompted by the conviction of an Ojibwa Lakota man, Leonard Peltier, for the murder of two FBI officers on the Pine Ridge Reservation in South Dakota. Matthiessen's attack on "the coalition of industry and government that was seeking to exploit the last large Indian reservations in the West" attracted a libel action (the longest in U.S. history) by the former governor of South Dakota. Although

The Long Coastline   143

Matthiessen and his publisher successfully defended the lawsuit, it cost them nine years and three million dollars; it also led to an infamous attack on Matthiessen's integrity in *Outside* magazine (July 1995), passionately rebutted by Matthiessen in the October issue.

Matthiessen seems to me the kind of man who fights hard but not dirty because he fights from deeply held principles. He regrets the time wasted and the money spent on the *Crazy Horse* matter, but he regrets none of his opinions, nor his decision to voice them so unequivocally. He despises bullying and oppression, and he is not easily cowed. He has an instinct for justice, which he feels called to defend. When I asked him at one point what moved him to write, he cited Albert Camus who, in his 1957 Nobel Prize speech, said that writers must speak for those who cannot speak for themselves.

Someone who has some insight into the Way—the just order of things—may, indeed *must,* speak out against actions that imperil that just order. And so Matthiessen, the Zen priest, the man of nature, the lyrical prose stylist, the son of privilege, does speak out, in his writing and in his public advocacy. In his person, in his life, the contrary aspects of his nature—toward peace, art, and acceptance on the one hand; toward engagement, argument, and resistance on the other— seem well enough at ease. In his writing, however, he has not achieved the same reconciliation. He has confessed that he was not able (though he says he knew how) to make his books of protest into good literature. He seems to feel that politics and literature do not mix.

But plenty of other nature writers, even within the constraints of nonfiction, have combined literature and protest—Aldo Leopold, Rachel Carson, Ed Abbey, Barry Lopez, Terry Tempest Williams, and Thoreau himself come to mind. Even Matthiessen manages it, on occasion, better than he seems to realize—in *Wildlife in America* and *The Snow Leopard,* most strikingly. And it is clear that all his fiction, especially his most artistic, is also deeply political. It ponders and dramatizes the same issues that run through his nonfiction: the plight of endangered species and human cultures; individual and institutional greed and violence. It is not pure art. There *is* no pure art.

Indeed, the purest art may in a sense be the most powerful politics, since it has the power to change the way we understand reality—and power and change are what politics are about.

Matthiessen may simply be articulating with excessive honesty a tension between politics and art, between activism and evocation, that is always present in this literature. At the gathering at Harvard, some nature writers spoke of the political nature of all true art and writing—how it aims to change the way we see the world; how it does that best when it does not speak the language of politics. That is to cast politics very broadly and to allow great scope for literature to play out as it must, ringing true, in the case of nature writing, to the nature of places and peoples and of one writer's encounter with them. Others suggested we need writing that provokes such change much more directly, that incites change in the world now. No doubt we need both. And Peter Matthiessen, as it happens, is pursuing both and letting the tension between them stand unresolved. He writes two kinds of books: literature and advocacy. But he does not try to mix them, for he believes that politics makes bad art and art makes bad politics. And perhaps he is right. But he is also anxious, as any writer might be, to be sure his readers understand the two kinds of work he does; he wants no one to mistake his ranting for his writing. Literature, for him, serves its own demanding god—a god of art, not of war. As in his life there is the sage and there is the warrior, in his writing there is lyric and there is protest.

Zen does not ask its practitioners to bring their lives into tidy order. It embraces paradox. The shore, too, more than any terrain, is defined and sustained by oppositions. It is neither one element— water—nor the other—earth. It is both, and they never blend, but constantly move and shift. Nor do the birds, though also part of its pattern of forms and sounds, adhere entirely to the place, for they belong equally to the sky and to coastlines far distant. The shore is not one thing or the other; it is not entirely here or there. It is both. Matthiessen, it seems, has grown content to let his art and his politics, his spiritual self and his political, stand separate—an argument never quite won. He is sea and he is land, but rarely both at once.

In his low-ceilinged kitchen before we set out for the beach, Peter Matthiessen told me a story. It pointed up the difficulty for all nature writers of finding the right pitch, the right set of words, to talk about what is wrong with the way our culture engages with the natural world, to talk about corporate greed, the profit motive, the problems of the extractive economy and economic growth.

"I rather disgraced myself with Marion Gilliam at 'Fire & Grit' last year," he confessed. Gilliam founded and funds the Orion Society, which sponsored the conference I have just been to at Harvard, and which ran its own big conference, "Fire & Grit," in July 1999. Matthiessen explained that he likes Gilliam, admires and respects what he does through Orion. When I visited him, Matthiessen had just returned, in fact, from a tour to Florida under the auspices of Orion's "Forgotten Languages" program, which sends nature writers and poets out on the road to read from their work and join conversations with community groups and schools about caring for the land. Matthiessen has also received Orion's John Hay Award for his work at the interface of nature and culture.

What happened at "Fire & Grit" was this: Orion had asked a spokesman for one of the oil companies to speak at the conference and to be part of the dialogue. He spoke for fifteen minutes or so, and, according to Matthiessen, he seemed a very nice man, but he just delivered "the usual corporate patter" about the work the industry now puts into mitigation and restoration and keeping the damage it does to a minimum. When the oil man was finished, Matthiessen stood up and "spoke sharply." It seemed, he says to me, that the man had delivered a well-rehearsed, oily presentation, empty of new ideas and not really honest. "I felt that needed saying," Matthiessen told me. "I may have gone in a little hard," but it is time, he said, to speak plainly with these people. He knows, and knew at once, that what he said offended some people there. He knows that it embarrassed

Marion. Other people, including a number of writers, came to him and told him they were glad he had spoken up as he had. "I meant the oil fellow no harm, of course," Matthiessen told me. Not personally. "But I don't think Marion has forgiven me—or ever will."

As it happens, I had heard the same story at Harvard, related by some of the writers who were there that day at "Fire & Grit." For some of them, the way in which Matthiessen responded had silenced, alienated, a man with whom the community of ecological thinkers needs desperately to engage. It was an opportunity lost for conversation across the ideological chasm. "We invited that man to come among us," said one of the writers, "and we treated him badly." But others spoke in defense of Matthiessen.

It does not matter who was right. Who is to say whether that was a time for peace or a time for war? Who is to say there is room for only one tone of voice in such discussions? To paraphrase Wendell Berry, if we are going to find solutions among ourselves, they are going to be human solutions; and therefore, we are going to need human beings to argue them out. Sometimes those human beings are going to speak and behave in a way we do not like, because they are human and prone to be themselves. Berry had Ed Abbey in mind when he said that, but he could as easily have been speaking of Matthiessen. Both Abbey and Matthiessen have been prone to speak their mind, but their integrity is unimpeachable. Indeed, one of the things most admirable about them is that they can be relied on to speak, on paper and (Matthiessen at least, now) in person, insistently as themselves— to paraphrase Berry again (1994, 23).

At "Fire & Grit," Matthiessen was doing just that: speaking as himself, out of his own experience. He is prejudiced fiercely in favor of freedom and truth and wildness, and against oppression, dishonesty, and mere civility. He does not spare himself from those prejudices, from his own critical glare—a trait that saves him from any charge of self-service or hypocrisy.

The story tells me that in his life as in his writing, Matthiessen understands the need for art and the need for war, the need for repose and for rage, but he understands also that he cannot do them both at once. He will attempt them both individually, however, and with absolute integrity. He will offend people. He will regret it. But he will not stop. The struggle to speak rightly for those who cannot speak for themselves goes on and on, and it lies at the heart of his work and at the center of the nature writer's challenge.

Perhaps because of what happened at "Fire & Grit," or perhaps simply because the world is changing, in the introduction to *The Birds of Heaven*, which appeared a year after my visit with him, Matthiessen writes this:

> Surely a lingering sadness is unavoidable for those who revere the natural world and must bear witness to the ongoing degradation of our human habitat, tragically sacrificed to such narrow ideals as "gross national product" and diminishing hour by hour, day by day. . . . And yet, to my astonishment, in the second summer of the new millennium, after four decades of lingering sadness and pessimism about the future and vain angry protest, a curious optimism has opened in my heart like a strange blossom. Paradoxically, in this scary period when out-of-date Western governments seem oblivious to any need except those of "big business"—and in particular "big oil" and the extractive industries—and just when the caravan of United States politics labors so heavily in its attempt at a U-turn back toward the past, signs of environmental heresy are appearing in the business world, a few thin cracks in the hard skull of the corporate mentality. For whatever reason, industry after industry and business after business are making a quiet shift toward environmental awareness. (2001, xv)

As we climb the dunes to leave the beach, a great blue heron rises from the fields and flies over us, heading into the southwest, toward the pond at Sagaponack. We stop and watch. This heron, its head tucked back against its shoulders, its wings wide, is a large bird. But the crane, Matthiessen tells me, is larger again, and it flies with its neck fully extended, calling its wild note as it goes. On just such a hard day as this, in November of 1997, a young sandhill crane turned up on this shore and proceeded to winter by the same pond at Sagaponack. Unlike that bird, which had strayed far from its course, the great blue heron is at home here at this time of year, and its flight above us speaks eloquently of the South Fork in this season.

Matthiessen is a man similarly at home in this place, and all his gestures, in prose and in person, speak of it. He belongs here as the waters and the sands belong, as the heron and shorebirds do: he comes and goes, flying far away but always coming back. His being here implies and includes his not being here. Like the heron and many of the other shorebirds, his voice and gestures carry a sad note and hints of other realms, as though a part of him is always elsewhere. Yet, also like them, he knows himself—at least part of the time—to be at home here, powerful and contented. Oppositions live inside him, define him, as they do the shore.

These oppositions contend, I think, in the body of his work as well, where one finds both lyricism and journalism; elegy and protest; literary integrity and political purpose; acceptance and resistance; the exotic and the vernacular; the physical and the metaphysical; the past and the present; the immediate and the remote. They contend, on the whole, with striking beauty; sometimes the music dies in the tension between them, but never for long.

Mostly I sense in his prose—and I feel in himself and his way of being present in his home place—the music of shorebirds. At the end of *The Wind Birds* I discover a passage in which Matthiessen relates how the curlew and the golden plover have been known in folklore as "harbingers of death," as singers of bad tidings.

> And in the sense that they are birds of passage, that in the wild melodies of their calls, in the breath of vast distance and bare regions that attends them, we sense intimations of our own mortality, there is justice in the legend. Yet it is not the death sign that the curlews bring, but only the memory of life, of high beauty passing swiftly, as the curlew passes, leaving us in soli-

tude on an empty beach, with summer gone, and a wind blow-
ing. (1973, 151–52)

Apprehension of the fleeting beauty of life floods the song of curlew and plover and fills the sad lyric prose of Peter Matthiessen.

I stand with him a while longer in just such a wind, the summer
also gone, the heron also flown, and then we turn and walk back
through potato fields to the house.

4 The Heart of an Arid Land

TERRY TEMPEST WILLIAMS

The Colorado Plateau

I write to the music that opens my heart.

Terry Tempest Williams, *Red*

Every man, every woman, carries in heart and mind
the image of the ideal place, the right place, the one
true home, known or unknown, actual or visionary. . . .
For myself I'll take Moab, Utah. I don't mean the town
itself, of course, but the country which surrounds it—
the canyonlands. The slickrock desert. The red dust
and the burnt cliffs and the lonely sky—all that which
lies beyond the end of the roads.

Edward Abbey, *Desert Solitaire*

Remember that the yield of a hard country is a love
deeper than a fat and easy land inspires.

Bernard De Voto, *The Year of Decision, 1846*

It is a country to breed mystical people . . .

Wallace Stegner, *Wolf Willow*

It was the only landmark in Moab she was sure I would find.

The night before, a map of the desert open in my lap, I rang Terry Tempest Williams from my motel room near the rail yards in Flagstaff, Arizona, to make sure she knew I was on my way. "I can make it there by two," I said, "if I get an early start." "Better make it three," she said "and meet me at the Double Arches."

She was allowing for my sleeping in or getting lost or meeting with some revelation on the way. Revelations there were, but speedy ones, and not enough to lead me astray. I made it to Moab on time, but I never made it to the Double Arches.

Terry's home lies close to Arches National Park, and "Double Arches"—the Moab McDonald's—was her apologetic joke. (There is a famous double arch—all slickrock red—within the park. I never got there either.) Right on two o'clock, I drove into town out of the desert and the purple sage. I passed the McDonald's, found the post office, parked the truck, and mailed some postcards home. I walked around the corner and found the information center. (Terry had suggested meeting there but gave the idea up because she thought I'd never find the place.) I was at the counter buying two of her books, *Pieces of White Shell* and *Coyote's Canyon*, when in she walked and caught me in the act.

So our meeting happened just where it was supposed to, though not where we'd planned. Little turns out as you expect with Terry— or in this landscape. Like her, this place has a mind of its own. It bewitches. It surprises. Magic and mystery attend Terry Tempest Williams, as they attend this landscape; and they are written into her works. Her realism is replete with magic, as the desert is alive with spirits and parables. Both of them sing a haunted, angular music of the heart.

I am in the West now. Four days back I put down at Denver on Thanksgiving, and I have driven, since then, down the spine of the Rocky Mountains, south through Leadville and the valley of the Arkansas to Salida, west through the Sawatch Range of the Rockies and out into lovely grasslands and cottonwoods along the valley of the Gunnison and its Blue Mesa; then south along the Uncompahgre on a morning of snow, and over icy roads through the San Juans to Durango, to stand in wonder among the ruins and vistas of Mesa Verde; and then southwest through the four corners, out into the Colorado Plateau and all its infinite deserts—painted, monumental, delicate, and deep—until I stand now above the south rim of the Grand Canyon itself.

This is not the same country—it hardly seems the same continent—I left behind in the District of Columbia. It is a place of natural drama and vast and silent space. (Washington's drama is all political and historical, its spaces full of human tragedy and triumph and urgent with voices.) This plateauland about me now is arid, sparely vegetated, thinly peopled, open to the sky. And there is snow. There is snow in the desert, and this is a miraculous thing to my Australian eye. It reminds me that winter is close; it reminds me that I am in latitudes where, even in arid places, winter speaks in snow. Snow storied the red-brown flanks of the San Juans as I passed through a day or so before, and it articulates now the ledges of the canyon of the Colorado, white among the black juniper and pinyon pine. I stand at six thousand feet and look down to a river running green in a narrow gorge four thousand feet—and many long eras of the earth—below.

The canyon opens its mouth ten miles wide to the sky, and walls and slopes and steps of sedimentary rock descend through five hundred million years to that tongue, the river on its bed of Precambrian rock, rock so old it suggests eternity. The space beneath my feet is silent but ample and suggestive with stories: of all that time and all that rock laid down in Paleozoic and Mesozoic seas, shifted about in dry spells and erosion between oceanic episodes, uplifted and cut deep by rivers during the Cenozoic. Most of what was laid down over such a long time has been lost—the Grand Canyon has been made—in the past six million years. That's fast in geologic time, and the drama of that rapid unmaking is loud in the silence of the canyon. What is gone makes the canyon, and the canyon astounds us. I'd need to enter into its mouth to begin to understand what it says. But all I can do is to stand here in the tepid sun and try to let it shape its space inside me. It is too large for me to hold and fathom in a morning—probably in a lifetime. But a morning is all I have. I register rawness and a profound vulnerability. Earth is laid open here, and the space where it is broken is swimming with time. The canyon discloses, it seems, the whole slow history of the earth itself. The West lays eternity bare in this way.

Ravens fly across this disembodied earth, down into the deeper zones of life on lower ledges, and back again to the present. I envy them their gift for riding inside time, for plumbing, with flight and song, with dance, the mystery of a space so vast, all in a morning's hunt for food.

The movement of plates that uplifted the Colorado Plateau also pulled it—and goes on pulling it—apart from the Great Basin to its west. One day the land may break apart here and let the ocean in again (McPhee 1998, 141–42). Half of the country—one geological province—that Terry Tempest Williams calls home is being racked and fractured into blocks, which rise at one end and sink into the mantle at the other; it is shaping itself into angular waves of basin and range. And it is being wrenched apart from the other half of where this woman lives. Terry's west is being torn from her east. If these lands are where her heart lies, then her heart is breaking in two.

I come to Terry Tempest Williams, this day, out of Navajoland. That is her name for the country of the Navajo, more or less the same stretch of ground as the Colorado Plateau, a province in whose northern reaches she now makes her home. On reflection, it seems altogether right that I should come to her out of this storied landscape. It was in the plateau, among the Navajo, their legends, and the magic of their stark and broken landscape, that her voice awoke and found expression in *Pieces of White Shell*. In that book—not her first, but the first she wrote for adults, the first that got noticed widely—she began to tell her own stories, which were the gift of the Navajoland to this

Mormon girl who entered it barefoot and attentive, alert for sharp rocks and revelation (1984b, 3).

This Monday morning in Flagstaff, my breath smokes the blue dawn air. I scrape the ice from my red truck's windshield and make north past Gray Mountain, into the Painted Desert.

The Painted Desert is a pastel badland of pink and gray dunes, a body without a form. It looks as though it might run away in the next decent storm—but I guess it won't. White Mesa rises on my left. Soon, to the east, Black Mesa, which has been keeping morning from us, lets the sun rise over its dark capstone, out of the deep yellow claystones, which have been lying here these past three hundred million years. Black Mesa runs beside me for fifty miles into Kayenta. Even these plateaus, their flanks harrowed by stormwaters, seem soft and temporary. The mesas, like all things, are contingent; they are remnant—terrains already radically reduced. Fallen rimrock skirts them. Cottonwoods, their trunks stained the same color as the rock, stand and draw forgotten rain from underneath dry streambeds, making a living by reaching down deep in broken ground.

But the morning belongs to birds. Ravens fly—in pairs, in raiding parties, alone—across the woods and rangelands. I watch them at their easy flight, shadows aloft, prayers in search of prey. They are birds of such tough and uncompromising elegance. Here and there they stand over a roadkill and make a desultory exit as my truck storms past, trailing its long morning shadow through the sage and juniper by the road. I upset in my passing a congregation of fifty tiny long-tailed birds—common bushtits, I think. They've been picking among the shadows at the road's shoulder, talking among themselves. Chatter, at my approach, gives rise to wild alarm, annoyance, maybe even joy, and they rise and swarm the air in a flock, then, fall to earth again, a community of souls, one mind, when I'm gone. A single red-tailed hawk, buff breast toward me, watches my approach from the top of a telephone pole, a hunter at rest. Just yesterday, close to here, I'd seen a mountain lion on rocks above the grasslands, considering the sunrise, drinking the morning in. A legend lying on the earth; a hunter at rest. I look for the lion again this morning. But she has gone, become yellow rock again. For this morning belongs to birds.

I reach Kayenta at 9:30, full of country, and pull in. The sun is up, and the day is warming. The truck needs gas, and I need coffee.

In town there's a McDonald's and a brand-new Burger King. And, next to the gas station, there's another place called the Blue Coffee Pot. That's more like it. I carry my satchel inside. It's nearly full, this ten-sided, new-age hogan, but I find a seat. I am one white man among Navajo. They receive me in dignified silence, which is to say no one seems to take any notice but everyone knows I'm there. A Navajo girl takes my order, fills and refills my coffee cup, and delivers a huge plate of breakfast, upon which I fall.

I eat. I take these notes at this laptop. I pay and leave. I walk back to my truck. I refuel and pull out of the parking lot, renewed. I leave these people in the heart of their country, among their legends and conversations, and drive north into a redder geography, a valley of improbable monuments.

Over the San Juan River and past the Mexican Hat, up around the latitude of three mountains—Linnaeus, Abajo, and Shay—I pull over to photograph a landscape of dry gulch, red slickrock, desert flats, and blue mountains covered in snow. I stop the truck on the gravel shoulder and throw it into park. Leaving the engine running, I wander off to capture the country. I shoot. And I hear behind me something moving over gravel. I turn. The truck is rolling back toward an arroyo. I run, and I open the driver's door and pull the brake, just before the truck finds the wash. And then I laugh. The gearstick has found its way into reverse, I notice. How could that be? Desert trick or human error? No doubt the latter, but out here, in this place that seems half underworld, who knows?

I drive deeper into Utah, through sage and field and the rise of the

La Sal Mountains, and I roll down into Moab's main street. There, a little after two, I meet Terry Tempest Williams. We greet each other with surprise and delight: the place had outsmarted us both.

Terry Tempest Williams is identified, and has identified herself, closely with the West—its landscapes, its people, the treatment both have had to suffer, the magic that endures in those savage and savaged lands. "One of the West's most striking new writers," proclaimed *Newsweek* on the publication in 1991 of *Refuge*. In a conversation with Robert Finch, Williams spoke passionately for the West, its spaces, the mystery it represents to the East Coast mind (in Leuders 1989, 41ff.). She has written and spoken ardently of her deep belonging to the geography of the Southwest, to the Great Basin and the Colorado Plateau in particular. I have come to spend some time with her in the country of her belonging, to see what it's like, how the place might explain, how it is carried on in, her work. "The landscape came before the words," she told Finch and the audience who'd gathered to hear their conversation in 1989, and the Great Basin, she said, is a landscape "perfect for draping ideas over" (ibid., 41). I wonder if she has done all the draping, or if the drylands have draped themselves on her, clothed her with language and ideas born there. I wonder whether this beloved place has given her ideas and sentences in return for her attendance upon it.

Terry Tempest Williams's writing is more intimate and personal in voice and focus than that of many nature writers, past or present. We get to share the country of her mind as well as the country itself—but this is true of many writers. With Williams, we get to share more of her body, feel more of her desire, taste more of her emotional responses to place. Her work explores connections between body and landscape, between desire, intimacy, and belonging; it proposes and articulates an erotics of place, in which land is lover, she, as inhabitant and poet, is lover of land, and touch is everything. From all this she derives a fierce politics of place.

Eroding the divide between self and landscape, Terry finds herself in the land: "I can look for my own stories embedded in the landscapes

I travel through," she writes in *Pieces of White Shell* (1984b, 3); "my basin of tears," she calls the Great Salt Lake in *Refuge* (1991, 280). Elsewhere, she becomes the land: she is arch and feather and bird and sage. She reads events in nature as signs for herself, as metaphors of her life's passage. And she aspires to speak the land's tongue, to know its red grammar. I come here wondering what that oft-repeated "I" and "my" mean when she speaks of her places. In which direction and in what manner does the possession in her pronoun run? Does she project her emotions onto land, taking a kind of psychological possession of her places; or is her writing an expression of kinship, of betrothal and passionate connection to the body and mind of a place she loves.

I come to see if I can't fathom how this weird and lean geography, in partnership with this gifted and place-passionate woman, might have fashioned the erotic, personal, and political, the fierce and fragile terrain of books like *Refuge, An Unspoken Hunger, Leap,* and *Red;* and I come to listen for what that geography may have to share, in its desert syntax, of itself and of her.

On a Wednesday night back in October, in a church by Harvard Yard, I heard Terry read a new essay, published later as "Labor" in *Red.* At the center of that essay stands a rock she calls the Birthing Rock. Late this November day, Terry drives me there—to a rock in the belly of Kane Creek Canyon, five minutes out of Moab. Terry stops the car by the side of the track, and we walk down to her rock. It stands on its own, a block fallen from the rimrock long, long ago, set on a natural platform above the pink sand of the watercourse. Each of its four blue faces is decorated with petroglyphs. Black figures, animal and mystical, teem over it, and in the heart of them all a woman seems to give birth to four youngsters. Stories emerge from the belly of the desert, long after their tellers, the old people, have vanished.

The space is a stage and a womb, a site for story, a theater for delivery, a place for recalling and starting again. Here new conceptions found—perhaps they still find—their way into the world. Here the miracle of animal—of human—life finds embodiment over and over.

Here the rocks are animated. They tell stories. The rock, writes Terry Tempest Williams in "Labor," is also "my private oracle where I hear the truth of my own heart" (*Red*, 2001, 154). Rereading this, I find myself wondering at that "my": How can this be *her* oracle only; how can it speak *her* heart's truths alone? Does it not speak its own truths, and those of the Anasazi women (almost certainly they were women) who found the rock, felt its holiness, and painted legends upon it? This "my" is not a pronoun of possession, though. This "my," and the "my" at the beginning of *Pieces of White Shell* where she writes, "I can look for my own stories embedded in the landscapes I travel through" (1984b, 3), and others—these sound like words of intimacy and connection, words of love. They do not deny the integrity of the place nor preclude the possibility that others may know it intimately too. They speak of touching, of connection—always a personal matter between two beings, in this case a woman and a rock of stories. It is not that this woman owns this rock or that it has been waiting here for her only; it is not that the narrative of her destiny has been lying buried in the sands waiting through time for her arrival. The point is, these places touch her, as they might touch others. They speak. They are animated for this woman, and in them she finds cryptic expression of how she might lead a life worthy of this landscape. Terry Tempest Williams's desert is oracular for her. She is avid for the mystical experience within places like this—and who knows, perhaps the place is avid for an attention such as hers, in which it is revivified.

Here I am now with Terry Tempest Williams at one of her oracles, the mother rock. Having written and spoken of it so passionately, she leads me to it now and stays silent. She has been faithful to it, I think. This feels like the same place she wrote of, and it speaks to me with power too—but differently, since I am not a woman; since I have not known the rock, as she has, since she was a young bride; since I have not chosen, as she has, despite all the promptings of her heart and body and culture, to have no children.

In the essay, she offers her own choice not to bear children as an image, a metaphor rather than a model, of how we might learn to live differently. She offers, out of her life's experience, out of her listening at this rock, another way of understanding kinship, fecundity, responsibility, and love: "Would you believe me when I tell you this is family, kinship with the desert, the breadth of my relations coursing through a wider community, the shock of recognition with each scarlet gilia, the smell of rain?" (2001, 157). And she draws a lesson from the redrock desert: erosion makes it the place it is, a place that "ignites the imagination" (ibid., 154). We need to give ourselves over to transformation, like the desert, she argues; we need to remake ourselves and our relations with the earth out of surrender, such as that which rock makes to water and weather; we need to give birth to new ideas of how to live, growing as fertile and as self-possessed as this oracle of stone. We might let the rock teach us to give birth to a new conception of ourselves and our world. We might reimagine kinship and maternity—learn to see the other beings around us as our children, our brothers, our sisters, our elders.

The essay is brave, outspoken, artistically elegant, and personal. It is about her, and it is about the desert; it makes each a metaphor of the other's life, and it makes a political statement of great sweep, drawn from the open legs of a woman etched on a rock. In "Labor," as elsewhere in her writing, Williams's poetic engagement with place spawns political commitment and advocacy. Her poetics gives rise to her politics. Both of them honor this place. She wants place to stir us, as the touch and memory of a lover stir us, to their passionate defense. This is one of the places that stirred her in that way; the message of rebirth is what she heard here.

The night that Terry read this piece at Harvard, a new friend of mine came to me with tears in her eyes and asked, "Do you think I might meet that poet?" I learned in that moment that Terry Tempest Williams has pushed the essay into a new lyric realm; and I saw that her art moved people. She performed it. It is a piece of dramatic writing, of shapely rhetoric, of oracles stitched together. Into a poem. It works—this essay and much of her writing—as this landscape works: through striking image charged with color, through fragments that throw our sense of order, stir us with their power and their odd but perfect juxtaposition. It works like rockfall and erosion, only faster. It is insistent, unrelenting. It moves to a jagged rhythm, stops and starts and stops. And starts. It sweeps you away or leaves you cold. There is nowhere to hide—you are in for the ride or you are out. It works like the flood at the heart of her essay, which she imagines sweeping down the canyon and carrying her turbidly away, down the birth canal and up, through death, to a new life:

> Erosion. I look up. Canyon walls crack and break from the mother rock, slide into the river, now red with the desert. I am red with the desert. My body churns in the current, and I pray the log jam ahead will not reduce me to another piece of driftwood caught in the dam of accumulation.
>
> *Who has the strength to see this wave of destruction as a wave of renewal?*
>
> I find myself swimming toward an eddy in the river, slow water, warmer water. We are whirling, twirling in a community of currents. I reach for a willow, secure on the shore; it stops me from spinning. My eyes steady. The land is steady. In the pause of this moment, I pull myself out. Collapse. Rise. (2001, 161)

Terry Tempest Williams works like this. She works this ground, brilliantly. She lets her writing, in its sound, flow, and image, encapsulate a place, and, in this case, she makes her phrases perform like—*adéquate*—a flood, like a speeded-up kind of erosion. Her words, in their image and music, are carrying a sediment of mind; these ideas of hers are in flood. There is no separating argument from art. You see her mind and her craft at work—the poetic becoming political, the poem becoming parable—particularly in her use of synecdoche. Her images—"dam of accumulation," "community of currents," "the land is steady," "Collapse. Rise"—are not meant to be merely descriptive; they stand also for psychological and social, economic and political processes. This is the work of a poet and of a polemicist. In the flood of her writing, the particular and the universal, the actual and the abstract, are caught up together. They are all one. One of the challenges of Williams's prose is to fathom where desert ends and dream begins, where place ends and prophecy begins—to know what, in her writing, is actual and what is metaphorical. For her, the boundaries are porous.

"Labor" does what essays are meant to do: it generates ideas of universal application from first-person reflection upon first-person experience. There is the rock; it is her oracle; it speaks to her (well, actually it picks her up and carries her away); she speaks to us; they (the place and the writer) carry us into a dream state; they pick us up and shake us; and we are moved, as she was moved. We are left with her conclusions, the only ones possible, as though they were the sediment the river of story dropped, as though they were all that erosion left standing.

Magically, the place seems to manifest the placards she waves: Transform yourself! Sacrifice! Be reborn! This may be bedrock democracy at work (a topic Williams treats elsewhere in *Red*). Her essay draws a credo from a stone. And her intimacy with the canyon puts us in her boots. We hear the stones saying what they say to her. Turbid with celebration and protest, lively with the feeling of bodies in motion and thoughts in freeflow, this is a lyric essay in place-based democracy and in ecological imagination. It speaks at once for these rocks, for the whole earth, for one woman, and, if we let it, for us.

This is artful writing. I feel Terry's hand in every phrase, wild though the writing seems. It is intended to rock us, to speak from her body—and from the body of this canyon—direct to our body and soul. Oh, and from her head to ours, but through the body first. This is the writing she attempted in *Leap,* she tells me later—"blood writing," written out of her sensing, feeling body, and *for* the body of her readers. Her phrase is like Thoreau's—his was "vascular"—for this kind of writing that wants to keep the life of the place and one's self vibrant in the sentence. Like him, Terry knows such writing is the child of hard labor (of thought and craft) as much as it is the suggestion of a place. The more thoroughly such writing is striven for, the more artfully it is made, the more the place may seem to speak in it.

But she is not manufacturing a prose unlike her own voice. This is not mere affectation and flourish. She speaks like this—except that the writing is compressed, made more intense by the erosional work of composition, just as this place is made intense, made utterly and essentially itself, by erosion. Standing in this womb of a canyon recalling her reading at Harvard, I sense that Terry has learned in the desert to place words, much as this canyon has learned to place rocks, so as to move us deeper than thought.

Her writing has always had that quality. Don't go to her for disquisition, for temperate exposition. Go to her for punchy, lyric prose that works the mystical moment and aims not to argue but to stir. You'll find writing like that in *Pieces of White Shell*, throughout *Refuge* (though that is perhaps her most conventionally narrative work), and in her essays. Its rhetoric is musical—and its music is all angles and syncopation—more than it is rational or linear. She favors short sentences of a simple form. And sentence fragments. Her prose feels spare and sharp-edged, spacious and rhythmic, but off the beat and irregular, staccato. If she wrote music, it would sound like Messiaen's star music, his "Quatre études de rythme" for example, or like Stockhausen's Klavierstück V—all fragments and intervals, all shattered cadences and scattered tones. And the rhythm of her prose is inseparable from its message. Take away Williams's music and metaphor, and you'd be left with a bunch of slogans; absent the stories—the natural history and archeology, the discontinuous narrative of erosion—from the red desert, from the Basin, and you'd be left with a bunch of rocks, saltbrush, and sage. Everything depends on the poetry, which is to say on the structure, the composition, and the patterned sound; everything depends, in Terry Tempest Williams, on hearing the ragged, broken music of her prose, just as an appreciation of this arid country depends on feeling out the rhythmic whole of which the rock, the saltbrush, and the sage are a few scattered pieces.

The writing in "Labor" is most like the writing in *Leap*, a book also born and nurtured here in the redrock. But in the essay, which reports her new beginning with her husband, Brooke, in the plateau, this wilder beat, this tougher aesthetic rings stronger, as though it is possible and even necessary to speak like this in such country. This place does not compromise or welcome compromise, though it houses ambiguities.

This place is delicate, though. We leave the rock and drive to the mouth of another canyon of red rock: Moonflower Canyon. Terry leads me into it, among bare cottonwoods, up a small stream running in a flat expanse of sand and tumbled mother-rock. We step across the water on stones. The surface of the stream has frozen in places, and the ice is a transparent mosaic. On the streambed beneath the crystals lie fallen leaves of Gambel's oak and cottonwood. We walk up the narrowing canyon, headed for a place where the walls close around a pool and the shallows hold broken red rocks and some pieces of the sky.

Halfway up the canyon, the soft song of a bird breaks into our conversation, and Terry stops me to point out the singer. "Canyon wren," she says in a whisper. His song comes down a sweet scale, down the canyon wall to us, followed by the wren himself, a compact bird with long claws, good for holding to slick rock, with a long beak, good for singing long songs. Canyon wren is a plain brown bird. But he wears black spots, and his chest is white. He darts along the rock-wall, and as we walk on toward the pool he goes on ahead, fleet and sure and full of song. While we sit and talk in the throat of the canyon, the wren's voice never lets up. It is a sweet and insistent sound, rolling like a chorus, stopping and starting up again, a voice singing the alto part. It's voice is a grace note, embellishing the canyon, decorating our own conversation.

It struck me that, in the canyon wren—the way it followed us up the canyon and included its voice in our conversation—Barry Lopez was with us. We were talking of him, as it happens: his truthfulness and purity, his earnestness and wisdom, his struggle through despair to contribute to a literature of hope. One of his books of stories, *Field Notes,* is subtitled *The Grace Note of the Canyon Wren.* In the opening fable of that collection, a lost man, seeking a way from his home country across canyons and deserts to the coast, encounters first some ancient pictographs—images, as he reads them, of a people's love and fear—on "the sienna rock" of a dry wash. Then in another canyon, as night falls and he stumbles toward hopelessness, he hears the pure, bare, descending call of canyon wren. The sound saves him. It leads him up the canyon, as our bird did, to water, to silence, to a holy place. In Lopez's narrative, it guides the lost man to the headwaters of a river he knows will take him to the ocean. The bird's phrasing, in the story, is the sound of hope itself. It is a testament to the forgiveness of water, an element in which it is easy to lose faith in these arid lands. Yet it is there, always there, somewhere.

It's not surprising we should have the company of such a bird and its song in this canyon. But it feels, all the same, like a blessing. The bird's song, so full of water, cold and clear, is a thing of beauty. It is a small and unremarkable coincidence, I suppose, that a mutual friend, a writer we both admire and who has influenced our lives, should have written of a similar moment of benediction and that we should just now have been mentioning him. Yet this is the kind of thing that occurs in Terry's company. It was right that Barry Lopez should have come to both our minds and to our shared words in such a place as this: his is a gracious and insistent voice, like this bird's, pure and tenacious and sadly hopeful.

Canyon wren sings in "Labor" too, I notice—in Kane Creek Canyon, which we have just left behind. It sang when Terry was there to reimagine birth, to give birth to a new self. It is here again now— another small coincidence, a humble but unquestionable intimation of meaning.

We say a lot sitting there on rocks, and growing cold. The place itself, canyon wren aside, keeps a diligent silence. We speak about the meeting of nature writers we both attended at Harvard in October, and we begin to talk about this literature of nature and Terry's practice of it. While we sit on those old red rocks, while the day pales, I watch half a dozen contrails pass high above in the thin blue altitude. Even this desert place is stitched into the fabric of the twenty-first century. It traffics—the moving world of machine and oil and flight and fume—east and west, north and south, through a desert sky that lies reflected here in Moonflower Pond. "Notice how the canyon resists the sound, though," says Terry. "It keeps its own stillness." In which the canyon wren keeps up its song and we our talk.

It is getting late now. But light still holds in the canyon. Terry marvels at the light, the way it reaches us indirectly, touches us and touches the rock as gently as birdsong. "Remember the intelligence of that light, of that moment?" she says to me later. Light is mindful in her world; moments can be wise. It has a lightness of touch, the Moonflower Canyon.

"I was drained by the Harvard conference," says Terry. "When I got back home, I came up here, I went up to the slough, and then I went up to the Birthing Rock, to connect with an order larger than myself, larger than the human. To become whole again. This country heals me. Land can do that. It is possible to participate bodily in landscape even though it cares nothing for us in any sense we understand as human. We can be intimate with it. We can love it."

Here in the canyon in this light, she speaks of her book *Desert Quartet,* a book of touch and place. In that work, prose poem in four movements—"Earth," "Water," "Fire," "Air"—with accompanying line drawings and paintings, Williams explores the intimacy and emotion, the desire, fulfillment, and replenishment, that are possible between a woman and a desert. "Earth. Rock. Desert," the book begins. "I am walking barefoot on sandstone, flesh responding to flesh" (1995, 3). It is a daring piece of writing, particularly for a Mormon girl. It brings to the page a language usually kept for the expression of desire between human lovers. "I stop. The silence that lives in these sacred hallways presses against me. I relax. I surrender. I close my eyes. The arousal of my breath rises in me like music, like love, as the possessive muscles between my legs tighten and release. . . . There is no partition between my body and the body of Earth" (ibid., 10).

What Terry Tempest Williams, lover of rock, says to me there in our moment of stillness is that places can speak right out of their bodies to our bodies, through eye and foot, through muscle. They can touch us and stir us to love, as they always have—as they did for the Anasazi. Our relationships with them can make us whole. Wholeness is our "unspoken hunger"—the subject and title of her 1994 collection of essays. Saving ourselves and our places on earth depends on our seeking wholeness—with, for, and within landscapes, within our human relationships, with lovers and family and community. Seeking wholeness demands vulnerability. We cannot love without vulnerability, without letting ourselves lie open to the lives of others, to change and pleasure and pain, just as this desert, this pool and canyon, have opened themselves to the weather, to geological transformation, to erosion. We need to lay ourselves open to places like this canyon, so that we might feel what it is like to be moved to the heart of our being. This is what she speaks of here; it is also what she elaborates boldly in "Yellowstone: The Erotics of Place," and in many of the essays in the masterful collection *An Unspoken Hunger,* in which "Yellowstone" appears. In "Winter Solstice at the Moab Slough"—an essay of hope written out of deep despair, she tells me a little later—she quotes D. H. Lawrence, and his words sound like the wellspring of her philosophy of intimacy with the land: "In every living thing there is the desire for love, for the relationship of unison with the rest of things. . . . Blood knowledge. Oh, what a catastrophe for man when he cut himself off from the rhythm of the year, from his unison with the sun and the earth. Oh, what a catastrophe, what a maiming of love when it was made personal, merely personal feeling, taken away from the rising and setting of the sun, and cut off from the magical connection of the solstice and equinox" (1994, 65).

A pale sun sets on cattails in the Moab Slough. This place, renamed prosaically the Scott M. Matheson Wetland Preserve, was preserved by the Nature Conservancy in June 1991, and Terry's essay "Winter Solstice" grew out of her attendance at the dedication. It is winter again, just short of the equinox, and we stand on the edge of this sanctuary, this saved place. The slough, thick in reeds and cattails, is dusky and serene at this hour. Wallace Stegner, a friend of Terry's and one of her elders, described it at its christening as "a geography of hope," borrowing his own powerful phrase, with which he concluded his famous "Wilderness Letter" of December 3, 1960.[1]

"My heart finds openings in these wetlands," Terry Tempest Williams writes in "Winter Solstice," "particularly in winter. It is quiet and cold" (ibid., 62). It is cold and quiet here now, at this place —a wetland in a worked-over desert—where love for land, where a miracle of survival and a metaphor of hope find expression. This is a place where it is possible for time to be swayed, as Terry is, by the conviction that "the land is love"—a love we have grown too hard of heart to return, a love for which we hunger.

The cold and the falling light bring on another hunger—for food—to which we surrender. Brooke Williams, Terry's husband, drives into Moab to join us for dinner. There, over tortillas, Terry tells me about a woman who came up to her at a reading and berated her for what she read as autoeroticism in *Desert Quartet*. It was an impassioned and angry attack, Terry says. "I weathered it, and then I told her what I told you in the canyon this afternoon": that the book was really about the possibility of intimacy, the need for love, between people and place. The woman calmed down, and later she wrote to say that when she had spoken to Terry she had been, she now realized, standing on the edge of the same kind of erotic relationship with place that *Desert Quartet* articulates. "What you said that night changed my life," the woman wrote. As an academic, she had been resisting that plunge into place, for fear of losing objectivity. Now she had let go, and she thanked Terry for helping her.

Desert Quartet was Terry's own plunge—into her own body, into a new erotic language for landscape. It was a breathtaking surrender to the actual world, one at odds with (though not utterly uninflu-

---

1. Stegner was a man, Terry writes in a recent introduction to his novel *Crossing to Safety*, whose own hunger for goodness, for beauty and justice, was never satisfied (Stegner 2002, xviii).

enced by) her Mormon childhood in Salt Lake City. It marked her coming into her own. It was a small death, a movement of the earth, an awakening to the desert, a finding at once of a new home and a new voice.

Terry Tempest Williams is the first child of Diane Dixon Tempest and John Henry Tempest III, and she was born to them in Salt Lake City on September 8, 1955. Three boys followed. For three generations before Terry was born, the men of her family worked in the family business, the Tempest Company, laying pipe. Now they are into their fourth generation, for Terry's brothers carry on the work. Tempests have always dug the desert. Terry was born with red sand in her veins. From her father, she learned the importance of the ground at one's feet; she learned the virtues of digging. I remembered this when I drove into Moab and saw on the outskirts of the town piles of yellow pipe, lying ready for burial beside the highway, lines of her biography resting, vulnerable and raw, on the red soil.

Her father knew about weather and geology, worked inside them; and he taught his children how to read landscape, something of its capacity to fool and test and sustain a person (Williams, in Leuders 1989, 43). Her family camped out on weekends in the Stansbury Mountains, by creeks that ran into the Great Salt Lake. Her family's faith included the tenet that God lives mostly outside, in creation. Family and divinity inhabited the outdoors, and her family's business worked in soil. It is no wonder that she learned as a girl that "our attachment to land was our attachment to each other" (Refuge, 1991, 15). Faith, land, work, and family were all aspects of each other in her childhood; and all of them were concerned with the actual ground. So it has continued. She married Brooke Williams when she was just nineteen. She was working in Sam Weller's Zion Bookstore when he came in and bought her favorite book, a field guide to birds. Birds and books brought them together. They married soon after. Brooke had a degree in biology, though he was still working then in his family's construction business. Terry and Brooke lived in Salt Lake City for many years until their shared love of the wild red country and their impatience with the city's haste, with the way its lights had extinguished the night sky, took them to live in Castle Valley, twenty-five miles outside Moab. This was in the mid 1990s, after the publication of *Desert Quartet.*

Although that book is a kind of love-child born of her union (reunion, really) with the redrock desert, and although she herself has been reborn as a woman by her plunge into the canyon country, Terry Tempest had learned already from her family, particularly its women, how to love the world as a woman—what that takes, what that costs. One of these women was her mother, whose life and slow, dignified death *Refuge* charts (along with Terry's own slow and painful healing). Another was her grandmother Kathryn Blackett Tempest, whom she called Mimi. With her Terry talked over many things. In Mimi she had a model of dignity and passion. In Mimi's company Terry learned a love of the wild, a love of water and of bird. It was Mimi who gave her, for her fifth birthday, a copy of Roger Tory Peterson's *Field Guide to Western Birds*—the book Brooke Williams bought from her the day they met. "The days I loved most were the days at Bear River," she writes in *Refuge.* "The bird refuge was a sanctuary for my grandmother and me" (1991, 15). Birds and wetland, sanctuary and the gentle attention of women, entered her life as ideas and events early, and became sacred.

Another womanly body that tutored her was the Great Salt Lake. She recalls in *Refuge* how, as a child watched over by her mother, she floated in its brine and learned the sky. In this way, she writes, the lake "flooded my psyche" (ibid., 33). What it taught her was how to beguile and seduce; how to cure oneself and heal. It got inside her skin, she implies; settled its sediments in her psyche's terrain; patterned her with salt stain and watermark. She floated in it, and it floats in her, she tells us. It taught her to be a mystic. Like the lake and the sky above it, Terry Tempest Williams uses a sensuous language that speaks to the body, where the mind and emotions dwell. She moves us, as the lake moved her, to faith and love. Mind follows, if it will.

At the University of Utah, Williams majored in English and minored in biology. She tells me that she approached the English department to see if they might let her do "environmental English" and the biology department to see if they might let her do "literary biology," and they both said no. Though she went to work later in the Utah Museum of Natural History, and though her writing is grounded in sound life science, she has continued to major in narrative, in story. If she is, as she says, "a naturalist first and a writer second," this is because "the landscape came before the words" (in Leuders 1989, 41). But they were always wedded, words and the world. Her master's thesis, in which storytelling prevailed over traditional scholarship, and mystical experience is described as a natural phenomenon, caused consternation at the university. Drawing on her time teaching among Navajo children at Montezuma Creek, Utah, and the wider Navajo-land, and "exploring narrative in Navajo culture" (Anderson 1996, 976), her thesis was at first rejected; but when the manuscript was accepted for publication by Scribners (eventually becoming *Pieces of White Shell*), the university changed its tune and accepted it as a work of scholarship. She was from the beginning a storyteller: a storytelling naturalist of the spiritual and physical world.

It is clear in *Pieces of White Shell* how the writings of Gregory Bateson and Barry Lopez, in particular, influenced Terry's thinking about story, land, and culture. These men, and other thinkers and teachers, helped her see what the land and its first human keepers, the Navajo, would then show her more directly. The Navajo with whom she worked taught her, by their lives and stories, that there is a way of living with land—and with each other in land—that proceeds by story. "Storytelling," she writes, "awakens us to that which is real" (1984b, 134). And in this, the land is the primary, the primal storyteller. From it, "stories come to us and sing the mysteries which surround us" (ibid., 137). It is for men and women to listen, and then to speak or sing what the land lets them know. Story as a way of life, as a way of knowing and passing on truth, begins with listening.

Pieces of White Shell received praise from writers, critics, and readers in the West. It also won her the 1984 Southwest Book Award for nonfiction. Shortly before *Pieces* came *The Secret Language of Snow* (1984a), written with her former teacher at the Teton Science School in Jackson Hole, Wyoming, Ted Major. It is an ecology, in free verse and story, of winter in Alaska. Just after *White Shell* came a children's book, *Between Cattails* (1985), which narrates, again in free verse, the ecology of a wetland. The book draws on her days with Mimi at the Bear River Migratory Bird Refuge. It invites children to enter through her words into the life of a marsh and then to step into an actual marsh of their acquaintance, and let it speak.

In *Coyote's Canyon* (1989), Terry Tempest Williams takes the next natural step after *Pieces of White Shell:* she writes myths of her own, drawn from the redrock landscapes of Utah. She becomes the myth-maker, not just the teller of other people's myths. Stories, though they come from *where* we are, tell us *who* we are, while relating us to the land and relating us and the land to our listeners. This is one of the themes Williams works in *White Shell.* Now, in *Coyote's Canyon,* a collaboration with the photographer John Telford, she lays herself open to the country, writing the myths that arise in her, through her, are of herself and of all of us. "The images and stories . . . from *Coyote's Canyon,*" she writes, remind us that "beauty is not found in the excessive but in what is lean and spare and subtle" (1989, 19). There is a fable about a woman like herself and a truck full of Navajo children and a mountain lion. There is one about a woman who lets herself, against her fears of what her family will think, wallow in the wet red clay of a wash; one about a man who writes poems and buries them in the Utah sand; another about the return to earth of the mythic flute player Kokopelli; one about a pilgrimage to an Anasazi cliff house; one, the centerpiece in some ways, in which a woman dances alone in the desert; and a finale in which a man and a woman make a spiral of colored stones in the floodplain of a desert river, dance and sleep and flirt and enact stories of creation, and then leap into the river and float "like a wish, downriver" (ibid., 91).

These fables have something of the naive wisdom, the power and polish, of Barry Lopez's stories in *River Notes*. They celebrate the life of the desert, human life at peace with all other lives, and the love one woman bears a place. The stories feel like blessings. Quiet, unremarkable magic happens in them; modest revelations occur. Nothing is explained. To call them fiction is to miss the point. These are stories in an ancient tradition—the one Barry Lopez talked to me about. They are true in the way that mythology is true: they elaborate truths encountered in the land.

The stories in *Coyote's Canyon* are gentle and assured. When she wrote them, Williams was grieving hard for her mother, who had died in 1987 after being diagnosed with ovarian cancer in the spring of 1983. In that context, the poise and peacefulness of her stories are remarkable. But Williams's search for meaning and hope after that loss, and the loss soon after of both her grandmothers, gave birth in 1991 to a larger and more remarkable work, her great book *Refuge: An Unnatural History of Family and Place*.

Refuge embodies all the ideas that Terry Tempest Williams had been rehearsing in her earlier books: that place is identity; that attachment to land is the same thing as attachment to family; that what we do to land, we do to ourselves; that what happens in our human lives happens also in the land; that consolation—the knowledge that we are eternal and go on and on, remade by death, healed by sorrow—is found in the places in which we find our stories of home. The book is brilliantly conceived and woven together with great skill. It is a narrative at once of a mother's death and a family's coping; a daughter's search for healing; the steady rise of the Great Salt Lake (the menace of that, and its challenge to the authority of a city); the slow inundation of the Bear River bird sanctuary, the flight of its occupants, and the refuge's resurrection as the waters fall back. Each chapter is named for a bird of the sanctuary; each chapter marks the height of the lake. Birds sing the chapters in; they count the story by. And the lake seems to choreograph the narrative. The survival of the refuge, the persistence of the birds, surrounds, echoes, and transcends the tragedy of a mother's death. And the lake rises and falls, rises and falls again, telling its own story of change and eternity while a mother sickens and recovers, sickens more deeply, finds peace, and dies. Family and land are one. Our stories are also the land's.

Refuge grounds a family tragedy, an ecological morality tale, and a memoir of loss and healing in the natural history those narratives share. Even a mother's death from cancer has its place in the story of the living world. It forms part of a larger story of birth and rebirth. Sadness and loss teach us what we love; they may even teach us how to love—generously, not fearfully; on and on in the face of everything. "Grief dares us to love once more" (1991, 252). In the book's final chapter, Terry Tempest Williams floats on the Great Salt Lake with Brooke. "There is no place on earth I would rather be," she writes. They float and you sense peace surround them and hold on. "My basin of tears. My refuge," the book concludes (ibid., 279–80).

Her mother's dying is as natural as the rise and fall of the lake and is subsumed by it. But Terry discovers in another sense—the one contained in her subtitle—that Diane Tempest's cancer is distinctly unnatural. In a powerful epilogue, "The Clan of One-Breasted Women," Williams writes of her discovery that she and her mother witnessed the explosion, one day before her second birthday in 1957, of one of the many nuclear warheads tested in the Nevada desert in the fifties and sixties. Her father tells her that they were driving home from California early one morning when it happened. Her father's revelation is a white flash to his daughter, as galvanizing as the one that eventually killed her mother. That discovery makes her an activist, though she never stops being an artist. She is engaged in a struggle; but she continues to engage us in story.

The epilogue finishes with a description of her incursion into the Nevada test area with a group of Utah women, and of their arrest. The women are dropped off in the desert, just short of the town of Tonopah, and told they should walk home from there. The officials mean it as a humiliation. "What they didn't realize," writes Williams, fusing poetics and politics, "was that we were home, soul-centered and strong, women who recognized the sweet smell of sage as fuel for our spirits" (ibid., 290).

Refuge attracted widespread critical acclaim and drew a national audience. In 1993 it won her the Lannan Foundation Award. Since its publication, Terry has found herself in demand as a speaker and writer. Her personal erotics, her drama and grace, the soft, strong voice and authority of experience that speak through her books, have made her now the most widely known and deeply loved of all contemporary nature writers. Not surprisingly, she has drawn the fiercest love from women, young women in particular. In some of her writing now she speaks directly to women, arguing that they have a special political role as beings who bleed, who give birth, who nurture and defend their young. "As women connected to the earth," she writes in her essay "Undressing the Bear," "we are nurturing and we are fierce, we are wicked and we are sublime. . . . We are the mothers of first words. These words grow. They are our children. They are our stories and our poems" (*An Unspoken Hunger*, 1994, 59).

These are bold and poetic words. Terry's politics have been feminine since they emerged out of her upbringing and more directly out of her mother's cancer; and they have been personal and writerly. She shows in her bearing, her behavior, and her prose how a fierce and vulnerable relationship with the world is possible; how it might be embodied and bodied forth in story. Story, as "Labor" shows so well, can be at once lyric and political. And it is women's work.

Since her mother's death and her own political awakening—though the Great Salt Lake entranced her in childhood, buoyed her imagination and bore her grief—Terry has found the redrock desert a more natural home for her politico-erotics of place. It was in the desert, after all, that she found the ground of her early writing, where she learned to tell stories, learned who she was and what the land wanted of her. That is where, in the red desert, she has gone to live.

I have vaulted over a book of Terry's just out when I was with her: *Leap* (2000). *Leap* is a book impossible to categorize, in much the same way *Refuge* was—but more so. It travels deep in her inscape, her spiritual life, and it moves slowly through the landscape of Hieronymus Bosch's painting *The Garden of Delights*, which hangs in the Prado in Madrid.

It charts her attempt to reconcile her Mormon faith with an aesthetic philosophy she discovers through this canvas—a way of seeing and being that values personal freedom and sensual depth, that finds divinity in the living world, that holds sacred all art that is itself both beautiful and truthful, regardless of the culture and faith it springs from. A painting—and a book too—may be a prayer, she concludes, though her family's faith tells her that that may not be possible. The assured, though grieving Williams of *Refuge*, and the sexy, passionate, and outspoken Williams of the redrock essays get lost in this book, though it is earnest and often lyrical and courageous. Her voice in this book is bewildered and modest, and that is apt, since this is a spiritual quest: "Let these pages be my interrogation of faith" (2000, 5). She has moved on from the City of Latter-Day Saints, she writes at the start, a city whose mountains were "hollowed to house the genealogy of my people, Mormons. . . . I have moved. I have moved because of a painting" (ibid.). And at the end she has arrived at a new home, in a landscape "where more is exposed than hidden . . . where the wind creates windows, windows that become larger and larger through time until they turn into arches one can walk through" (ibid., 266).

Leap, then, is the book that describes its author's leap from the basin to the plateau, from the salt lake to the red river, from the wisdom of her fathers to the wisdom of the earth. It is not clear where her Mormon spirituality ends up, though it is clear that some of it persists: the part of it, I suppose, that holds the desert sacred; the part that cannot be separated from the soil in which it found home. If the writing feels sometimes thin, it may be because the land is not present in this book as much as it is in all her others. It was important to her, though, to spend time in the country of her mind. If the book seems fuller of sky than it is of earth, that may be because in it she is leaping—she is, for its duration, airborne between one home and another. Where she lands is the redrock desert.

It is my second afternoon in Castle Valley, and we are sitting on the pink banks of the Colorado, talking. The river rolls past, green and blue and slow, and the sand is patterned with a frantic text made by the feet of birds—the three long prongs of the great blue heron, the flatter marks of migrating geese—and the delicate arches of deer. Our feet have made stories too among them; we sank quite deeply in the fine-grained mud of the floodplain as we walked to the river's edge. The day is still, but the river keeps on moving, cutting the country deeper. "Writing is a spiritual practice," Terry tells me. As in intimacy with another person, we do it best when, with the best of our self, we seek to know the essence of the other, to honor the actual thing, the form, the being they are. Just as in love we love the body of the other and hope to draw out the spirit that animates it, without copying it, so in art, our production—a canvas, or a text—should not aim to *replicate* the thing we study, but to honor it: to express the god in it, as it were.

Later in my truck as we drive to Moab for dinner, she expands on this idea. She reminds me of the story she tells in *Refuge* about the Shoshone moccasins crafted for the feet of a woman's dead grand-mother (1991, 234). The boots, she says, are beautiful because they are made in honor of that one body; they are made, indeed, to serve that dead person, that they might be fit to hold those feet alone, just that one beloved person's feet. They are holy because they bring to mind the feet themselves, and the loved one whose feet they were. They remind us of the feet by making a space that might house them, but does not. The thing they honor is not there; they do not replicate it. That, she says, is what the best art attempts: not to replicate the thing itself—in this case, the body of the loved one, the reality of a moment or a life—but to bring it to mind, and to honor it through the care taken in the work's production, the aptness of its shape and ornament. The beads sewn on the soles of the moccasin celebrate the life and remind us that these boots are not made for walking but for recalling a life once lived and now carried on in death.

I think about this as we drive by the river in the pitch dark. Above, the black sky is beaded with stars. Each moccasin makes a space before our eyes. A text makes a space, I am thinking, in our imagination through its sounds and the images they make, through its story's arc and weave and form. In text, the work will be good, it will be truthful—and, in Terry's conception, holy—if it is adequate to shape a space in the reader's mind fit to house and hold the place (or person) the writer had in mind; not the actual place (or person), of course, but its spirit, its genius, its essence. And it does not matter that the reader has not felt the place. She will be moved by the writing, as Terry in *Refuge* is moved by the burial moccasins, if she can discern in its craft that it is made to honor and house the beloved.

To speak in the language of her beloved place would, for Terry, be to write about it in a way that honors its truth and suggests its form. For Terry, I sense, the piece of art—the writing, say—must seem to a reader to *come close* to the thing itself. That is, it must seem to have been made out of intimacy with the place: the author must seem, to the reader, to have *touched* the place. Only if that is so can the place, in its essence, touch the reader.

The land tells you things about itself and about you—you, after all, are part of the land if you are intimately present in a place. Whatever it tells you, even if it is nothing so exact as an idea, your task as a writer is to honor the source. These are my words for Terry's thought, and they come from long reflection on what she said by the river and in the cab of the truck. This is what, I think, she has come to understand about stories. It is one of the things she knows about them, anyway. The better they resound with that one place on earth, the more powerfully they may also protest and celebrate and warn. All those things are the work of telling the truth about beloved places and their people.

Living in an eroded landscape has fashioned inside Terry Tempest Williams a thought about the way a mind shapes a piece of prose, and why the finished sentence, if it's good, seems to imply so much more than it actually says. Her notion is an aesthetic of exacting restraint, such as the redrock desert knows; an aesthetic of erosion. Just as the rocks that ornament and articulate the desert—Castle Rock, for instance, the thin minaret rising from sage plains, onto which her study window opens—take whatever form they take because of the editorial work of weather, so the good sentences or lines of poetry a writer is left with in a finished work, Terry says to me, are what is left of the imagined landscape of thought and image and sound that settled and built up in the basin of the writer's mind—they are what is left of that possible world of text once the wind of consciousness, of discernment, of spirit, has gone to work and carried away most of the original terrain of sentence and paragraph. The finished piece of writing—the work—is what the "erosional mind" leaves intact. That remnant speaks for all the rest of the country; it is the stuff of our whole life deposited in that great lake of imagination, formed into a large terrain, uplifted in hope, and swept away by the creative/destructive force (let's call it creativity) that operates in the mind with the same will and power as weather exerts upon land. This may be why works of great beauty make us weep. Like the moccasin, they always speak of loss. They are what remains.

Terry was working at her latest book, *Red*, when I was with her. A collection of new and old pieces, all set within the redrock country, the book is, she writes, "a gesture and a bow to my homeland" (2001, 19). This book is an enactment of both defiance and gratitude—a defense of this place (and all places) and a love song to it. It is here she coins her phrase, her slogan, "bedrock democracy." "Each of us," she writes, "belongs to a particular landscape, one that informs who we are, a place that carries our history, our dreams, holds us to a moral line of behavior that transcends thought. And in each of these places, home work is required, a participation in public life to make certain all is not destroyed under the banner of progress" (ibid.).

Here in the canyons of her new home, though, I find myself wondering where Terry Tempest Williams's heart lies—which is the particular landscape to which she belongs, the one that informs her, her politics and her syntax? Is her story written in sage, in redrock, in swift (though dammed and diminished) river, in dissected plateau, in Great Salt Lake? In the blood of which place, mixed with her own, does she write?

For she comes from two countries, not one. These provinces—the Great Basin and the Colorado Plateau—border each other in America's West: a sagebrush desert of basin and range, and a high red sandstone plateau deeply dissected by the Colorado and its tributaries. Though they border each other, they are distinct. She has roamed over both terrains in her life and work and writing. In the one she was born; in the other she now lives. Which of them speaks in her writing; in the likeness of which of them are here sentences formed?

In her writing, beginning before *Refuge,* Terry Tempest Williams has been moving steadily east, out of the Great Basin and into the canyons and arches, the old, eroding sandstones of the Colorado Plateau, until she can say that this is where she is at home, where her spirit is animated. She announces her arrival home in the plateau, as we have seen, at the end of *Leap.* In many essays in *Red* she speaks of her new home among the canyons and wonders, in "Changing Constellations," whether she is not "returning to the place where my animal body resides" (2001, 123). Strikingly, in this essay she uses Brigham Young's pronouncement, *"This is the place"*—italicizing the words to tell us she knows where they come from and to what they once referred—to describe how she and Brooke felt on finding their new home in Castle Valley (ibid., 122).

At the heart of *Red* lies an essay of the same name, "Red." In it, firmly setting herself down within the red plateau, she writes: "I want to learn the language of the desert, to be able to translate this landscape of red into a language of heat that quickens the heart and gives courage to silence, a silence that is heard" (ibid., 138). "How," she asks, "do I learn to speak in a language native to where I live?" noting that for the people indigenous to the Colorado Plateau—the Ute, Paiute, Hopi, Zuñi, Diné (Navajo), Hualapai, Havasupai—"vocabulary is based on kinship, shared stories, and a long history of inhabiting the desert." She goes on: "Native people understand language as an articulation of kinship, all manner of relations" (ibid., 136–37).

Language, then, articulates relationships, and not only those at play between the human beings. And the pattern of a local language is akin to the pattern that holds among the community of beings who live in that place—who *are* that place. The geography of the language native to a place is apt for—it fits—the geography of the place. "The relationship between language and landscape is a marriage of sound and form, an oral geography, a sensual topography, what draws us to a place and keeps us there. Where we live is at the center of how we speak" (ibid., 136).

But where does she live? Now, she lives in the red desert. But, as she well understands, she is not indigenous, as the Diné, the Hopi, the Paiute are indigenous to one place. She travels. She has given her heart to a lake. She gave it to a basin. Now she gives it to a desert. She has entwined her love, over time, around them all; and all of them live in her language. She may have to choose one geography to participate in the politics of place, but two geographies, at least, have colored her poetics.

Williams's nature is porous, curious, mystical. She surrenders to places, has done so all her life, and so she is shaped by them. It is impossible, therefore, to separate her development as a writer from her movement from one terrain to another within the arid West. She is a trickster and seductress, like the Great Salt Lake; her writing itself is still a kind of "dreamscape," like the Great Basin, lean and miraged, haunted by distance (Leuders 1989, 51). But, in her last few books—books born and composed mostly on the plateau—it has grown denser, more angular, less pastel, more deeply toned.

Both terrains that shape Williams's work belong to one climatic zone, and it is dry. She finds her stories, she finds healing and meaning, in dry places. Aridity is the bed of her imagination. "Aridity, and aridity alone," writes Wallace Stegner in "Living Dry," "makes the various Wests one" (1998, 216). The country in the rain shadow of the Sierra Nevada, the land of little rain where most of what falls from the sky is light and legend—this dry place teaches her aesthetics, schools her in rhetoric. Aridity is what unifies the neighboring provinces she inhabits. They are dry lands scattered with miraculous plants and animals, surreal rock forms, deep colors, and great holes in the earth. Space reigns, and in it each thing seems distinct and peculiar.

Both the Great Basin and the Colorado Plateau belong to the same weather; they are dry and full of sage. They are full of distinctive lifeforms, all of them gifted at surviving where there is too little water. Each of them, by adapting themselves to tough country, adorn it, decorate its underlying starkness, quicken and animate it. In people— those who survive it—such broken and spare country breeds mysticism, stoicism, and deep love; it turns out autodidacts, adventurers, poets, and singers. The arid West has shattered many dreams that people brought to it, too, and it has been mistreated very often because those dreams, though akin to it in grandeur, were unsustainable in it, being excessive, ill-adapted. But those souls responsive and adapted to its forms, to its dryness and intractability, sometimes become its poets. And the "forms and lights and colors" (ibid.) of the arid West—its extremes of temperature, its rain and dry, its scarcity and abundance, its spaciousness and improbability—find their way into the language of those people it claims, and into the forms and lights and colors of their lives and writing. Stegner was one such man and writer. Abbey another. Williams is another yet. And strikingly in her writing, the beat of the place seems matched to a human heartbeat, measured out in text. The arid lands have found in Terry Tempest Williams a woman and a writer ready to listen, to adapt. They have found a sage listener, a storyteller vulnerable to the magic and mystery as well as to the naked truth of these dry lands. And she speaks as they do; she speaks for them, for herself, for life as it is lived here.

"The West is a region of extraordinary variety within its abiding unity," writes Stegner (ibid., 213). This is true of the neighboring provinces of plateau and basin—they are two parts of one arid whole, each distinct from the other. Drama inheres in both of them. But in each it is differently disposed.

Drama in the plateau is express. Though the sediments that compose the plateau where Williams now lives are old, the uplift and deep, deep erosion that give it its form are quite new. They happened fast.

Drama as well and ancient magic inhabit its canyons and ridges. Terry's spirit—both oracular and dramatic, both restrained and expressive—is well housed in such a landscape, as is her prose. She runs like a river through her places, cutting fast and deep, picking up stories like sediments and running red with them, adding their histories to her own. Her essays and stories are deep and sudden, passionate affairs, meant to last forever. They change your life; and then they are over. But they are performed with swift, sure, condensed phrases and clauses that imply more than they say—like oracles, like this country. Like the plateau, she is the master (or mistress) of compression; of the sudden dramatic, heartbreaking, or breathtaking gesture in the midst of endless space and light:

> Just then, we hear the garage door open. Dad and Brooke are home. A few more breaths . . . one last breath—Dad walks into the room. Mother turns to him. Their eyes meet. She smiles. And she goes.
>
> He kneels by her side, takes her hand, and says, "Diane, finally you are at peace." (*Refuge*, 1991, 231)

Drama in the Great Basin, by contrast, is inherent. It waits to spring. The crust of that country is being stretched by the movement of the plate on which it sits. Tension runs through it, has thrown up its ranges and pulled down its basins. Its skin is thin and it threatens to break open, fracture, change the face of things, lay open its heart. Occasionally it does, and steadily another part of the sagebrush ocean rises, another sinks. Power and danger here lie barely hidden; they live within the earth, just below the surface. The Wasatch Mountains are the most easterly range in the province of the basin and range. Terry and her family grew up digging into the soil of that country, a country coiled tight with life waiting to articulate itself.[2]

Terry's prose has always been alive with a quality like that of the

2. I rely for my geology chiefly on John McPhee's *Basin and Range* of 1981, reproduced as the first part of his *Annals of the Former World* (1998).

basin, too. A book like *Pieces of White Shell* has about it the same restrained, deceptive calm. It's a composed and quiet sedition, a revolutionary plot hatching underground. Its surface is still, but it feels as though it is drawn thin, as though at any moment it might fracture and give rise to a sudden range. The surface does occasionally give, in that book; and what arises is a story, some magic, a revelation—and then the calm of the sage resumes. In her later writing, she lets the country (now mostly the more voluble plateaulands) rise in weirder shapes, in the daring, edgy phrasing of *Leap* and the more recent essays of *Red.* In these pieces her prose surrenders more to the drama of eternal re-creation that she sees written about her now in red—but it does not surrender completely. Even in the more daring works, including *Desert Quartet,* the skin that holds the body of her text remains taut with a habit of civility and poise, learned in the basin, practiced in a Mormon home.

Until *Leap* (and possibly still), her life, like the basin, contained fundamental tensions, and you felt them in her prose. In her case, the tensions were not tectonic, but they may as well have been. She was, she once said, a "radical soul in a conservative religion" (quoted in Anderson 1996, 973). As Lorraine Anderson puts it, "She is . . . a feminist in a patriarchal religion, an environmentalist in one of the very few American religions that in the 1990s has not embraced ecological values, a woman who has been arrested for civil disobedience in a religion that holds obedience to civil authority as an article of faith, a childless woman in a protonatalist religion" (ibid.). She is a sensualist, an eroticist, in a society that frowns on the body's desires. All these years she has harbored these contrary forces, just as the Great Basin has harbored its tensions. She made a jump in the end and became, if not a range, then a plateau.

In his book *Basin and Range,* John McPhee travels into the Great Basin with geologist Kenneth Deffeyes. Their conversation in the Nevada desert gives a palpable sense that the basin is, beneath its apparently quiet slumber, alive. "The earth is moving," says Deffeyes.

"The world is splitting open and coming apart. . . . It is live country. This is the tectonic, active, spreading, mountain-building world" (McPhee 1998, 45–46). And though its silence is profound, this country has a powerful rhythm, coagulated in its ups and downs, which express that ongoing energetic dance of rise-fall-stretch-rise-fall. It goes like this: "Basin. Fault. Range. Basin. Fault. Range. A mile of relief between basin and range. Stillwater Range. Pleasant Valley. Tobin Range. Jersey Valley. Sonoma Range. . . . Ondographic rhythms of the Basin and Range" (ibid., 42).

Just such a rhythm—just such a surge and spread, jump and rise and fall—runs through Terry Tempest Williams's prose. She could almost have written that passage of McPhee's. She has written this: "Heat. More heat. My face flushes red. The fire's hands are circling. I sit inches away from something that tomorrow will not exist. The blue-eyed coals I gaze into will disappear. Ashes. Ashes. Death is the natural conclusion of love" ("Fire," *Desert Quartet*, 1995, 43).

This is one example, but I could find you thousands more. Terry has, I think, the rhythm of a highly strung and lively terrain inside her. Even when, nowadays, she sings a landscape whose genius is for lying still and, quite unstressed, surrendering to the work of erosion—I mean, of course, the Colorado Plateau—the same pulsing rhythm persists, though it shifts, now and then, into something more like the turbidity of flood waters: "Where I live, the open space of desire is red. The desert before me is red is rose is pink is scarlet is magenta is salmon. The colors are swimming in light as it changes constantly, with cloud cover with rain with wind with light, delectable light, delicious light. The palette of erosion is red, is running red water, red river, my own blood flowing downriver; my desire is red" ("Red," *Red*, 2001, 136).

Old lands live on in Terry. They live on and shape both thought and expression because she is a human animal, a woman, and memory and family tie her to a basin and a lake, even when she finds her home and grounds her work in redrock canyons. For there is no leaving the landscapes of our childhood, even though we may come to belong—where perhaps we have always belonged. Who we are is where we are and where we have been; and it is whom we have been there with.

Over both basin and plateau, the same sky holds, and the same weather, more or less, does its thing. And I think Terry works under the influence of that sky. Her writing is not dense. It is light. It darts and suggests flight. It alights here and offers a quick song, flies and finds another perch, and sings again. Birds unify *Refuge.* "I am a woman with wings," she writes in that book; "the birds and I share a natural history" (1991, 273, 21). She flies, as a feather, in *Pieces of White Shell.* She soars like an angel in *Leap,* a book of airiness, of spirit and mind. Though her newer work—particularly the new pieces in *Red* like "Labor"—dwells on ground and feels rockier, still it has a lightness, a quickness that is her character as it is the character of the Utah air. Even on ground, she dwells and moves and sings like a bird—like a canyon wren.

But in person and in prose, she also moves like water—desert water. In the desert, water is a god. Water is the magic of the place. Everything depends upon it, scarce and ephemeral though it is. A woman so native to arid ground knows this, and she loves wetlands, lakes, and rivers—the places the waters are. The waters she has known—Bear River, the Great Salt Lake, Moab Slough, the Colorado River—have taught her about flow and buoyancy, about nurture and stillness. She has these things in her nature too, but she found them spoken in water, and when she writes, she seems to recall the things that water knows, the importance of simplicity and transparency, for example.

You will find these qualities in her prose. Sometimes her words lie easy, go slow—transparent, if, like water, not always easy to get to the bottom of. Open *Pieces of White Shell* at any page, and you will find this intelligent languor. It is there in the stories of *Coyote's Canyon.* You will hear it in the melancholy of "Winter Solstice at the Moab Slough." Sometimes waters rage through the desert too, and then her words storm with them—in the flood sequence in "Labor," for instance, and in "Undressing the Bear." Terry's words engulf you or buoy you; they carry you along; they embrace you. Even when she rages or grieves, she finds a soft diction, like water in the desert, whether lake or river or rain. Her words on the page, like her voice in the canyon, come out sweet and smooth.

Listen to this passage, for example, from a new essay "River Music," which puts me in mind of our afternoon on the same river bend, November 28, 2000. (The river ran red past Terry the day she writes of here, whereas the river we shared ran green. Its mood was the same, though, as it is in this essay, as it always is.)

> River. The river is brown, is red, is green, is turquoise. On any given day, the river is light, liquid light, a traveling mirror in the desert . . .
> May 28, 2000—a relatively uneventful day. A few herons fly by, a few mergansers. Two rafts float through the redrock corridor. I wave. They wave back. One man is playing a harmonica, the oars resting on his lap as he coasts through flat water.
> Sweet echoes continue to reach me.
> I sit on the fine pink sand, still damp from high water days, and watch the river flow, the clouds shift, and the colors of the cliff deepen from orange to red to maroon. (*Red*, 2001, 148–49).

Terry wrote this piece for a CD cut by local musicians and activists in Moab to raise money for the ongoing campaign to save and restore the Colorado River. Her reading is the final track—a kind of epilogue. But she reads as though she knows her words make music too. So here is music again—a community of voices—put in service of a local cause: poetics as a vehicle for a politics of place, a redrock democracy. Terry gave me a copy, and I played it as I drove among the sandstone arches that day and then all the way out of Utah. I have seen the river run blue and green, and I have heard it read. I have heard the river red. Always a kind of water, sometimes red, sometimes blue, sometimes a torrent, sometimes a pool, runs through Terry Tempest

Williams's prose. You will hear it if you listen. It is in her voice. It is there on the page.

Terry Tempest Williams has drawn her voice from the desert, then. Her voice is not the desert, but it suggests the desert. Her writing honors this dry country and touches us with it because her body— her voice's house—leans into her places, past and present, basin and plateau, lake and river, range and canyon, and is touched by them. The arid lands are places where the elements are starkly present—earth, water, fire, air. Terry's prose is an aptly elemental expression of the arid zones she loves. She writes in many colors, but most of all in red. It is the color of many things—passion, heart's blood, slickrock, erosion, birth, river, bird, coyote, and sunset.

Four o'clock. This is the place. Here, in these sage fields, within an astonishing landscape, sits the house where Terry Tempest Williams lives. It is built from a Frank Lloyd Wright design. Walls of windows facing east, north, and south carry you outside and bring the mesas in. And I am sitting, as the world grows dark, in Terry and Brooke's living room, looking north through wide windows, over their patio and across gray-green sagebrush to Castle Rock, a monument on a mesa.

Around the house on two sides runs a stone rubble wall colonized by sage. This, Terry has told me, is to keep floodwaters out—for the house is set down in a floodplain. If you are not careful, you could get swept away.

Castle Rock is red, the color of rust: a tall, strong, sharp-edged spire on top of a pyramid of sandstone atop a mesa. Its color fades as I watch it in this falling light, in this rising cold. But it seems to glow as though it held the memory of the day, its gentle warmth, longer than you'd expect against the coming night. Dense green Utah junipers hold to the slopes and valley floor, while Mormon tea and Russian olive and rabbitbrush run up into the wash. Terry pointed them out to me earlier when we walked with her dog Rio among the slickrock and sand.

This is not a place of trees. The road into the cluster of widely spaced houses that is Castle Valley crosses a dry creek bed, and that crossing is held by the most massive cottonwood I have ever seen. I stopped beside it as I drove in this morning, and I marveled. But I can't see it now; it's behind me. Most of what I look out on is rock, rockfall from ages of slippage, and soft red earth.

I am looking up to the ridge where, in the midday, we sat in cold sand, making figures and lines in the earth and talking, bathed in light and looking down into the next valley. Now, night is coming on.

Up on the same mesa where Castle Rock sits, west of it, run the Nuns and the Priest—spires made by long erosion. The redrock erodes to sharp edges. It tells tales, always has. Below that storied ridge, a jagged spine of stone runs east with junipers on its flanks. It looks like a crocodile. To the west of the house rises Adobe Mesa, a plain old massif of more red stone.

East of the house the La Sal Mountains rise, their northwest flanks covered in snow and ponderosas. These are mountains formed by volcanic activity, not part of the long geological story of the sandstone, and very much newer. In front of them, only a mile from Terry's house, Round Mountain sweeps up from the flat land to a low peak, like a teepee. It looks like a holy mountain, a shrine. A walk around its base is a meditation, says Terry. Up in its basalt crevasses hawks and eagles nest. Behind me, so to the south, running east-west, the other side of Castle Valley is a long flat-topped mesa, whose gently undulating strata the snow spells out. Its skirts are spotted with green.

It's 4:25 now, and Round Mountain and the mountains behind it have surrendered their color. But Castle Rock still holds its warmth and light. While I have been here making notes on my laptop, Terry has been working in her study, a shed like a container that sits outside the house. She comes in now and flicks a switch. "Look at you sitting here in the dark," she says. Then, urgently: "Can you smell gas?" I hadn't noticed. Terry smells it straight off, and now I smell it too. She is alarmed. She switches off the light and suggests I turn off the computer. Then she calls her father. "He's been laying gas pipe all his life," she says. "He'll know what we should do here." Her father, John Tempest, suggests we turn everything off—light and power and gas—and get ourselves outside. So we do. "My father said I might have blown us up when I turned that switch on," she says.

As we sit there on the patio in the falling light, the doors wide open, letting the gas out and the landscape in, light plays in the sky. The sun has dropped behind the mesas, but even as it sinks from sight, the light swells again in the sky and falls on the rocks all around us. This is secondary light, muted, luminescent, reflected out of cloud that looks like river shallows above us. The clouds turn vermilion; the sky behind the rocks to the north goes from violet and blue to purple. The tip of the tallest of the mountains to the east—the one called Tukuhnikivats, "the peak that keeps the light the longest," which I remember from Ed Abbey's *Desert Solitaire*—turns electric blue and then yellow. And still the glow rises and rises and stays and rises again. "It was like a multiple orgasm," Terry said later, and I'm going to have to take her word for that.

In this long twilight, this drawn-out blessing, Brooke, who's been out jogging, comes running home through the sage fields. "I startled some deer out there," he tells us. "I heard coyote too, and I'm afraid the deer ran from me right toward them, to their death. But"—he looks us over—"what are you guys doing sitting out here in the cold?"

Terry explains. I stand out in the drive agog at the light show, glad to be alive to see it. Terry and Brooke decide to forget about grilling the steak and drinking the red wine. That had been the dinner plan. Brooke will sit with the house and wait for the gas man to come and check for the leak. But he sends Terry and me into town for dinner. "I'll come along later," he says.

Terry is astonished by the light. "I've never seen it go on so long as that," she declares as we make for Moab. The gas in the house, she reflects, forced us outside to witness this display of sacred time. Inside, profane time held in the dark. "Propane time," she quips; "and you were the caretaker of the light."

"Is it possible to make a living by simply watching the light?"

Terry asks at the start of her essay "Ode to Slowness" (*Red*, 2001, 141).
If it is, this is the place: Castle Valley, blessed by light and slow time.

"Perhaps I shall be an arch tomorrow," Terry writes in *Pieces of White Shell* (1984b, 30).

And tomorrow, the day after the erotics of the desert sky, Terry
sends me off to walk among arches on my own. I drive north toward
Arches National Park, where Ed Abbey spent so much time. The road
runs along the line of the Moab fault. To the east the rock layers lie two
thousand feet lower than those to the west. After paying my entrance
money, I drive up into a landscape scattered with monuments, balancing rocks, windows, petrified dunes, gold-colored pinnacles—a
spectacular ruin of an ancient order of stone. It is poised, this landscape, in its present moment of decline. We catch it just like this, in our
time. It is poised between its solid past and its future fall. It almost
seems to hold its breath. Change is written all over this static landscape—written into rock by wind and rain, storm and gravity. Here is
the story of the stones, lying all about: plateau becoming mesa; mesa
becoming arch; arch on the point of collapsing into rubble; rubble
becoming desert floor. It is poised. This is the moment you turn the
page between chapters; this is the silence between the notes. And here
I am in that moment within a landscape of fragmented narratives, of
overlapping orders of time.

I park at the head of the trail to Delicate Arch. I take the path, and
I pass no one coming or going. The track wanders by an old settler's
hut, over a bridge, across soft sand and expanses of naked yellow
stone, and I go with it. It cuts through juniper, sage, and pinyon pine,
unwinding toward Delicate Arch. I am there. I climb over the lip of red
rock and behold the arch. It is unaccountable, an elegant mystery. It
stands like a huge red whale's jaw upon this slickrock, solitary on the
edge of a bowl, a thing made by the fiat of winds. I can see right
through it, through the eye of god, across a red desert to the snowy La
Sals. At the feet of the arch, facing west, is a great elliptical basin of
stone, hollowed also by the wind, an arena for spirits, surely. This is a

holy place—Terry's words. And a palace of the winds. No winds play today, just an assembled silence, a pool of lost time. To the southwest, monuments and ridges form a city on the horizon.

The north wind picks up as I make my way back. The day is growing late, and I have another arch to visit yet. Halfway back I meet a man and woman in their sixties, walking with a dog toward the arch. "Is that your wife who passed us just now?" she asks me.

"I'd be surprised," I reply. "My wife's back in Sydney."

"Well, if you get a move on, you might get lucky," her husband says. "She was pretty good looking, I thought." But I catch no one on the trail, and there is no one waiting at the parking lot.

What do I make of this? There may have been a woman, of course—perhaps a woman who had been an arch yesterday. Who did these people see, and why did they take her for my wife? Coyote in drag?

I follow my love into the desert. My beloved leads me on, just ahead of me and out of sight. I think of Terry's saying to me the day before: "The writing I need to do is always just out ahead of me. Just out of reach. I reach for it; I follow it."

At the head of the trail to Landscape Arch (the one pictured against a deep summer sky on my copy of *An Unspoken Hunger*), I find a coyote. Another one saunters in the middle distance, her mate. A woman is getting close to her to snap a photograph. "She snarled at my wife when she came out of the toilet," the woman's husband says to me when I leave the truck and walk over. Raven sits on the roof of the pit toilet and caws. Another trickster and harbinger. The man points up the trail I am about to walk. "I'd keep my eyes open if I were you," he says. "A wolf, or maybe it was a coyote, crossed the path halfway up there as we were coming back."

Coyote has a powerful reputation in the redrock country. His name is synonymous with trickery and seduction, with shape-shifting and elusiveness—the same qualities you find in the landscape itself, "its chameleon nature" changing from one moment to the next, tripping you up with surprise just when you thought you knew it well. "The trickster quality of the canyons is Coyote's cachet," writes Terry in *Coyote's Canyon* (1989, 19). And Coyote's message is that it is the desert that matters, the desert that goes on, the desert that can teach us what we need to know. Coyote pricks pomposity, fools and disconcerts us. Coyote reveals the desert:

> Coyote knows we do not matter. He knows rocks care nothing for those who wander through them; and yet he also knows that those same individuals who care for rocks will find openings—large openings—that become passageways into the unseen world, where music is heard through doves' wings and wisdom is gleaned from the tails of lizards. Coyote is always nearby, but remains hidden. (ibid., 18)

I set off through a slot canyon, beyond which a wide, flat expanse of red-gray earth, sagebrush, and juniper opens out. The light is falling, but the sky is clear, like yesterday. I walk over patches of rock-hard snow. A gilded flicker—black and white and flashed with red—drums out some message on the silver trunk of a juniper. I am thinking about the coyotes behind and the wolves, or whatever they are, ahead. I look behind to see if I am being followed. Soon I just start seeing this wide and lovely desert woodland, and I am lost in it still when the long lean reach of Landscape Arch emerges right here beside me out of the thinning light. It has stayed hidden against the rocks behind it until I shift and see a patch of sky beneath its slender arc. There it stretches, poised a moment before its fall. Perhaps it will be a pile of rocks tomorrow, perhaps in a thousand years, or a hundred. It seems to compose a fragile gesture of resignation. I feel an immense, deep stillness up here among the weathered bodies of the old Utah junipers, the arch's haunting note above. I stay awhile and find myself asking the place to remember me. I sense mystery collapsing into sentiment. It is time to leave.

I take up a stick to go back with, remembering the "wolf." Five minutes later, an animal, slick and gray, all tail it seems in that fast moment, slips across the path and disappears into the sage. My whole body awakens with fright and wonder. I bristle, feel my shoulders rise, my pores open, all my senses kick in. The animal made no sound, and when I pass the place it crossed the path, I can make out no sign of it. As I walk on, I keep turning, sensing it behind me. I am wide awake.

I reach the old juniper where the flicker tapped, but she is gone. I stop and peer ahead into the canyon, trying to make out the shape of waiting coyotes. At my side a gray-brown animal slips from the sage, and I jump. My heart falters. It is a jackrabbit. When my heart is back in its proper place, I find myself laughing, and I enter the canyon without fear.

But fear, I notice, has woken me to the land. In my fear the whole place quickens. Fables walk, and animals change their shapes and play their jokes. I am so easily beguiled.

The coyotes are gone from the parking area, but as I drive away into the glow of the rocks, into a sunset that is turning the shoal of clouds crimson, another coyote comes from the sage toward me. I stop the truck. This animal is much more golden than the other two, and smaller, more delicate in her movements. She comes right up to me, and I wind down the window to ask her what she wants. She doesn't say anything. I'm a little scared to leave the cab, so we sit there regarding each other in fear (I'm fearful, anyway), in fascination and desire. She looks gentle and beautiful to me. I want to know what this coyote knows. I'd like to look that good in a desert sunset. I'd like to feel so at home here. I'd like to know what she wants of me. But we are lost to each other. It almost breaks my heart to press the pedal down and move away. She stands watching me go.

My beloved? Coyote out of drag? *It's a coyote, Mark, get a grip.* She seems so complete and entire, utterly herself. That is magic enough. I feel called to stay, but I don't stay. It is growing dark and cold; the sky is dying to embers. And I feel as hungry as she looks.

I call Terry when I get back to Moab. I tell her what happened to me among the arches, and she tells me I have been showered with revelations and desert magic. The animal encounters sound like blessings to her. She has had a small blessing of her own this evening. Brooke was out picking sage for her to take to Washington, D.C., on Friday, where she will read a "Liturgy for the Earth" she has written. ("I can crush its leaves between my fingers and remember who I am," she wrote of sage in *Pieces of White Shell* [1983, 1]. It smells like home, this desert plant of basin and plateau, of all the arid West.) Along with the sage, Brooke found a quartz arrowhead out in the red sand, a relic of the Anasazi. The ancient ones have gone now, but these were their hunting grounds once. Their stories still lie in the desert from which they (stories and people both) rose. What they have left behind, in stone and figures on stone, in cliff dwellings, speaks of them and their desires, their belonging here. It is part of the grammar of the West, the language of red—arid, angular, and broken, eloquent with loss and departure. We can almost touch these people in the bodies of their work, made with their hands out of desert. Profane time stops, sacred time starts, in that touch, and the memory of their walking in this land becomes another story that deepens our own belonging here.

It deepens Terry's belonging anyway, and it might deepen mine if my being here did not end tomorrow, when I head north, up through Salt Lake City and on to Jackson Hole, Wyoming.

On the road, I find myself thinking a lot about magic and revelation. Nothing that happened around me in Terry Tempest Williams's country is beyond explanation, of course. I saw no actual ghosts; I witnessed no authentic miracles. The magic I speak of, the magic Terry writes of, is a kind of experience of qualities in things that surpass or defy our expectations. These are, understood one way, the erotics of place—to use Terry's own metaphor. Those sunsets, those coyote encounters, the accompaniment of canyon wren—these are the rare rewards, incidents of grace, that happen now and then when you hold yourself present in the land. They are pieces of a story, a story that seems to include the listener, but a story that went on long before we stumbled by and will go on long after. They are small parts that hint at a whole.

Maybe Terry has schooled me in presence, and I have been blessed in return with a few outbreaks of wildness. Erotic encounters, with people or with places, open up emotional realms—in the other and in ourselves. They reward intimacy with sudden moments of unprecedented sensual experience. They reveal aspects of ourselves and the other that we have never seen in decades of thinking we knew that person or place, or even our self.

Stand close, make yourself vulnerable, let go of preconceptions, and unexpected music and light, emotion and coincidence, may occur. In life and in prose, Terry Tempest Williams leans toward such wild, erotic, magical moments, and she finds them now and then. She has a gift for intimacy, with people and with places. Perhaps that gift invites marvels and sudden revelations. Intimacy demands emotional engagement. It may be that when we bring to an encounter with the land the kind of presence that we bring occasionally to a lover, we make ourselves ready for aspects of the land that otherwise would be lost on us.

I find myself thinking ahead to the work of James Galvin. His writing offers up the idea that the real world has a face it mostly turns from us. This may be, I'm thinking, the magic realm, the inner—or other—aspect of a place, that Terry has a gift for coming into intimacy with. Occasionally, people who have learned how to pay attention to places, who have stayed and wondered long, are visited by moments in which they realize that the world is not what it has always seemed. Magic and mystery may be the rewards for learning to witness long and deep and hard—like a geologist, a poet, and a lover, such as Terry Tempest Williams; or like Galvin's Lyle Van Waning, who has worked a single stretch of land for fifty years. In a literal sense, much more goes on inside the life of a coyote or a cloud than we can begin to imagine; ancient realms are contained within the sediment that composes desert rocks. Everything is not as we come to imagine it through conventional, fact-based perspectives. Let go of those—let go, as Terry puts it in *Coyote's Canyon* (1989, 16), of "society's oughts and shoulds"—and we may be allowed, now and then, to walk through that window or arch into the inner nature, the musical heart, of a place.

Williams's writing dwells often on the extraordinary and inexplicable, and it moves outside linear and orderly modes of expression to shake us out of fixed positions, to stir us into intimacy, to shatter the shell of the familiar that surrounds the extraordinary inner life of the world. In words, she animates landscapes whose teeming mysteries might escape us otherwise. And in the flesh, who knows, perhaps something of her discipline of intimacy, her way of apprehending reality, rubbed off on me, and the real world turned its other face my way a few times.

Shape-changing and out-and-out magic occur mostly in Terry Tempest Williams's fictions, not her essays—the stories in *Coyote's Canyon*, for instance. In *Pieces of White Shell*, a work essentially of nonfiction, she describes a council of desert animals just as though it actually happened; in *Refuge*, she sinks into the bosom of the salt lake. These are moments of magic realism, to be sure; but it is clear she wants us to understand them as metaphors. They are stories, miniature myths—the kind she studies among the Navajo and the kind she says we must make for ourselves. Very largely, Williams respects readers' expectations of books that purport to engage with the real world. She does not falsify or fabricate. She does, however, imagine the real a little more deeply than others might. And she tells stories, even when she is not writing fiction. Stories are a way of seeing reality—its insides, its essence, its patterns of connection—and they see it not so much literally as poetically, often expressing it as dreams, fantasies, and parables. They see design and texture; they hear rhythm and harmony. Stories concentrate on moments that may be of little interest to science and are surely far beyond its reach.

In the prologue to *Pieces of White Shell*, Terry Tempest Williams tells the story of a weaver finch that came down the chimney of her family's home on the weekend after Thanksgiving, flew through the fire and alit on the Christmas tree just as her grandmother was telling the season's story of new life. She had begun this story, as usual, with the words, "You see, this tree is alive." This is a tree so crowded with ornamental birds and angels the Tempests had taken to joking that it moves. Suddenly it was a living tree with a living ornament, this bird.

The event is extraordinary, if explicable, and touched, in the telling, with awe. It is a marvel, if not a miracle or a sign. Earlier in the prologue, Williams explained that Mormons share with the Navajo a belief "in a power that moves us, directs us, cares for us. . . . We are a spiritual people, Mormon and Navajo. . . . The Navajo have their sacred mountains and we have our sacred groves and temples" (1983, 3–8). The story of the bird belongs in such a cultural setting. Terry's own culture disposes her to a worldview and language that allow for the existence of magic and miracle in the world. She was schooled to expect them even before she moved to that miraculous place, the red desert.

If you live in the desert, you will see ordinary miracles every day. Terry grew up with a lake that rises and falls, shifts its shape, merges with the sky, and allows a girl to defy gravity. She lives now within a valley of extraordinary light, near a river that has carved canyons of impossible depth. She lives among birds and mammals and reptiles that need to learn the trick of invisibility and other acts of guile just to stay alive in a land of little rain. It is a land that teaches the possibility of magic, the necessity of illusion.

Terry Tempest Williams writes landscapes in which, as one of her narrators puts it in *Coyote's Canyon,* "the lines between the real and the imagined [are] thinly drawn" (*Red,* 2001, 54). She has also learned in the Great Basin and the red desert that places are dynamic, composed of lives that are fast and slow, enduring and changeable, where sands fly, rocks fall, landforms alter, rivers run red, run blue, run high, run low, canyon wrens come and sing up water and go. Her writing—all of it, but particularly her fables and her poetic riffs, her narration of miracle and magic—tries to show us, through its many devices, that her places are animated, are made of energies at play, most of them beyond our senses' reach. To reach for and grasp them, one needs imagination, specifically an ecological imagination; one needs to be present, listening and letting oneself be moved. Her writing tries to move us, its readers, from a position that imagines places as finished and inanimate, as silent and still, as disenchanted. Her writing is a song of, and a dance with, places she experiences as lively, mysterious, and rhythmical.

Magic attends Terry Tempest Williams. She belongs in the red desert— a place where little is as simple as it seems, an erosional landscape that, in its present form, is an expression also, an apt memorial, of a departed country, a former world. You can sense what is no longer here in what remains; the past lives on, enfolded in and celebrated by the present.

Terry has a gift for intimacy with people and with places, an intimacy that makes them deeply and immediately hers. She hungers much for country, and she writes out of her earnest desire to know the ground she stands on, and to be known by it in return. She wants to learn a language spoken among the red rocks and sage, so that she can make sentences composed of words first spoken ages ago, and still spoken without sound in the landscape she loves. She wants most to honor and protect this place on earth and all who live within it, not excluding rock and river and light. The politics of nurture and restoration begins in intimacy, arises in erotic encounters with the wild, and speaks itself in stories true to such encounters.

I was worried before I walked out with her into her country that she found too much of herself in it, that she didn't leave the land enough space to speak for itself. But I realize now that her writing enacts her love and contains the country in the same way a wife holds intimate secrets of her husband, and sometimes, respectfully, speaks them. In the same way Shoshone burial moccasins honor the life of the man or woman they are made to fit. The making of the moccasin requires and speaks of intimacy. And so it is with writing like Terry's. Terry's "my" is an expression of love—a mother's, a lover's. Her identification with the arid country of Utah speaks of intimacy, not ownership or projection. She is a woman, above all, of heart. And her heart is incapable, like this country, of playing false, though it is fast to passion, and given to playing games to trip up the self-assured and fool the predator. All of them, these games, are really a dance, and they lead you deeper into the nature of what is real here at the heart of a dry land. The prose you read is the dance she makes with this ample and arid, shape-shifting place.

Navajo and Mormon worldviews are both rooted in magic. Terry Tempest Williams inherited a feeling for magic, and it is fed by her country. The magic here, in the red plateau, is quite real. And in Terry's writing it is no affectation. It is a quality of the place and of her dance with the place.

6   *The Real World*

JAMES GALVIN

Boulder Ridge and Sheep Creek, Wyoming-Colorado Border; Iowa City, Iowa

> Beauty and grace are performed whether or not we will
> or sense them. The least we can do is try to be there.
>
> Annie Dillard, *Pilgrim at Tinker Creek*

> Some people never stop wanting to disappear into
> the mountains.
>
> James Galvin, "They Haven't Heard the West Is Over"

> A poem should be equal to:
> Not true . . .
> A poem should not mean
> But be.
>
> Archibald MacLeish, "Ars Poetica"

It is early spring 2002, and I hang twenty thousand feet above the real world. Well, if you count the sky—as one ought to here—I'm moving inside the real world already.

    Wyoming and northern Colorado lie stretched and buckled below me. Snow holds the higher peaks of the Wind Rivers, the Uintas, and the Neversummers; it dusts the tops of the entire ragged front range behind

Denver. It is Denver we're making for, descending now into air shaped by the mountains. This country is scarped and hogbacked, bluffed and bouldered, lined and weathered; its basins are scoured, its rivers braided and gestural, its ranges bunched chaotically and articulated sparely among all this tawny ground. Dark standing timber decorates the folds where gullies run, where high ground picks up from the grassy flats, and they reach, these dark lean pines, right to the ridgetops.

I sit within the most overwhelming element of this landscape— the open blue sky above it. And as we draw close to Denver airport, the plane is set upon by that other element for which this part of the world is infamous—the wind. It touches us in motions as random and forceful as those slower, larger rhythms of mountain building evident in the ranges below, whose peaks are, of course, the reason any descent into Denver is bound to be rocky.

Set within shallow depressions, between the fingers, as it were, of the granite ridges close below me now, I can make out, ringed by black-green pines and spruce, high meadows, some drifted still with snow, others pale green with the start of spring. It is a meadow that brings me here—the meadow on Sheep Creek below Boulder Ridge.

I am coming to Wyoming because of a meadow and its book. Eighteen months ago, in the Shenandoah, the poet Laurie Kutchins put that book, *The Meadow*, into my hands. It was a book I hadn't known till then, and when I read it I was changed. I have come now to find the man, James Galvin, and the places that made so fine a thing. Reading it led me to Galvin's novel *Fencing the Sky*, also set among these meadows, parks, prairies, and ranges below me; and then to the poems that have been most of his life's work. They are fashioned, all of these works, out of the country of Larimer County, Colorado, and Albany County, Wyoming—mostly out of Boulder Ridge and Sheep Creek and the Snowy Range.

Laurie pulled Galvin's book from her shelf in the yellow study in Singers Glen, Virginia. "You need to read this," she said. "I wonder what you will think of it as a piece of place writing." I didn't read it until I was home again in the blue plateau, when, maybe, I was ready for it, but when it was too late to go and find its source. Laurie was right: reading *The Meadow* altered my sense of what a literature of place might be. What I learned from it, and from Galvin's poetry and fiction, about form and composition, about the wild music of places and the capacity of words to find and sound it out again, has made me rethink and recast my own book *The Blue Plateau*. I have learned from Galvin's writing about the power of orderly chaos in a book; about the musical arrangement of apparently—but only apparently—random fragments of text and how well such an arrangement seems suited to the task of overcoming the limits of linear and narrative, largely visual, perception and how well it seems given to the business of witnessing the other order of time and space in which land goes about its life.

I learn another thing from Galvin's writing. The lives of men and women might pass, as he puts it to me when we meet later, like so much weather through a place (or through a book of that place), and yet we can love them, those men and women, as though they were weather we have been longing for; and we can love and write the place more truly the more care we take with its human meteorology. I learn from James Galvin's writing that a writer may best find the place he seeks to sing—its lives and landforms—in the lives of the people who love that place, who belong there and have worked and known it long and deeply. So if we want to render country, one way—maybe the best way—to do it is to write some pieces of the history of some human lives that have passed through the place. One can bring a place to life most truly on the page by writing the work of men's and women's hands and the turning of their souls within a landscape.

Like weather, people in their passage may do good or they may do harm, may come like welcome rain or like a hundred-year flood; but viewed in landscape terms, all of it passes, all of it shapes the place and, while it's there, may be said to be part of the place. Landscape makes no judgments; it simply receives what comes, accepts it, and goes on. So if we learn to imagine like a meadow or a plateau, we can learn to love, or at least to render truthfully, those who pass like locusts through it or set in like a drought, just as we can love and render those who live like a blessing in the land, as Lyle did on Sheep Creek.

One more thing I learn from James Galvin's work: an author may leave himself almost entirely out of his narrative and yet write a book of place that is a description of his soul.

A chance has come to me now, after a stay in Alaska, to visit this place and this man. And so I come to the country that does its best to hide the Colorado-Wyoming border. Its pale spring sky, its high winds, its unbearable lines of fault and uplift, its pared-back, planed, and scoured poetry bring Laurie Kutchins's work to my mind, and a traverse I made across Wyoming, a little north of here, in the winter of another year. Ten thousand feet above all this now, buffeted by wind, I find myself longing for the ground, and for a meadow.

The country encompassed by two rivers, the Laramie and the Cache la Poudre, that rise in the Neversummer Mountains has given rise also to nearly every word James Galvin has written. Sitting across a table from me, when I meet him in Iowa City, Galvin imagines the map of Larimer County, Colorado, and Albany County, Wyoming, blackened with the paths he has walked, the contours he has ridden, since he was a boy. He has known this land, and it has known him, since he was two. More than most writers, James Galvin is steeped in one place on earth—this high and arid landscape and the sky from which it fell. ("Who ever doubted that the earth fell from the sky?" he writes in the poem "Misericord" [1997, 101].) His life and all his writing have their center here; their roots are sunk into its meager soil, and deeper, and down into the thirty dense miles of granite beneath. This is his subject—all his writing speaks of it. And this is his home—his whole life expresses it and what it has taught him.

Here is that country in his words. This is how *The Meadow* opens:

> The real world goes like this: The Neversummer Mountains like
> a jumble of broken glass. Snowfields weep slowly down. Chambers Lake, ringed by trees, gratefully catches the drip in its tin
> cup, and gives the mountains their own reflection in return. . . .

The real world goes like this: Coming down from the high lake, timbered ridges in slow green waves suddenly stop and bunch up like patiently disappointed refugees, waiting for permission to start walking out across the open prairie toward Nebraska, where the waters come together and form an enormous inland island, large parts of three large states surrounded by water. The island never heard of states; the real world is the island. (1992, 3)

This makes a bold beginning—"annunciatory" and musical, as Franklin Burroughs put it in a review of the book (1994, 145). This passage—the whole opening section—is a recitation of metaphor for one place on earth, a liturgy, a chant of "dicta about the real world" (ibid.). It is also a sustained challenge: What is real? Why is it real? Why is it real *here?* The opening section, just a page and a bit, rises and falls against those questions, sketching at the same time the country of the story, its themes and players.

Within that realm, that tract of river-enclosed range and prairie land, there is an island, which is the meadow, "the highest cultivated ground in this spur of the Medicine Bow," "offered up among the ridges, wearing a necklace of waterways, concentrically nested inside the darker green of pines, and then the gray-green of sage and the yellow-green of prairie grass" (Galvin 1992, 3–4). This is Lyle's meadow— Lyle Van Waning. He is not named yet, but it turns out he belonged more than anyone else to the meadow. And the book, like the meadow, is more his than anybody's; though it's clear to Lyle and to Galvin, and to all of us by the end, that neither a stretch of level terrain nor a book of ordered sentences belongs to anybody really.

James Galvin has known that meadow since 1953, when his father bought a cabin on Boulder Ridge, which rises behind Lyle's place down on Sheep Creek. Jim was two then. In his poem "What Holds Them Apart," he writes: "Long/afternoons I fished in the creek that runs through Lyle's/meadow. I knew that water down to the bottom stones" (1997, 140). And he knew—he knows still, better than he knows anything—all the country that rims the meadow round with spruce and pine and granite mounds, and the wide, gaunt grassland of the Laramie Basin, all the way north to the Laramie Range and all the way west to the Snowy Range astride the Medicine Bow. For this is the landscape the Galvin cabin looks upon. Lyle, while he lived, and the meadow have been Galvin's neighbors all his life.

> The story of the meadow is a litany of loosely patterned weather, a chronicle of circular succession. . . . It's the highest cultivated ground in this spur of the Medicine Bow, no other level terrain in sight. There have been four names on the deed to it, starting just a hundred years back.
>
> The history of the meadow goes like this: No one owns it, no one ever will. The people, all ghosts now, were ghosts even then; they drifted through, drifted away, thinking they were not moving. They learned the recitations of seasons and the repetitive work that seasons require.
>
> Only one of them succeeded in making a life here, for almost fifty years. He weathered. Before a backdrop of natural beauty, he lived a life from which everything was taken but a place. He lived so close to the real world it almost let him in. (1992, 3–4)

The real world is not, for Galvin, an unpeopled, pastoral, antique realm. It is, in a sense, the landscape free of our ideas of it, but not free of us. It is what is actual, what can be grasped through the senses, absorbed into one's life through the body's long encounter with the body of the land—in his case, the Neversummer Mountains, the Snowy Range, two rivers, a lake, a meadow, and the litany of seasons there.

I suspect Galvin means by "the real world" also the first principles, the pattern of true notes, made manifest in the forms we encounter on earth—or, perhaps, dancing between them. He tells me when we meet, "I write about what I *don't* know about what I *do* know. That is the realm of literature, of poetry." The mysterious within the familiar, he means; the ineffable whole expressed in these material parts. The French poet Paul Éluard once wrote, "There is another world, and it is in this one" (in Hirsch 1999, 9). That divine, essential realm, of angels and dreams and frozen music, of familiar mystery, may be what Galvin means by "the real world": the reality that explains the world we see, the world that escapes our apprehension, even when we are looking, but which is expressed by the phenomenal world; the order to which long slow attention and moments of grace sometimes give us entry—the real world that almost let Lyle in. "The meadow's a dream I'm working to wake to," Galvin writes in "Against the Rest of the Year" (1997, 147), a poem he wrote as Lyle lay dying, a poem that locates the real world within this one, the real river below and above the river we see—the secret they suggest. And so *The Meadow* is less about one high mountain grassland than it is about the miracles, and the dreams of the earth, manifested there. The real world, the province of literature, is the mysteries that hold, the world that is suggested within the forms you grow intimate with—if you work at it—somewhere on earth.

But I'm guessing. Galvin is not going to give such a secret away easily. Nor is any place. What he means, what any place really is, moves under and over the words on the page, the landforms on the ground. You learn to apprehend the real world by staying put.

This much, though, is clear as creekwater from his writing, particularly *The Meadow:* the real world includes all the lives that start and stop within the body of a place, within its reach; that pass through it like Lyle's and App's and James Galvin's and even mine; that rise and fall within it like mountains and rivers, rock walls and hay barns and beaver dams and trout, fast and slow. Whatever they may signify, the real world is all of those particular things, nowhere else but here. It is *this* corner of creation, never mind who created it.

"The real world goes like this," his book begins. The real world goes like this book goes, like this place goes. "This is the real world, indifferent, unburdened" (1992, 3).

James Galvin does not say, beyond that, what the real world is made of. He tries to show us and to sound it out. It is made of works and days of men and women and a place. It is made of weather, and the way men and women differ little from it, in their wildness, in their seasonal patterns and their fast passage. These are the things—these fragments of the real—that his poems and his prose works witness. And Galvin puts that "real" there, right at the beginning, as a challenge to conventional wisdom, which uses "real" to mean politics, human society, the state of affairs, the state of the economy, the interest rate, the war in Iraq, the free trade deal—the things that matter; the things the news is full of; the things you can count. Those things too are part of the real world, for sure, Galvin implies, but only part, and only fleeting. Something much older and deeper enfolds them. That is the real world. The real world begins with land and sky; it is the mystery embodied in a place.

Seven hundred miles of prairie lie between Tie Siding, Wyoming, where Galvin lives and the meadow lies, and Iowa City, Iowa. It's May, and Galvin's still teaching there. He told me I was insane to drive all that way to talk with someone (himself, he meant) I wouldn't find that interesting. I told him I'd come anyway.

Just past Aurora, Nebraska, four hundred miles into the journey, I'm beginning to think he was right. Not that there is anything wrong with this fertile country, or the day, which is sweet and warm. It's just that seven hundred miles is a hell of a long way to travel anywhere by road. But I press on at seventy-five miles an hour. It's as fast as they'll let me go. And it's not fast enough. This is a pilgrimage I'm on, in the company of semitrailers and SUVs, recreational vehicles and Buicks— but mostly semis. The prairie, thoroughly tamed, intensely husbanded, undulates about me, strung with irrigation gantries, green with young crop, brown with plowed field, contoured with strips of grass meant to stay the erosion that has carried away ten feet or more of this rich soil in one hundred and fifty years—soil, most of it, brought here in the first place out of Wyoming on the wind. It's on a pilgrimage, too. Nothing stays still for long, though everything about these waisted barns, this industrial complex of tractors and irrigation technology, suggests it should. The orderly fields, these dignified and workmanlike barns, the sometimes beautiful wood-frame houses, are trying to button down—to button up—the prairie and hold this cultivated territory in place and time. But everything—the wind and the soil especially—is traveling east faster than any of us would like. Everything but me, that is. But the real world goes like this.

Every pilgrimage begins in insanity and depends upon grace. You don't get to choose your company, and you go where you have to go. I am glad, despite its madness, to be on this one.

"If I could draw you a picture of my soul, it would be the Snowy Range," James Galvin says to me. By now, I have walked by myself in the meadow; I've driven Boulder Ridge and stood and watched the Snowy Range sitting very still in the wind; I've driven the prairie to Iowa City. And here is James Galvin drawing me a picture of his soul in the Prairie Lights bookshop.

He means the hard but tender-toned range topped in quartzite upon which the Galvin cabin looks out. He means the qualities of the landscape that became his home—became indistinguishable from his sense of self—from a very early age. "The Snowy Range" is also a synecdoche for all the country of home: that particular bit of geology, that particular outlook, but also the larger geography the range inhabits—the meadow, Boulder Ridge, the Laramie Basin lapping against the feet of the ridge to the north; the whole long range of the Medicine Bow, which makes the horizon to the northwest; and Laramie Peak, one hundred and twenty miles away in the northeast. He means, I think, a certain stringency, angularity, toughness; the tenderness and improbability of white quartzite atop darker granite; the everyday miracle of soft red soil beneath prairie grass, of snowdrift among lodgepole pines. He means qualities of sternness and delicacy, brokenness and endurance you will find there. The ground of that place is the ground of his being. Understanding the place, you will understand the man.

"If I could draw you a picture," Galvin says to me, "of my soul." He uses words carefully, so let me take care with them, too. The landscape of home, the one he has spent his life looking upon, coming to know better than anything, than anyone—drawing that, rendering its form, he would represent the poem of his life so far, his soul's terrain. He is telling me that the form that expresses most truthfully the nature of his life is the landscape of the Snowy Range and the Medicine Bow. He is telling me something else, not unconnected: that his idea of who he is includes the land he grew in; he is telling me that he is who he is because he has grown attached to a place.

Galvin says to me as we sit and talk, "You know the writer Wallace Stegner? Okay, well, he's got this great little aphorism, which I sort of live by: 'You can't know who you are, if you don't know where you are.'" We are talking, as it happens, about wolves, right now. But it is no different for wolves than it is for men and women, he is saying. We know what to do, we find our calling, we live rightly—like the wolf, we know what and how much to take from the land, where to roam, whose stock to leave alone, how to stay alive—when we know our terrain as part of ourselves.

If, then, James Galvin knows his terrain in that way; if he has grown akin to this place of mountain, meadow, and prairie; if he is made in its image; if it has (almost) let him in; if it has turned him into who he has become—how did this happen?

"I became attached to that landscape," he says. "I just looked at it my whole life." "Just looking" is no slight thing for James Galvin. Done properly, it is witness, and it changes you. Witness is the real work of poetry, he says to me. It is largely a kind of staying present; it is looking hard and long and letting the language arrive out of, well, the real world. He writes that landscape because that is where he is, that is a thing he knows, and it has about it a mysterious reality that calls for poetry, for a fitting, a dignified, response. He is no different from the wolf; and his poetry, as he sees it, is no different from Lyle's work—caring for the meadow or building a barn there. Witness depends on looking well, on learning to know a place (or any fit subject): how it works, what it demands of you, how you are to see it for what it really is. But it is a skill for life, really. Learning to see, he says, has been the art he's spent most of his life pursuing; and it was, it is still, through art, through poetry, that he schools himself in that kind of apprehension of the world—in witness. "Just looking" constitutes a good part of a good life; it is a practice, an ethic, a discipline of belonging. Lyle—the man, in Galvin's experience, who got closer than most of us to the real world—did a lot of looking. *The Meadow,* among other things, is the story of the vigil Lyle kept—though Lyle wouldn't have put it so fancily. For Lyle, seeing was a prosaic matter, but an essential kind of prose.

"The way people watch television while they eat—looking up to the TV and down to take a bite and back up—that's how Lyle watches the meadow out the south window while he eats his breakfast. He's hooked on the plot, doesn't want to miss anything. He looks out over the rim of his cup as he sips" (1992, 5). Like all spiritual pursuits, witness yields revelation parsimoniously, though it breeds an unfakable and unsentimental kind of familiarity with one's country. The place itself seems doomed to elude us, though we ourselves are changed by the looking.

> But this morning the cold air hangs still down in the meadow, and there is enough haze in the air to filter the sunlight so Lyle can lean on his elbows over a cup of steaming instant and smoke a Prince Albert and gaze out the picture window he now spends most of his life perched in like a hunched up old raven. . . .
>
> "I've been staring at that confounded meadow and those idiot hills and lodgepole stands for over forty years now. I'm about done for and I'm still not sure I've ever *seen* any of it. All I know is I'm damned tired of looking at the sonofabitch."
>
> He thinks about how completely the meadow changes with respective seasons, how much it can change under light and clouds between two times he raises his eyes from his book and looks over the top of his half-lens reading glasses. (ibid., 53)

You see in Galvin's writing how the meadow has, in fact, revealed its subtle nature—some small secrets—to this old man, hunched near his death, in this passage, like a raven, the meadow's gruff, grave witness. You sense in this moment, the end of a lifetime's watching, what Galvin means by these words from his poem "Rintrah Roars":

"Another friend said,'I am chained to the earth to pay for the freedom / of my eyes'" (1997, 240). The toll exacted—and the reward surrendered—for such close noticing is a kind of attachment that approaches inclusion. It is connection, authentic and reciprocal. It is a kind of transparency you accomplish ("Misericord," 1997, 101); a successful disappearance into the mountains, such as App Worster aspires to, nears in life as Lyle does, and pulls off fully only in death (1992, 159; and "They Haven't Heard the West Is Over," 1997, 136).

Lyle's accomplishment, the outcome of all that looking at those "idiot hills," is to "raise his consciousness almost up to coyote level," so that those artful creatures give him their respect and friendship (1992, 14); to achieve a touching and remarkably tender acquaintance with the barn swallows (ibid., 5–7 and passim) and the snow (ibid., 43 and passim); to have the weather inside him and know it as exactly and rawly as the meadow does (ibid., 224); to hear the stars singing, each in its own pitch, on cold nights (ibid., 221); to feel the wind just once or twice cut right through him as he walks among timber, just as though he were not there at all (ibid.). To know a place is to intrude so little upon it you do not get in its way; you haunt and are haunted by it. You are as local as the light. You may be allowed odd glimpses of its reality—the way it is when our backs are turned ("Getting a Word In," 1997, 59), in which moments we do not recognize it as the place we have been looking at all these years at all, but as itself:

> Lyle hoists the rafter to his shoulder and climbs the ladder with it and sets it in place, driving in one tenpenny nail to hold it. He climbs back down and sits on a sawhorse. He fishes out his tobacco. As he lights up, the sun is setting, turning the sky as many pastels as you see on the side of a rainbow trout. The reddest clouds are the fish cut open. Aspen trees are peaking with yellow. . . . Up over the opposing hill he sees the snow on mountains west of Laramie. Another breath of wind comes up and starts the aspens chattering like nervous girls, and they catch the last low-angling rays of sun and flare. The dark tops of evergreens are red, almost bloody, and for a good thirty seconds he

knows that the world is something altogether other than what it appears to be. (1992, 121–22)

This view, as it happens, is the one from James Galvin's place. In the scene I quote from, Galvin imagines Lyle at the work he did there in October 1963, extending the old cabin Galvin's father had bought ten years before that, up on Boulder Ridge. That looking and seeing the sun's fall change everything might be James Galvin's, but in the book it is Lyle's. And it is the emphemeral payback for his hard work (that day and every day of his life) and his dignified attention to the world. It is also—this sudden and fleeting awareness of the strangeness of the familiar—what a poet, what a writer, hopes for, and sometimes gets to see.

The end of all this watching, Galvin implies, is to know a stretch of land as well—and as little—as you know your own soul, and to know that both of them will elude you and survive you. In the end, each of them will resemble the other, so much does the land change and inform its witness. In the end, it is possible to feel, as Galvin writes of a woman he calls Sara (and who sounds a lot like Lyle's sister, Clara), how "the valley can't imagine itself/without her" ("Sara," 1997, 127). It is possible to feel how the meadow, when Lyle died, was unable to imagine itself without *him*. It is possible to sense, reading *The Meadow*, how the meadow changed Lyle—the more he looked and the more it seemed beyond him—into another true expression of itself, all the while making him more truly the man he was born to be. And it is possible to sense how the Snowy Range, the timber, and the weather over the prairie have changed James Galvin, their witness, into the man he is, the writer he is—vernacular, brutally mystical, smart and delicate and sage.

Just who each of us *really* is, and what this place that grounds and becomes us *really* is, will escape us most of the time, and so it should. It is the work of poetry, of art, of a good life like Lyle's, of hard work at the forge like Lyle's, to seek and try to express what is real, what is true, without ever capturing it exactly or defining it. Witness—practiced in poetry, in farming a meadow, or in simple attention—is "a conversation with the way things are" ("Homesteader," 1997, 34). To witness is to lean toward the real world quietly and wonder hard; and it shapes a man's soul.

If we can imagine a place as all those interconnected stories, relationships, energies, and forms of life at play somewhere, including one's own being there, the memories, dreams, and desires one had there; and if it is true, as Jeff Malpas has argued, that it is those complex structures of place that make an experience of self possible at all;[1] and if it is then true, as Malpas continues, that "to have a sense of one's identity . . . is to have a sense, not of some simple underlying self that is one's own, but rather of a particular place in the world" (1999, 152)— then to witness one's place, to articulate something of some few pieces of the complex structure that composes that place, *is* to draw a picture of one's soul. One of the lessons I have learned from *The Meadow*, indeed, is just how truthfully a writer may make a memoir of himself—may *adéquate* himself—by witnessing the place of his attachment, barely mentioning himself at all.

James Galvin does not exaggerate when he says he has looked at this spare high country all of his life. "I was born in the air force in 1951, right after my father got back from Germany," he tells me. "He was working in counterintelligence. I have an older sister born in Germany and a younger sister born six years after me. Anyhow, the first two years of my life were spent bouncing around air force bases, and then my dad quit the military and took a job out west. He was a physician. He was supposed to go out to Denver where his job was and find a place for our family to live. So he drove out there in his convertible Hudson

1. Malpas seems to have largely human-generated attributes, such as memory, desire, connection, and so on, in mind when he speaks of "complex structures," so I may be stretching his words a bit to accommodate what I want to say. I use his elegant phrase to include the many interconnecting pieces of narrative, human and nonhuman, that compose a place.

Hornet"—he looks at me and interjects, with boyish enthusiasm, "great car"—"and he got the classified ads, and somehow his eye fell on this piece of property, six hundred and forty acres—that's a section, one square mile—sitting on the Colorado-Wyoming border. Twelve thousand dollars. And he bought it. As a result, we also had to rent a bungalow down in Denver. My mother was, to say the least, not pleased."

This was the section Pat Sudeck from New Hampshire homesteaded in 1923—"half-timber, half-pasture, with five springs, but no bottomland," and a side view of prairie and range (1992, 127). The section borders the three hundred and twenty acres—"that almost imaginary thatch of peat bog surrounded by low hills and tall stands of lodgepole pine, with its own ocean of sage-gray prairie lapping at its shores and the whole Medicine Bow Range to drink in every day" (ibid., 159)—that Lyle Van Waning's mother, Hazel, bought in 1938 and where she still lived in 1953 with her two surviving children, Clara and Lyle. Pat was the Van Wanings' neighbor until he sold the place to James Galvin Sr. and moved away to Fort Collins, then down to Arizona. It was then that the young James Galvin started being Lyle's neighbor.

"You know," Galvin continues,

it's two and a half hours from Denver to Boulder Ridge. We did a lot of driving. And back then, in the early fifties, that country was extremely remote. That Cherokee Park Road you drove up the other day to Lyle's, that was a two-track back then. But my dad had this vision of that place—he wanted to be Ernest Hemingway. He wanted to kill everything that moved. Fishing, hunting, the whole thing. And so I was raised from a very young age to kill whatever moved too.

I killed my first antelope when I was eleven, first deer when I was twelve, first elk when I was thirteen. That's a child, right? And during the summers, starting from the age of eight, when my father had to go back to work during the week, he took my mother and my sisters and left me up there. That first summer he left me up there from one weekend to the next with a juvenile delinquent to look after me, and after that it was just me.

There isn't anything I can't tell you about loneliness. I know all about it, have known it from the age of eight. But I can tell you what it was like to be nine and ten and eleven and to watch my family drive away on Sunday. I had no telephone; I just had a twenty-two. The nearest neighbor was Lyle. If a tree fell on me or something, you know, no one would have known for a week. What I was doing up there was working for my dad. I was putting up his firewood. I was painting his house. I was building retaining walls. And he was paying me every time he showed up with a cardboard box full of powdered milk and spam. My supplies. He thought he was making a man out of me.

The only communication I had with the outside world was the radio. There was this station out of Laramie, KOWB, Cowboy Radio, and it would have this thing at noon every day, the ranchers' party line. Mostly it was stuff like, "Slim, your chickens are in. Come get 'em." But sometimes it was something for me, like, "We're not coming up this week."

So I survived, and I thought it was making me strong, and it probably was. In my childhood I idolized my father, as most children do. You don't question anything. You just go, okay, so this is what is happening.

And it went on happening like that until James Galvin reached his late teenage years. Apart from getting him used, in a very raw way, to the litany of weather and the cycle of repetitive work, all that time up there alone threw James Galvin into Lyle's company and kindness. And it gave him to the mountains and the meadow, which was, in the days Lyle cared for it with his network of timber irrigation flumes and his haying in the fall, "a kind of Eden," Galvin says. The meadow, lying just downstream from a reservoir made some years before by the damming of Sheep Creek, went like this in those days:

> Full, the reservoir looks all right: a mirror Sheep Creek dies in, timber straight and still along the edge, and sky swimming through its face. . . .
> Just below the outlet Sheep Creek resurrects itself in an instant. It leaps from the outlet into boulders, tangled willows, and

tall grasses. Below the gunsight rock outcrops that pinch the valley into a waist, Lyle's haymeadow opens like a proper afterlife.

In spring the new grass grows in standing water. At sunset the
white mirror-light shines through the grass. That's when the
beaver ponds light up, too, and the rising trout make bull's eyes
on the surface.

A doe that has been drinking lifts her head to listen. Done irri-
gating, Lyle heads home across the shining field. He has a shovel
on his shoulder that looks like a single wing. (ibid., 142)

And there's Lyle, a broken kind of angel, at work in the field,
hardly disturbing a doe for long, so much is he a part of the place. "He
was so completely moral, noble, you know," Galvin says to me. In the
1984 poem "What Holds Them Apart" you can see them together,
young Jimmy Galvin and Lyle, building a retaining wall. Lyle is teaching the boy that even a mountain is just "a slower kind of river," that
a wall is "a puzzle with one ideal order that doesn't make / a picture,
and whose puzzle-parts weigh fifty pounds each" (1997, 141); Lyle is
teaching the boy that the hawk in the sky who seems to the boy to have
the easier lot is working hard, like them, at the life-and-death business
of staying alive.

With Lyle and without, Galvin got his education in the world in
this way—bodily, emotionally. It was performed with his hands and
eyes. It was suffered. It was grounded.

"All the hunting, the massacring, and everything—I finally just got sick
of it," he says. "That coincided with the time when rebellion naturally
sets in anyway." The war in Vietnam was on by then, and his father,
who still worked for the military, pressed his son to enlist. Young
Galvin refused, and there was "a falling out." "At the same time," he
says, "I decided I was done with killing things, and that broke his
heart. And we never really did come back together."

Galvin's father suffered a stroke when he was fifty and could no
longer work. He became destitute, and lives now with Jim's sister. He
is aging without much grace. In the meantime, the Boulder Ridge

property, which Galvin never stopped knowing as home, even in the years he was away at college, was seized by the Inland Revenue in lieu of the taxes his father had failed to pay. But Galvin managed to find the money to buy the place back.

And so a piece of land, surrendered by a father, returned to a son who'd never really left it. When Jim Galvin tells me this, I am struck by a coincidence I'm sure is not lost on him. Among the stories *The Meadow* tells is one about how the upper part of the meadow, once App Worster's, dear to him but lost to hard times and debt, found its way back to App's son Ray. And so, two pieces of neighboring land, lost by two fathers, are returned, in time, to their sons, whose souls were formed there. As though the meadow could not imagine itself without them.

Galvin, who had already earned the right to the place, you would have thought, through work and loneliness, had to pay for it a second time in cash. Galvin's father almost lost the place through the misfortune of his illness and the arrogance of his believing he could cheat the taxman. Ray's father lost the meadow because he lost a wife he'd loved, and had to pay for the medicines that had failed to keep her alive. Ray grew up, after that, down the bottom of Boulder Ridge, on the northern side of what became the Galvin place, at the edge of the prairie that rolls on into Tie Siding. Ray went off swamping on ranches and ended up getting married to a girl called Margie and working in her father's plastering business in Laramie until, in 1972, out of the blue, he got a call from a man who worked for the company that ran the reservoir on Sheep Creek.

Ray's father, App, had first dreamed up that reservoir. App owned the entire meadow in those days, and his plan was to flood the top half and sell off the water to the dryland farmers in eastern Colorado. "App intended to sacrifice the upper meadow to save the rest. . . . It was supposed to pay off the doctors and set him up for the rest of his life" (1992, 94). But it didn't turn out that way. A businessman called Eaton stymied App's plans with the bankers and decision-makers down in Fort Collins. That man then bought the top half of the meadow from App, when App was desperate for money, and he built the dam himself. It still bears his name—the Eaton Reservoir. And there it still was, in need of a new manager, and there was Ray, whose knowledge of that country the Divide Ditch and Water Company had somehow gotten wind of. Ray took the job and returned to live "on his father's homeplace, his father's dream, which was now half-drowned and half-owned by some fellow named Lyle Van Waning." (App had sold the bottom half to Lyle's mother in 1938; and Lyle took over the title when his mother died.) "So Ray became a water engineer, my neighbor, and Lyle's" (1992, 96).

Land, in the real world there along Sheep Creek and up on the ridge, is hard-won and hard-kept. It makes you work for it, and for the right to stay. And it makes its own claims, impossible to forget, on those men who grow up within it.

James Galvin, meanwhile, did not return to the place his father had dreamed of—that is, he returned to the same *place,* but not to the same *dream.* He returned to a place without which his own life's story is incomprehensible, without which he would not have become the man and the poet he already was. James senior had imagined the section on the ridge as a hunting paradise, and possessed it in that spirit. His son had found himself, as a boy, apprenticed to the land, and now, returning to it as a man, he had to find a way, as Lyle and App had to find a way down in the meadow, to live with it and to draw a living from it, while as far as possible letting it be.

Working that country exacts a tough-minded love for it. It went that way with the younger Galvin, and it went that way for the other men his writing tells of. They express their love without sentiment, and mostly by just looking. Lyle expresses it like a surly father in his grudging affection for coyotes in the field; in his caring for the birds; in his knowledge of the weather; in his staying put through every storm. This is the way it is with all the (good) men in Galvin's writing. The relationship those men, and Galvin himself, arrive at with the meadow and the ridge is both robust and tender. It is stoic and dignified—and I would say sacramental, if that were not too pious a word for those men. For their love for the place and their life within it is sometimes cryptically, even meanly, expressed, as though fondness were too vulnerable a thing to feel, affection too untrustworthy an emotion to express. The men are parsimonious with their affection as the place is parsimonious with water. Their hard words are not meant to hurt—they just come out that way. The place delivers a heavy snow in winter, almost enough to kill a man like Lyle, whom it loves, when all it means is to guarantee water for the summer. The place and its men are contrary, short-tempered, unfair, democratic. There is no place among them for pity but plenty for respect. In this place you persevere. No one prospers here.

Galvin writes in his poem "Three Sonnets,"

There is no philosophy   of death where I live
Only philosophies   of suffering. (1997, 88)

It was through his father's misguided impulses, his regimen for making young James a man, that Galvin, as he puts it, "got seduced into loving that place." Then, as a man, he found he loved it for real, and he knew it as if it were a property of his mind, as if it were a place that lived inside his imagination, as if he were made on the same design it was. "I had to leave home to discover that I had been raised in an unforgiving paradise," he observes (Holt 1998). And once that place was also, in the worldly sense, his property, "when I got grown up enough to know what I wanted," he says to me, "I turned it from being a hunting paradise into an agricultural entity." He summered cattle on it and ran horses. He learned to rope so he could help his friends drive and manage cattle. He still does these things. He's not turning a profit on the land. He earns his money teaching poetry at a university, and a little from his books. No one could make a living from such a parcel anymore, he says. "But I can almost pay the taxes, and I can keep it." As it keeps him. "There's a forest lost in me," he writes in "Left-Handed Poem" (1997, 159)—the lodgepoles and spruces of Boulder Ridge. And there is a man lost in them.

He built himself a log cabin there, using trees from the site and others Lyle gave him. "I didn't want to use living trees if I could help it," he explains. "So I spent a lot of time walking around my timber looking up for straight dead trees. What I discovered then is that there is no such thing as a straight tree. And in the end I had to fell some, just to get enough wood. I spent two summers and two falls dropping and skidding timber, and two more summers and falls building that house." He lives inside his own timber, worked by his own hands into a house; and the timber, worked by the wind and time, lives inside him.

Galvin has a feeling for timber—the trees of the ridge, in particular. His first book of poems, written in graduate school in Iowa City, was named for them: *Imaginary Timber* (1980). The trees stand for home. They stand for endurance. They are holy and humble. They live and they die. They are real.

> The pines never stop praying.
> They pray best in a drizzle.
> The pines pray up a drought.
> They pray snowdrifts and sheet lightning.
> They get everything they pray for . . .
> Here in pines under ashen sky
> I am. Reason is
> To join my prayers
> With theirs.
> ("More Like It," 1997, 206–7)

These lines tell me that presence is prayer. This is what the pines do—they stay. They relate with and articulate every kind of weather, and the relationships they form are holy because they are enough in themselves. Everything, every kind of weather, is welcome among the trees. Drought and snowdrift, for trees, are not a disaster, not a matter of regret. They are answers to prayers: they come in time, if you stay put. This is the stoicism Galvin reads in the trees. He joins them in it. To be present—to be "here"—is to *be*. And to be is reason enough. To stay put and suffer the conditions that make a place what it is: this is a kind of prayer that gets you everything you could ask for, since you ask for nothing other than what is true, what patterns the place. Acceptance is belonging, is prayer; it is the ethic of the place that James Galvin calls home. Places last; people and trees pass. To accept this is to come to belong and to find the only comfort one can find. This was the way Lyle lived; it was what he learned from the meadow. It is what you learn from witness, I suppose. It is what the timber says to Galvin, the timber lost in him, the timber he used to make a home among the trees, upon the ridge, above the meadow, in sight of the range.

In the early eighties, Galvin brought a wife, the poet Jorie Graham, to live with him here, in the pines. Until recently, when they split, the two of them spent part of each year on Boulder Ridge, working the land and writing poems; the other months they spent teaching in Iowa City. On Boulder Ridge (and in Iowa City) they raised a child together— Emily, for whom James Galvin wrote *The Meadow.*

There was an education Galvin had beyond the timber and the meadow, of course, and it culminated at the Iowa Writers' Workshop, where he met Jorie Graham. But there were years of it before that. Galvin went to school in Colorado. It was cruel in a way nothing in the meadow—except perhaps for his father's dreams and ambitions— was cruel. "I had seen cruelty to animals but never child to child," he says. "It was very *Lord of the Flies.*" He had one fine teacher at high school who introduced him to literature, to *Moby-Dick* and *Heart of Darkness* in particular; and another teacher, one of the founders of Outward Bound who was also a mythic figure in mountaineering, and who led him into alpine climbing, an enduring passion of Galvin's about which he has scarcely written. "So the two good things that happened to me in high school were getting into alpinism and getting into literature."

But no one yet had suggested that he write a poem, that he witness anything in lines on paper. "You can grow up as a male child in the American West," he says, "and you can live your whole life and no one is ever going to ask you to write a poem. They'll ask you to kill things. They'll ask you to get into fights. But they won't ask you to create anything." Then he went college at Antioch in Ohio, a Quaker school, and there he was encouraged to learn, through the arts, to see; he was asked to create and found that he could. "I was astonished to meet people who had bearing, who were not sissies, but they were making art. They were painting and drawing, making sculpture and photographs and poems." He got seduced by Zen Buddhism "for a while there," he tells me, and saw how his spiritual development required him to learn to see the world with the same kind of detached intimacy and discipline, with the same kind of attention the arts also called for. At college, pursuing the real world, he tried photography and drawing and lithography. Painting frightened him because he is partly colorblind and "was just overwhelmed by the idea of color." He discovered that he had to work in black and white—in word and sound.

Antioch asked its students to work while they studied, and Galvin took a job as an apprentice to a man who made guitars. He became skilled at the craft, loved the making, and got quite good at playing the instrument. But there, as with Zen and painting, he reached a plateau ("and it was a pretty low plateau"). Galvin has a good strong voice well suited to singing. He admits he loves to sing and play guitar—this passion, this pastime, plays in a minor key through *The Meadow*. But he realized that making music was not where his artistic calling lay either. He was never going to be good enough at it.

So, as he tells it, he ended up with poetry and found that he could do it. He had spent his life reading, and he says he wound up writing, "by process of elimination." He also says to me that if he could play any better, he would much sooner have become a musician than a writer. I'm not sure he means it. Music matters to Galvin; he writes about it, uses it as metaphor, often in his poems. But would he really rather be composing and playing? Perhaps in his writing that is really what he is doing anyway—I'll say more about this. His point, I think, is that writing is tough. "For one thing, a writer needs a new idea every line," while the other arts can make a single idea go a long, long way.

Anyway, Galvin got good enough at poetry, he found enough new ideas line after line, to get into the Iowa Writers' Workshop, the best graduate writing program in the country. I sense that, though the ridge and the meadow, and the years with Lyle, made Galvin the man he is, fashioned his soul, attached him in kinship to that country, something more than that living and that looking was necessary to make him the witness to that country that he is today. He found that extra quality—the mortar to hold its puzzle-pieces apart, the craft to shape his country in sound and image—at Antioch and Iowa.

Imaginary Timber (1980) came out of his graduate years at Iowa. The poems in it, though they are youthful, are astonishingly accomplished works. Out of those years and that poetry came a job teaching poetry at the Iowa Writers' Workshop, something he has done ever since. So did his marriage to Jorie Graham, whom he met at the workshop, where they were both students, and who went on to teach there too. "Our souls recognized each other," he says to me. "I knew destiny when I saw it. And it wasn't until twenty-five years later that I realized I was wrong about everything."

His recent divorce is still hurting Galvin when I see him. He is sad about everything that is over. He is wounded by having been forced by the split to fight again to keep hold of the place on Boulder Ridge. He is anxious about losing his daughter, who has gone to study at Harvard, where Jorie is now teaching. (These anxieties, along with the consolations of sky and country, flood his latest book of poems, *X*, which appeared in May 2003.) Through this hard season of his life, his work and a place sustain him: poetry sustains him, a new colt to practice care and attention upon, and a home place that goes on and on through every kind of weather. He is still surrounded by the weather and the praying pines, and in that he finds solace.

Shortly after my time with him, Galvin published a poem called "Depending on the Wind" about his loss and about the ultimate consolation of places—of trees and wind, which last. It is a poem again about timber and a timber home, about the relationship of wind and wood and window. It understands that there is little comfort to be had from these things, from the real world, for the kind of grief a man (or a woman) can suffer; but it knows that there is a truth they speak of, among themselves, upon which one can depend, a truth that is "chaotic, senseless, wise" ("A Portrait of My Roof," 1997, 205). "Depending on the Wind" appeared first in the *New Yorker* in May 2002. (He included it in *X* with some small changes; I quote from that version.) Its lines are long, a lilting elegy, their sound stunned, barely accepting, quietly raging:

> A score of years ago I felled a hundred pines to build a house.
> Two stories, seven rooms in all.
> > I built my love a home
> . . . .
> > Where once I was not alone, now each
> closed door is panic, and spaces grow immense with memory, like
> shadows at dusk.
> > Gone that arrangement of allegiances called *family*
> we never really know before it ends.
> > Like love itself, it isn't true till
> then
> . . . .
> > Wind still blows through open
> windows like it always used to do.
> > What did I love that made me
> believe it would last? (2003, 46)

Think of his life's trajectory to this point. Alone among those trees, he began the life that has made him this man. His life was, among other things, an often lonely deepening into the body of that ridge, a deepening of love for it. And then, later, after learning to write, learning another love (of poetry), he brought to his beloved place a wife, with whom he learned that one might have a place and yet not be alone within it. It was for Jorie and their love, it was for their daughter, Emily, who was born there, but it was also for this transcendent love of life itself—the kind the pines understand—that he built that house of timber. And now, feeling abandoned again, recalling how bad abandonment used to feel, even here, when he was a boy, all that boy who is now this man has is the house, the trees, the wind—and it is enough, though barely. Everything is *barely* enough on that ridge near that meadow and that range. Yet it lasts; it is true; it is dependable. Two things, in fact, are dependable, and they bear each other the same kind of relationship the wind bears to the windows: place and poetry. Windows frame the real world; they let us see it; they let it inside. Poetry frames the real world and lets its chaos, its sense-lessness, its wisdom speak.

I am sitting in the meadow now. The wind is coming down hard from Little Bald Mountain and Deadman Hill on its way to Lyle's house. It's rattling the rusty willows and the yellow reeds, distressing the dark mirror faces of the beaver ponds along Sheep Creek in its hurry to get there. It doesn't seem to know that he lives there no more. It keeps on coming anyway. I'm having trouble, too, imagining this meadow without Lyle. He died in 1988. He's lying beneath a taciturn headstone in the Fort Collins Cemetery, beside his mother and his sister, who lived here too and knew this wind. I've plucked a bit of sage from the ground beside me, and tomorrow I will take it down to them and leave it where they lie.

On the snow fences Lyle made to keep winter from burying the small township of wood buildings he put up over the years around the house—workshop, lumber shed, garage, barn—the Sheep Creek Ranch has posted a sign: *Keep Out—you will be prosecuted.* They've strung a wire fence along the county road, too, to keep Lyle's meadow in; and they've hung more signs along its length to keep the people out—pilgrims like me, and fishermen, like the guy just downriver, waving a shining line above the beaver dams. I am sitting squat on the pink-brown earth among the gray meadow grasses and the sage. I am sitting in the wind between the road and the fence, on a bit of the meadow that got out and is also on its way to Lyle's place. My truck sits behind me, just off the county road, which is made of this same red earth. It slumps here and there, this track, the county road that runs west off Cherokee Park Road; it gives way a little beneath you—patches of soft and waterlogged gumbo (Bentonite, geologists call it) that grab at your tires as you pass over them. Stay, says the ground, now and then; hold here a little. There is something hidden here. And beyond the road sits Lyle's place, not hidden but daily lost a little more to its past.

Winter is over. It is the last day of April, and the grasslands look dry as old parchment. Up on the ridges, there's no sign of snowpack. Winter brought little snow, and April brought no rain. The pines have prayed up a drought. But see if the wind cares. In the Fort Collins paper a weather historian says that winter moisture levels are way below average. "I guarantee the grass and trees know it," he says.

So I am witnessing Lyle's meadow in a lean season, as he did, I suppose, plenty of times. Upstream the Eaton Reservoir is standing almost bereft of water. It is a gash in the heart of the meadow App Worster fell in love with, the small-waisted form of it. I was up on Boulder Ridge Road, above the granite rocks that make the meadow's waist an hour ago. I stood looking down on the blond haymeadow and the empty reservoir from among Engelmann spruce, lodgepole pine, white fir, and some red cedar, until the wind blew me down here. The trees encircle the meadow, but it is the kind of jagged, uncertain circle trees make. The pines encroach upon the grassland down the line of some of the streambeds that fall from Deadman toward Sheep Creek. The meadow is the place where everyone wants to be—water, wind, fisherman, student, and tree.

A number of Galvin's poems ("Three Sonnets" and "Navigation," for example) explore the shifting border between forest and grass. Just why mountain meadows like Lyle's keep themselves free of trees remains a lively mystery. Fine-textured soils seem to travel to such bowls as this in the high country and pool there. These soils drain all wrong for evergreens—some say they stay too wet too long into summer to give hope to conifer seedlings; others say they are too dry for trees. The soils—like this soft red ground I sit on—give more encouragement to grasses and herbaceous plants, which outcompete the slower-growing pines. So meadows form in places like the shallow valley along Sheep Creek. Snow drifts in deep and stays ("memorizing the landscape," as Galvin puts it in *The Meadow*) much longer than it does on the ridges. This, too, works against the trees. And then there is, of course, the wind, which rushes too hard across flat stretches of ground for anything taller and less supple than sedge and grass, sage and willow, to hang on. Beavers may have something to do with meadow-making too—they dam the creeks and flood wide areas, and drown the roots of trees.

The ecology of mountain meadows is deceptively complex. If there is one thing that makes them just what they are, one thing that deters the trees, the ecologists have not yet decided what it is (Knight 1994, 193ff.). That's how it goes in the real world. Although only the landscape knows the real reason meadows are meadows, Galvin puts it down to the wind:

> Evergreens have reasons
> For stopping where they do,
> At timberline or the clean edge
> Of sage and prairie grass.
> There are quantities of wind
> They know they cannot cross.
> ("Navigation," 1997, 71)

Out of the wind, the day is mild in the meadow. Some fair-weather cumulus sails in from the south. Close to the ground, some white flowers—stemless daisies and phlox—try their luck among the sagebrush and fescue. The sage has already bloomed. Spent flower heads droop about me. The whistle of a bird rises above the thrum of the wind. I saw mountain bluebirds, a Steller's jay, swallows, and a kestrel on my ride up here, but I cannot spot the bird that makes this sound, sweet and pitiless. I wonder where Lyle's white-crowned sparrows are. I wonder if this is one of them.

When I drove up here late this morning I recognized Lyle's house, sitting so close to the road, by the bay window facing south. Before that, I knew I was getting close when I noticed the beaver dams on the creek. I had passed the old sagging barn beyond the creek. Then ahead, south of the road, I saw the big barn Lyle built late in his days, the creek's course marked by orange willows flaring from the grasses behind it. The barn looks as if it were built yesterday. I knew from *The Meadow* what skill and care and persistence Lyle had exercised upon it, as if he were raising a cathedral, and the real thing stopped me dead. It was then I saw that I had pulled up in front of Lyle's window. Boulder Ridge rises, timbered, behind the empty house. Granite outcrops among the conifers. Small creeks run off the shoulder of the ridge on both sides of the Van Waning place on their way to join Sheep Creek. One is Trout Creek; the other has no name on my map.

Later in the day I make my way around Green Mountain, east of Lyle's, and up to Boulder Ridge where the Galvin place hides, then down to Tie Siding on the prairie to the north. And back to Fort Collins in the last light. I have traveled fast around country Lyle and the others lived in long and slowly. I can understand how they fell for it and why they stayed, and why one's hold on it is always tenuous, its hold on you tenacious. It is the kind of country I love too—simple, austere, lightly timbered, grassed, arid yet discretely watered.

I can't know it as Lyle did, closely and steadily witnessing it and disappearing into it as he did. Nor, of course, can I see its human-sized stories unroll through time, the stories Galvin's neighbors and their ancestors enacted and recalled in this sweet, spare country, stories Galvin grew up with, inherited or collected like the fallen timber— none of it straight—he turned into a house for his love. A place includes the memories and storylines of the people—perhaps of other beings too—who have lived and been formed there. It includes the stories of the place itself—of the things that mean themselves behind our backs ("Getting a Word In," 1997, 59). Galvin made a house from found and felled pieces of native timber; he made another such house, *The Meadow*, from the many told and untold pieces of narrative, bits of life story and weather, he found there. From these things, too, he has fashioned most of his poems and most of his life.

The turning of those stories into works of words—if it is done with humility, knowing that they are just small pieces of what makes this place real—wakes the poet, and the reader as well, to the dream of the place. Without these fragments of song in "ordinary language" ("Navigation," 1997, 71), the land will sleep on, and we will be unable to enter its dream. Works like Lyle's barn, like Galvin's book, are what let us in. The rest is up to us.

The way Galvin tells it, he never set out to write *The Meadow*. This is true, in one sense, of all writing—all literature—in his conception of it. No work is the child of intention; no work, if it is any good, is merely the product of one man's or woman's skill and desire. "None of us is smart enough to write a poem," he says to me. "The language is smart, though, smarter than any of us. We need to tap into it. That is what form does. It is the wall socket. We plug in, and, sometimes, the language writes itself through us." Form is the shape of an idea; it is poetic structure—sonnet, blank verse; certain prose forms, too. Like a pair of earrings; like a barn.

But in the case of *The Meadow,* even the form was not a thing its author chose. Galvin did not sit down to make anything. He meant to *write* something, of course, when he sat down to bang out the stories of the meadow and ridge onto sheets of white paper in his typewriter. He knew it was not poetry; that much was certain. "I had no idea at the outset of this thing as a book in any genre, that anyone else might read," he says. It was an exercise—with two purposes.

One purpose was to set some of those stories down, the ones he'd grown up with, the ones he felt someone should record before they sank from memory. Ray was dead, and Lyle was dying. Hazel and Clara had gone to the grave years ago, and App was an even older ghost in the meadow. More recently, another neighbor, Frank Lilley, had passed away down on the Chimney Rock Ranch. The old places were steadily falling to corporations or being divided up into ranchettes. The West was slipping through their hands. Galvin thought he should write down the stories he could remember, so that they would not disappear with the place he had known so long and so that Emily, his young daughter, might know the ground out of which his poetry grew. So that the place would be real for her. "I wrote this book for Emily," he writes, simply, at the top of the acknowledgments page.

The second reason Galvin wrote what became *The Meadow* was to kick-start his poetry. "I have always known that poetry is a conversation with silence," he tells me. "And the silence was winning." This was around 1990, between the volumes *Elements* (1988) and *Lethal Frequencies* (1995). "I wanted to try something different to get my poetry going again."

"I was at the house I used to share with Jorie in Italy," he goes on. "Each morning I woke and had three cups of coffee. And then, wired, I put one sheet of white paper in the typewriter, set it so there were no margins at all, and rolled the paper in so that I began right at the top. My idea was that the white paper was the silence and I would just write it out. So I covered whole sheets in black type, and when I was through with one page, I turned it right over and did the same on the other side. I was making all these blackened pages, writing out the stories I had of the place, of Lyle and the other people I knew there."

After four months, he had eighty pages covered in black type in this way, and he felt done. Jorie commented, sensibly enough, that no one, especially not Emily, could read what he'd written in that shape. So Galvin began a second draft, this time with margins and double spacing, typed on one side only.

"While I was working on that, Jorie would read bits of it, and she got interested and said to me, 'You know, you should see about publishing that.' I didn't think anyone would be interested in it at all. It was so personal. But she spoke to some folks here and there and nagged me about working it up and sending it to someone." And one day, he got a call from an agent in New York, Abigail Thomas (Lewis Thomas's daughter), who said she loved his poetry and had heard he was working on a kind of novel. She asked if he would send it to her when he was finished. "Well, I told her it wasn't a novel, and it was not for publication and definitely was not the kind of book that would make anyone any money. 'Now you really have me interested,' she said. And so, in the end, she seduced it out of me."

Before he sent it, though, he had to convince himself that it was indeed a book anyone would want to read. So he sent it to two writers he knew, very different men and stylists, William Kittredge and Allan Gurganus. Both told him it was working, and so he mailed it to Thomas. "She shopped it to Knopf, first," he tells me, "whose editor wanted less of what made it strange. An editor at Holt [William Strachan], on the other hand, wanted me to include more of what was weird about it. So I guess I had found my editor."

He had set out not knowing where he was going or what he was making, intending nothing except to get some stories down and to talk the silence down. Some ideas of form and structure, important ones, emerged, though, out of the writing itself. And as he wrote, he realized that these ideas about the shape of the work served well what he now discovered was the true subject of the writing: the landscape itself. "I realized that the landscape was the main character," he says. "But how do you speak for the landscape? You can't. But, still, I wanted it to be there." The main challenge of writing narrative about landscape, says Galvin, is that the landscape does not run to human time. It transcends our short attention span, which is defined roughly by the length of a human life; it defies our sense of a human life as a long time; it refuses our linear sense of causality, and it baffles our eternal hunting for cause and effect, for meaning itself. Landscapes last a long, long time. A hundred years is nothing for them. "There is not the same passage of time," he says, "for the meadow."

He tried to write the landscape—to give it lines and shape, to be true to its antiquity and slowness—by his choice of form and structure. His form (that is, the shape of the finished work, the body of the thing) was a conglomerate of text fragments, of prose poems. His structure (the way these parts arranged themselves, the pattern of the work's articulation) was discontinuous sequence, spliced fragments, mosaic. Broken song.

So, after the first writing frenzy, a kind of exorcism, he worked his prose fragments into an orderly chaos. He begins with the meadow—no accident, that—and splashes landscape pieces throughout, juxtaposing episodes of weather and landform memoir with tales of people's fates and fortunes, deliberately not allowing any human story to run on from beginning to end. He disturbs the passage of human time, running back and forth from Lyle to App to Ray to Pat Sudeck to Frank and so on. He breaks their stories up and scatters them about the meadow, the ridge, and the prairie, trying in this way to be true to the life of the landscape and the human lives within it—"as though each story were just an event, like the weather's passage, in the real world." As though each human life, each story, were "just one of the points of view, among many, in a place." This arrangement attempts to catch the complex patterning, the interconnected narratives that *are* that place, that landscape; and it moves his narrative forward in approximation of place-time, not human time—discontinuous, many-tempoed, never ending.

Galvin tried to imagine ecologically the human lives and the life of the place that contained them, that expressed them. He tried to write, though he does not say so in just these words, like a meadow. "Lately I have come to think that the landscape may be nothing but a bunch of points of view," he says. He confesses that this idea remains mysterious to him, but he senses its truth. To write a book of lives, human and nonhuman, from a dozen points of view—Lyle's, App's, Ray's, the coyote's, the snow's, and also his own as Jim Galvin, his own as author—and to write it from many points of time, all out of (human) sequence, was his way of writing the *landscape's* story.

In a poem in *God's Mistress* (1984), "To See the Stars in Daylight," James Galvin expresses a closely related thought about landscape, imagination, and point of view. This poem speaks of the need to go down deep (into the earth, in this case), to leave your own fixed and usual position, in order to imagine the world right (here, to see the stars, which are present all the time, but hidden to us in the daylight)—in order to see the real world:

You have to go down
in a deep mineshaft or a well,

down where you can imagine the incomparable
piety of the schoolbus,
the wherewithal of bees,

down where you can be a drawer full of dust
as night comes on under full sail,

and the smooth rain,
in its beautiful armor,
stands by forever. (1997, 110)

Form, then (a book of fractured prose), and structure (this kaleidoscopic arrangement)—artistic choices that were part accident, part design—became Galvin's writerly devices for expressing the place. He set out, though, to do nothing but bear witness to that place. True witness—if it is to be more than the articulation of an argument, a recital of conclusions about a life or a place or a self—may work best in such a (half-accidental, half-chosen) mosaic, wild, unfixed, but always attentive. Particularly where what one witnesses is something so complicated and neverending, so far transcending our sense of time and order, as a place on earth.

"To See the Stars in Daylight" goes on to express something like a personal ontology and aesthetics, in which the poet imagines the real world as just such a musical mosaic, scattered and hard to fathom:

I believe
there's a fiddle in the wings

whose music is full of holes
and principles beyond reason.
It binds our baleful human hearts

to wristwatches and planets,
it breaks into fragments which are not random. (ibid.)

These fragments of music, full of holes and resounding with meaning beyond reason—are these the scattered points of view and time, including our own (wristwatch time), that compose a landscape? Is the real world made of music, fragments of which speak in lives and landforms, seeming random and without meaning, and yet composing, if you can imagine their connection, the order we long to join? I don't want to reduce a poem to a theorem here. But I am taken by the resonance between this poetic idea and the thoughts about the representation of land and life Galvin spoke of when we met, and which he embodies in *The Meadow*. He has come upon a structure of prose that is beautifully apt for the structure of the real world, its broken music perfect for catching the broken music of the world. By "music" here I mean not just soundscapes, but the chaotic, multiple, and dissonant interconnections of lives and energies that make a place itself, and never stop. If the world expresses itself so, then a book of broken music, of fragments, of coherent tendencies not tidily linear, is well made for witnessing it. A strange, beautiful order, immanent in each phrase and paragraph, orders the apparently random mosaic of Galvin's book of place; just as, in his conception, a strange and barely coherent musical form orders the world we experience here or there, makes sense of its fragments. This music is, if you like, that which we do not know within the world we think we do know; hearing and joining that fractious music of the real world, somewhere, is what literature is for. Getting the world right is a matter of catching its lyric and somehow rendering that in writing. Whatever you say, whatever you make happen in your pages, you must catch the lyric or the world will elude you, your work, and your readers.

Galvin resists being seen as a poet of the West. That is because the West is a fabrication, an abstraction. "It's not a subject," he says. He also resists being seen narrowly as a writer of landscape, a writer of meadows and prairies. Like Lopez and all the other nature writers, he insists that his places and people are just what he knows, and writing of them is his way of engaging in the enterprise of literature. "I don't think Robert Frost writes about Vermont," he says. "I don't think Melville writes about whales. It is a way of writing something we might recognize as literature." What concerns him is what is mysterious, musical, strange, and, most of all, real about those places and lives. That is what he goes after in poem and prose.

Galvin does not see himself *merely* as a writer of place, as the poet of the meadow. Yet a place and the lives that pass within it are his subject, because he knows them and because he loves them. And from attention to this place, perhaps, he has learned something that he works hard at expressing in his writing: the idea that the landscape, though it encompasses and subsumes human lives, runs by a different order, plumbing which we may strum the mysterious strings of existence itself.

You can only write truly from *somewhere*. Only work that is grounded somewhere in particular can express part of what is real. Writing that speaks out of "no place," as Galvin puts it, "is actually a kind of antirealism." So Galvin writes his strange, fragmented realism, a musical and linguistic articulation of the context of all human experience—place. The real world needs to be known somewhere on earth, and it will have a certain weather and a certain music. The meadow participates in this reality; so did Lyle; so might a poem or a book of broken prose. So might a reader, if the real is witnessed well in the work's music.

"There is a line from Heidegger," says Galvin, when we are talking about the business of witness and reality. "He uses the word 'work'— I think he's talking about art. He says this, or something like it: 'The work lets the world be a world.' He was a pretty smart guy. He takes things so far, and he's so smart, of course, that in the end all you can do is change the subject."

Which we do, after letting Heidegger's adage sit with us a bit. But I can't get the words out of my head. They come from an essay, "The Origin of the Work of Art" (1935). In fact, the better translation of the phrase is "The work lets the Earth be an Earth." My sense is that Heidegger's idea of Earth includes not only the physicality and complexity of the places of the world, but also their inherent mystery. In this sense, his meaning is close to Galvin's term "real world"—the place itself, as we see it and as it eludes us; the fragmented music that plays inside the familiar.

The German phenomenologist has been taken to mean by these words, and others like them, that the rest of the living world has no being until it is apprehended and sung by the poet, expressed in a work of art. In *Being and Time,* Heidegger says that we draw things into being through language, which brings them into the articulated world. "Only the word grants being to a thing," he wrote in *Underway to Language* (1979, 164). Jonathan Bate (2000, 283) concludes from Heidegger that poetry saves the world because the poet sings it forth (see also Rigby 2004). "Things need us so that they can be named," Bate unashamedly transcribes Heidegger's thesis (Bate 2000, 265; Rigby 2004, 433). The "human racism" implied by this thesis, the sense that the poet is the god who conjures the world in song, that the rest of creation depends upon humankind for its real life, is not what Galvin has in mind at all, even if it was what Heidegger imagined. Quite the contrary. For Galvin, the world is always much larger and more actual, more truthful even, than the work—which only transcribes small pieces of it into music a guitar can play, into poetry a reader can share, or into, perhaps, a barn. Some of the real world is sometimes transcribed through work that, in the case of a poem, say, or a painting of a landscape, intends nothing other than to be well made and worthy, perhaps, of its subject matter. "Work" in the sense Galvin means it, I think, is just a humble act of witness—not of creation by invocation. It is just a conversation with silence, conducted in darkness and confusion.

Recently, the Australian ecocritic Kate Rigby (tentatively but hopefully proposing a new basis for an ecopoiesis in which poetry may reanimate the world and so serve the earth) has suggested a reading of Heidegger's writing on the artistic work and the nonhuman world that would allow us to understand the German phenomenologist this way: that the role of the poet is so closely to attend to the world, to the experience of being here *(Dasein)* in it, that the resulting work of artistic witness sings along with—is fully in tune with—that piece of the apprehended world (Rigby 2004, 431–32, 435). The poet, in other words, sings *with* the world; she does not sing it up, she does not sing it into being. The material earth doesn't need poets to make it real, to let it sing. But poets need the Earth, and may sing with it, joining the earth's chorus and disclosing something true about it in their singing. The earth only needs our songs, Rigby reminds us, to the extent that they may help save it from our further depradations (including our bad poems about it).

The real world—the fragmented music—is finally unsayable, so Heidegger thought (ibid., 436–37). Heidegger felt that what distinguishes poetry from technical creations such as a barn is that the poetry concedes the unsayability, the mystery, of the real world and preserves it intact (ibid.). So a poem evokes the essence of the real world, writes Rigby, drawing a reader's attention to that essence of things while letting the world keep hold of that essence, by understanding and avowing that the real world will always elude the poem. In this way each poem saves the earth by expressly or implicitly affirming the unsayability of the earth. *I have made a thing in which the place I evoke is not enframed or expressed and never can be:* this is what, among other things, each poem says (ibid., 436–37). And so, Rigby insists, a nature poem is not a new embodiment or even an embodiment for the first time of the essence of a place. A work of art lets the world be by attempting the impossible, knowing it will fail: the poet sets out each time to express what is inexpressible somewhere, all the while knowing that the world cannot be formed into words. A poem that may save the earth will do what Galvin's poems and prose works often do: it will concede that what the world is made of will not be caught by these words, and that the world will go on without the poem. The poem, though it reaches for the real world, will always fall short of it, in other words. As an example of a poem that expresses its knowledge of failure, Rigby cites a poem by Robert Gray that includes these lines: "If no-one saw all this, its existence would go on just as well?/And what is really here no words can tell" ("Very Early," 1998, 159; quoted in Rigby 2004, 435). Galvin expresses a similar sentiment in a line I quoted earlier: "The meadow's a dream I'm working to wake to" ("Against the Rest of the Year," 1997, 147).

Certainly, in that heroic seeking and falling short of the world lies some of the beauty of a work of art such as Galvin's: its power to return our eyes to the world itself that lies beyond the page; and its capacity to witness the autonomy of creation with which all of us, like the poet, need to go and seek intimacy. "There is no substitute," writes Rigby, "for our own embodied involvement with the more-than-human natural world in those places where we ourselves stray, tarry, and, if we are lucky, dwell" (2004, 440). The poet celebrates a place and articulates an act of witness and calls on us, by its example, to go witness, go reinhabit the world ourselves.

Kate Rigby, you see, is trying to redeem Heidegger's idea—the one Jim Galvin put to me—from the "overvaluation" Heidegger and his followers have put upon "the poetic word" (ibid., 435). She wants to save ecopoiesis from anthropocentrism; she wants to find a way to honor the ecopoet's work while rejecting the Heideggerian idea that the poet somehow makes the world real by putting it into words. She argues that the poet may serve, if not save, the earth, while letting it be, by falling, in her poem, knowingly short of the earth and leaving us readers free (and, if the poem's any good, inspired) to go out there and find the earth for ourselves. Rigby makes her case generously, thoughtfully, rigorously—even beautifully. But in the process, you notice, she reaffirms the radical disjunction of the poetic work from the world it engages with. She ends up insisting upon the "nonequation of word and thing, poem and place" (ibid., 437). Now, I share with Rigby her instinct that the best poem must remain modest in its relationship with the world. The poet needs to understand that her poem can never say what the earth says, and that it can never be what the earth is. The poet (or the lyric essayist) who *tries* so to save the earth by saying it will surely fail—and she will fail to make a decent work of art, too. But you can let the place come and find you and lodge itself in your poem. And sometimes it does. A place on earth and a written work that witnesses it do not, I believe, remain disjunct. Sometimes something about the word and the thing, the poem and the place, is essentially the same. Poems and other literary works sometimes move, I believe, as meadows and forests, shorelines and deserts do. There may exist some equation—or some *adéquation*—between them.

So Kate Rigby sells the poem short. If Heidegger claimed too much for the poetic word, Rigby claims too little. Despite the elegance of her exposition, she misses something (in the poetic word and in the world), and what she misses matters. What she misses is the music, though she's not alone in missing it. In fact, she mentions singing quite a bit and explores at length the idea that a place may be a choir to which the poet adds his voice (ibid., 435). But she doesn't draw out just what that might mean, that "singing," and in reaching her conclusion about the necessary disjunction of text and world, she lets the aural nature of the poetic enterprise, of the witnessing of the world, slip back into silence. Instead, she overemphasizes in her conclusions the materiality of the text. She ends up speaking of texts as artifacts (ibid., 437), which stand, by definition, separate from the world they refer to, unable to take part in whatever it is that the world beyond the page is making of itself. As though the poem were at best a response to the place of a very different nature than the place itself—a kind of humming along beside a place, pointing at it, hopelessly. But works can do more than just refer back to a place, acknowledging their failure to get what they sought. Some works are part of the land. They do, deep down, what the land does. And they do it to us (their readers).

By emphasizing the musicality of writing (of *The Meadow* and Galvin's poems, in particular) and the musicality of places, I want to carry Kate Rigby's argument forward. I'd like to suggest that ecopoiesis *is* possible. The poet does not make the earth come true by singing it. But she *listens* to it, and then what she makes in response—her poem or lyric essay—continues and joins something the place began (and perpetuates, with or without the poem). I want to suggest a way in which a work really *does* express and participate in the nature of the place, in which the work really *does* sing what is unsayable in the place. If the world gets into the work and yet remains itself, this is because each of them—work and world—really *is* a song. If the forest and the poet, walking through it and (later) responding to it in verse, really are "a choir," as Robert Gray writes (ibid., 435, citing Gray 1998, 239), then is it not the same music they perform?

Though a piece of prose or poetry is material, a form, or a set of forms, what it makes is music—patterns of sound—and it is through its music that it works upon a reader. All meaning comes to us out of the sound that words make—whether that sound is imagined sound (as when we read a text without voicing it) or actually heard (as when we hear a work read or read it aloud to ourselves). Without sound, the thing means nothing. It *is* nothing, or at least it is not a work. The rhythm of the syntax of a sentence speaks to us. Patterns of sound—phrasing—prepare a reader for meaning to arrive (Voigt 2003, 147). Music, in prose and poetry, precedes meaning, then, and precipitates it. But more than that, it is through their music, a quality that transcends their visible and material form, that works of words touch us and carry to us, it is as patterned sound and rhythm that they shape again in a reader's mind, what is more than merely meaningful, what is not merely material in the places and people they speak of.

In their lyric element, some works of poetry and prose may be said to sound like, to join and reiterate, the unsayable quality of a place on earth. The music of the place—the quality that makes it what it is and yet, like actual music, has no form we can hold, since music passes in time and does not coagulate in space—is what I think the place writer listens for and hopes most to express in words. Never will a writer find words equal to that essence of the world. The song of the text will never *be* the song of the earth. Yet perhaps it may echo it, ring true to it, always in a human voice, always shaped by letters on a page, while letting the fragmented music of the real world sound on, out of the poet's ultimate hearing. The work of art—poem or essay, and perhaps even the barn or irrigation ditch, the rifle or earring, if they are works of art—may stand apart and sing in tune with the place from which it arises, to which it looks, whose soul it shares, whose chant it is a response to—call and response, call and response, making one song.

"In music," wrote Victor Zuckerkandl in his classic *Sound and Symbol: Music and the External World,* "what is inmost in the world is turned outward. . . . What, elsewhere, can be made accessible only by laborious speculation, and then only uncertainly and insecurely—so that it always remains open to doubt, opposition, and rejection—

music brings us patently" (1956, 348). *Talking* about the essence of a place, *arguing* about what makes it what it is, in other words, will never discover, or if it does it will never express (and carry to a reader), that inmost quality. For that you are going to need music or a lyric essay or a poem.

While of course there is no literal music in a place, there is, as Galvin writes in "To See the Stars in Daylight," a music in the wings, a musical order giving shape to this silence, and it is that fragmentarily manifest order that one's writing, in its sound as much as its image and thought, is making some sort of a guess at, some sort of an approximate articulation of. The work attends to and then attempts a tuneful response to what Zuckerkandl calls the "tonal world" of the place—the musical order at work in its silence (and also in its sounds). The poet's response will not, of course, express everything that is going on in the complex music that is a place on earth. But if the poet has listened carefully, the rhythms and tones of his singing will be utterly in keeping with the place; they will form part of the complex music it performs. It is not that the writer gives the place a voice, but that he responds to its music, its tonal world, to what is inmost in it, with his own fragmentary music. He tries to catch in his cadence the very music of the place.

A poem or a lyric essay of place is, then, an attunement to place. It tries to discern the soul of, the music of, a place on earth; and in the work, if it has listened well, we readers hear the place, or hear it as it manifested itself to the poet, listening. The listening and the witnessed place then become ours. The poem or the piece of prose, at its best, is a choreography in words of an act of careful listening; and through that listening we may hear the place express itself. We may catch the lyric of the country. We may catch the tonal world, the metrical quality, of that place—depending on how well the writer has listened, and how tunefully we read.

"Lyle taught me," Galvin has written, "that the principal character in our life's drama is the land. He was properly humbled by his surroundings. He knew the land to be un-ownable, that, indeed, it owns us. He lived in harmonious and reverent conversation with his sur-roundings" (in Holt 1998). Lyle's whole life was a listening, an attune-ment to place, a silent conversation with it. A work of prose like *The Meadow* is another such conversation. It listens humbly to a piece of the world, knowing that it has the melody of which one's own life is a small expression, and then it offers some reverent and harmonious sounds in response: a joining in song, an act of witness.

Through its music, a work of prose or poetry may form what is essential, yet unsayable and unhearable, in the world into a song—a thing of patterned sound, a kind of invisible dance, which a human body and mind may experience. A work in words does not only point to, enframe, disclose the world and take its own tangible form. It also sings—and what it sings is sometimes the music the place also sings—the particular pattern of that place's self-disclosing, to use Heidegger's term (Rigby 2004, 433): the way it goes on and on making itself up.

Let me say a little more about the nature of music and the rela-tionship of music to form—landforms and texts. Music, having no body, exists in space. It lies between forms. And its sound is shaped by the space it inhabits as it sounds out—cello, room, human chest, ear, canyon, cathedral. And music has a way of implying space—the nature of the space in which it seems to move, from which it seems to come. Music gestures spatial volume and the texture, depth, and history of the space in which it exists, or in which we can imagine such a music living. We seem to know that music needs a body in order to reach us, to become real. And so when we hear music played, say by an orches-tra or on a CD, I think we imagine the kind of body that is being expressed by it—the kind of landscape or room, as well as the partic-ular instrument or singer, from which it comes. Music always implies, for me at least, a certain kind of space, and a certain kind of body (the cello's body or the body of the land it refers to). It implies a certain kind of place. Music conjures spaces and forms in our minds.

In the same way, the music of a piece *of writing*—the particular pat-tern and quality of its sounds and rhythms, its musical forms and structure, its voice—always implies a quality of space from which it might have been born, to which it belongs; and that space will not only be the character of the author's mind. The voice and syntactical rhythms—the music, that is—of a work of words shape a world; they re-enact a particular kind of tonal world in the mind of the reader, an embodied space characterized by a certain frequency and energy. The work implies in its tonality, in its music, the kind of space from which it arose.

So the music of a symphony or a chant, and the music of a work of prose or a poem enact a tonal world—and place the listener within it. Music implies place. And in a sense the opposite is true: places imply a music of which they are an enactment. They imply the kind of music that such a set of forms, such an amplitude, would be fit to contain. They embody music. Just as, when we hear music, we long for the kind of space, the kind of body, it belongs in, so, when we enter into a landscape, we long to hear the music that its forms suggests—the music that makes sense of such a place.

And this is what the witness—Galvin or I—listens for in the land; it is what we want to find rhythms and tones of written speech apt to express. And sometimes, I think, we succeed—or, I should say, the land succeeds. So it may be that the kind of space a book like *The Meadow* makes through its form and structure, the shape and pattern of its sentences, bears a qualitative resemblance to the space at play in the place it bears witness to. One of the elements of a landscape I would expect to enter the imagination and memory of a writer—particularly a writer like Galvin, whose purpose it is to bear witness to a place, and who has a feeling for music—is the kind of music that landscape implies. And I would expect that music to find expression in his words and phrases. It is that music, silently dreamed by a landscape, that a place writer's work may intuit and express in its own lyric—in how the work sounds, more than in what it describes. In this way it may catch the lyric of the country.

A play of form and formlessness, substance and absence, recurs like a dance through Galvin's poetry. In one, the afternoon's light tries to become tangible. In "Misericord," which strikes a note of lovely sadness, a man wakes after camping out all night with his lover in the snow beside a half-frozen lake, and he wants to tell her that "small frogs were singing from the lake as if / we had become transparent in our sleep." Lack of separate human *form* would be a sign of belonging in a place, of belonging even in its song—frog song here. In "Against the Rest of the Year," the sky is "cut out for accepting prayers": as though the land longs for the space above it. The music of the place may be the sound we cannot hear of that longing of form for complementary space, and of space for complementary form. Again, in "Misericord" Galvin writes:

> Who ever doubted that the earth fell from the sky?
> As though it had traveled a great distance to reach us
>
> and still could not reach us,
>
> though we held our hands out to it,
> some vague intention, some apprehension
> occurred between us. (1997, 101)

In this imagining, earth is the child of the shapeless sky, still and always falling, its dream of form sent like a prayer—to us, this time. We cannot hold the sky's wish; what earth really is does not quite reach us. All we pick up is a sense of the longing of a void for a form. The "vague intention" is sound or sometimes the silence in which the sound is implied. In the poem, "We heard the earth cloud over, clear again, / the low voltage of granite and ice." The place reveals its true self in sounds beyond hearing, but not beyond apprehending.

That metaphorical yet transcribable music arises from the play of form and space in landscape. For places are dynamic spaces, as Paul Carter reminds us; they are networks of interactive forms and frequencies and actions, of time registers as slow as the life story of a mountain range and as fast as the beating of a sparrow's wings. We can perceive it. We can participate in it by listening and making a piece of writing; and that work of words, in its metrical, in its musical characteristics, might continue the place, might reenact, that dynamic space.

Landscapes make real music, of course—the frog song, the creak of tree, the sound of the wind, birdsong, passing cars, and so on. But I am not talking here just of the soundscape. I am talking about the dance of relationships that is the place, the defining character of that dynamic space—the pattern of how it expresses itself, on and on, becoming what it will become. That kind of music is the one thing that a landscape does not, materially, sing or speak, and yet getting that musical quality right is the object of our witness. The music of a place, then, is that which it expresses without saying anything, that which is implied by but not literally uttered by its forms. It is also that which gives it meaning—its patterns of interconnections. The music of a written work, too, is what is not literal about it; it is what its forms (letters and sentences and paragraphs) express, the pattern of sound that arises from it—without which it, too, has no meaning.

And so to return to Heidegger and Rigby, to the relationship of work to world. My rumination upon the work of James Galvin and those words of his in conversation, which set that rumination off, leads me to this point: in its singing (and in its listening), a work does more than gesture at—that is, point to—the world. It accompanies it; and it transposes it. In its music, a work of prose or a poem draws closer to the world than Rigby, for one, allows the work to do when she imagines it as an artifact (though I note that Rigby, following Michael Haar, herself gently proposes what she calls a Rilkean poetics in which "poetry sings the sayable world" (2004, 11).[2] What makes a work a work is what makes a world a world—not the materiality of each, so much as the unique song, the defining and intangible quality or pattern, at play within and expressed in and between its material forms.

Each—place and work—is really a process: endless, while ever there is life and listening, but with a characteristic pattern. And it is in

<hr />

2. I note, however, that Rigby (2004, 437), following Michael Haar (1986, 123–24), gently proposes what she calls a Rilkean poetics in which "poetry sings the sayable world." It is, however, poetry's capacity to sing the "unsayable" world—what Galvin calls "the real world"—that is at issue here.

their lyric quality—the inner life that each expresses, that arises from each—that both may sometimes be said to express the same vernacular truth, the same reality. The work sings what is sung in a place on earth—at least as one poet hears and transcribes it. The work does not make the world's music; it makes its own. Yet it seeks, if it is a work of witness, to form into syllables stressed and unstressed, into patterns of sound, what the writer has discerned in the world. The song of a work takes a reader as close to the world itself—to what is distinctive about it—as any work of human hands and mind can take us. A reader might even sense, though she could never prove it—it being a matter not susceptible of proof, only witness—that a quality of the place is also a quality of the work, and present in the way the work's song unravels in her head.

If the work sings in a lyric that is faithful to the music of the place, then it serves the place by calling attention to what is true about it. It serves the place, while letting it be, by resounding the place's genius in our minds, by transposing what may not be merely *said* about that piece of world, may not even be apprehended in any other way, into music that can play in human time, may be apprehended by the body. The work, through an act of human witness, elaborates the same music, perhaps, that the place makes, though each of us will hear and sing it slightly differently, just as a piece of music sounds uniquely in each of our heads. A work's lyric, its tonal world, its dynamic space, is in this sense the music both of the place and of the work. They sing the same thing together—or at least, they sound out.

This is the truest and humblest *adéquation* a piece of literature can perform—its best service to man and to place. The place is there in the work's music—as the tune is there in our heads—while remaining exactly where and what it always was: itself, complete, mysterious, and entire.

This is close to the (lyric) project Galvin imagines for the poet, I think. You stand and pay attention to the world somewhere. You let it dawn on you. You let it change you. What you write should ring with what it was you learned in that encounter, and it should ring with the quality of change wrought within you. Your job is to hear the music that runs through the place you stand in, and to sing it as best you can, in your phrases, lines, or paragraphs. You choose word structures befitting what you heard, fit to let that music—all those scattered notes and voices—sing again out of the body of your work. Your job is not to interpret or to offer too many conclusions. Your job is to let the world be what it really is; to let it occur to you as it will; and then to express the pattern of its being in the form and sound, the shape and of course the ideation and the imagery of your work. Then your glimpse of reality might also live for a reader through your work— though you must also help the reader to understand, through the humility of your voice, that what might be apprehended in your writing is not the meadow itself, but just an image of it, an image (or I should say an echo) of its truth (in which its whole truth, its entire music, is nonetheless implied).

The point is to tune your writing to the music of the place, that community of lively subjects (including yourself). When you do, you leave the place alone—you let the world be what it is, to go back to Heidegger's phrase. You do not colonize it, take possession of it, enframe, imitate, or sample it. You do not compete with it. You simply let it be, and it goes on and on without you. But you also allow it— some tiny phrases of it, implying the whole musical form—to sing itself; you allow it to appear, through your work, to others by virtue of your honest witness of it, your careful musical rendering of your own experience of it. Your work then lets the world, the real world, be what it is, free of your narrow take on it, free of your assessment of its merits. Although what it is at heart will always be beyond you and beyond your work, even that will somehow be suggested between the notes in the lyric such a work expresses. As the real meadow is sung and present in *The Meadow*.

So, here I sit, in the meadow, making notes in pencil in the blank pages at the end of James Galvin's book. In my hands I have one of the songs this place has sung. Though I hear nothing in this amphitheater of weather but the wind and a bird, I know that I sit inside the meadow's recitation of itself. I look up from my own writing and from Galvin's, and I wonder if *The Meadow* lets the meadow be the meadow.

The book, one man's act of witness here, has led me from a text to the very place, the one place on earth, to which it bears witness. I didn't have to come here to know that the book's music would be true to the place itself, but I find that it is. I am not thinking of music, though, as I sit here; I am thinking that much of what this place really is would be lost on me if I sat here without the book's fragments of story and, yes, its cadences and the mood they make, the imaginal, dynamic space, lodged in my body. The book wakes the meadow to me; wakes me to it. I see the grasses Lyle hayed, the treeline he contemplated, the road the beavers ruined, the creek's afterlife where it emerges from the reservoir App imagined. The work has storied the place, made it mythic, made it rhythmic and metric, has articulated its truest patterns (some of them, anyway). It has given it a life in my mind independent of its real life. And yes, I recognize it as though I have been here before, as though I return to the meadow.

But the more I sit here, the more the place grows around me, into its geological past, into its present season of drought, into the shape it has taken since Lyle left. It grows into the place it seems to me. The book stops and the place starts, all on its own. I see how much of the meadow escaped the book's covers. The book plays on, not out of key nor discontinuous with the place. If it fell short of the meadow, there is music going on in that gap. But the meadow is, I see, doing just fine without its poet, Galvin. His book, his witness, gave me the meadow and then let it be. "This is the real world" in front of me, "indifferent, unburdened" (1992, 3).

Each thing—work and world, *The Meadow* and the meadow—is made of the same vernacular: a spare, austere, angular, and broken ground, with a creek, now hidden by willow, now mirroring sky, now running, now dammed, coursing softly, haltingly, something like an everyday kind of libretto, through the middle of it. Each is an image of the same set of stoic truths, each is the product of weather and work, a song of endurance chanted over and over beneath a miraculous sky. To read the book or to sit here in the meadow is to occupy two spaces, fragmented and full of holes, in which the same kind of aesthetic runs, the same wind moves, the same kind of music plays— true and sad like that bird I heard, or like music played well on a handmade guitar.

The Meadow was—still is—a prayer. Like the prayers Galvin imagines the pines send up to the sky, the book expects nothing, attempts nothing but presence, asks for nothing except that what is real might go on being real. It gets the meadow. Its reward is to express the place as unselfconsciously as the pines do. It is a sustained act of love for a place; and it has led me not only to this place but deeper into my own. It schools me in a kind of witness that occasionally can do the kind of justice to a place that Galvin's book does; the kind of justice that transforms a place into a work of art without changing a thing. Not only the meadow but the whole world is better and more enchanted somehow because of *The Meadow*, Galvin's prayer.

In *The Meadow*, James Galvin may have found his way, without even trying, to the literary form most apt for what he was attempting— showing what a small piece of the real world looks like, letting us hear how the meadow sounds, charting its weather, giving us episodes in a few of its lives, washing us awhile in its light. For it is a lyric essay. And lyric essays are well made for work like that—for making music of the actual world. Not that Galvin had ever heard of a lyric essay when he began. Indeed, he didn't hear the phrase until the book was out in the world, finding readers and mystifying booksellers, who didn't know whether it was novel or prose poem or natural history or what. They had never heard of lyric essays either. Few of us still have. The term came into use only in 1997, though it is just an attempt to give a name to a kind of writing that, as a strand of essay writing, has a long history in that great and overlooked tradition, stretching back to the Greeks and Romans.

It was a student of Galvin's who conceived the name and gave it to *The Meadow*. John D'Agata, now associate editor at the *Seneca Review*, got himself two MFAs at Iowa, one in poetry and one in non-fiction. His dissatisfaction with the narrowing of creative nonfiction to memoir and personal essay, along with his own poetry practice, led him to think hard about other kinds of factual prose; and his meditations and his own writing led him to the form he called the lyric essay. The name has been adopted now by the *Seneca Review* and celebrated in two special issues (vol. 27, no. 2; vol. 30, no. 1). D'Agata has published his own collection of lyric essays, *Hall of Fame* (2000), and an anthology, *The Next American Essay* (2003), which traces the lyric essay back to Cicero and gives special mention to Emerson but also argues for its status as an emerging contemporary form.

While he was a student at Iowa in the nineties, D'Agata told Galvin he thought *The Meadow* was a lyric essay. "I thought about that," says Galvin. "Because you know, when I go into bookshops, I never know where I am going to find it. I find it in fiction, and it is not that." He tells me later that the book has the ISBN of a novel. "I find it in nonfiction, and it isn't entirely that. I find it in memoir, I find it in biography, and it isn't either of those. I find it in natural history, and it's not that. There are so many things it isn't—but what *is* it? Well, it's a book. But I was drawn to that idea of the lyric essay."

It occurred to him that in music the lyric is the words, and what we call the lyric in writing is its musical quality. "So I thought that maybe all 'lyric' means is something that is trying to be what it is not, or something that is trying not to be what it is." He went back to D'Agata, he says, and reminded him that an essay—from the French *essayer*, to try—is an attempt. "So I asked John, 'Do you mean that *The Meadow* is an essay that is not trying?' And he looked at me and he said, 'Yes. That's what it is.'"

But both Galvin and the book *were* trying. "I was trying very hard to do certain things writing that book: to be precise, to be truthful, to get it right, to get the landscape in. But I guess I wasn't trying to write an essay or to say anything or persuade anybody of anything. I was just writing." Just that kind of "not trying" is what distinguishes a lyric essay.

As the editors of the *Seneca Review* define it, one thing the lyric essay does not do is try to explain, to confess, or convince. It does not make an argument—not deliberately. "It elucidates through the dance of its own delving. . . . The lyric essay does not expound. It may merely mention. As Helen Vendler says of the lyric poem, 'It depends on gaps. . . . It is suggestive rather than exhaustive'" (D'Agata and Tall 1997, 7).

"While it is ruminative," the *Seneca Review* editors go on, "it leaves pieces of experience undigested and tacit, inviting the reader's participatory interpretation. Its voice, spoken from a privacy that we overhear and enter, has the intimacy we have come to expect of the personal essay. Yet in the lyric essay the voice is often more reticent, almost coy, aware of the compliment it pays the reader by dint of understatement" (ibid., 7–8). It does not have the voice or use the rhetorical techniques of declamation and persuasion. Very largely this is true of *The Meadow,* which offers up fragments of weather and story and dream, smaller and larger prose poems, and leaves them for a reader to sew into a narrative, if she chooses. It puts the reader on a horse and lets her ride through thoughts as shapely and lean as conifers, past stories like beaver dams in which a hundred conclusions lie. But it makes no pitch. It does not even try to be complete or neatly made.

Lyric essays work hard at singing, at letting worlds be worlds, but not at telling; they work hard at looking like they are trying nothing. This is their art, and it is a poet's art. "They forsake narrative line, discursive logic, and the art of persuasion in favor of idiosyncratic meditation" (ibid., 7). In their witness, they respond to and embody "principles beyond reason," to put it as Galvin put it, speaking of poems at the time. Like the essay, they cleave to the world of fact. But unlike the essay—and most like the poem—in their exploration of the actual, in their exposition, in their wondering, they proceed in rhythmic fragments, shapely phrases, and distilled, enacted ideas; they unfold in riffs and what may sound like improvisations. Their logic is a poetic logic; they are shaped by cadence, not argument, by breath, not reason.

The lyric essay—to borrow Mary Oliver's words for the lyric poem—"is a pattern made with sound just as much as it is a statement made through sound" (1998, 6). It is a dance more than an oration. It depends, as a poem does, on particularity and texture, a "musicality of language" (D'Agata and Tall 1997, 7). The lyric essay is an utterance, a song, a chant, even a liturgy. It is voiced, particular, strange, alive.

Galvin says nothing about his own prose's music, but there is no question that it is written for its cadence and voice as much as for its story. His poetry is strewn with musical references: violins, in "Getting a Word In," that crack from trying to "exist," for instance, and the sound of a fretless guitar his neighbor made him, in "Hell to Breakfast." He reads for the music in other books—the books he loves ring with music, as different as *Moby-Dick*'s Shakespearian meter, Faulkner's dirt music, and Cormac McCarthy's brutal cantillations. We speak about music we both love, including the cello and the tenor voice, their restrained, raw emotional power and edge, and he says, "One wants to write that way too. There's form reining everything in, but as well as the reins, there's a whole horse there." We speak more about his musical training and his singing and playing, the plateau he reached. "It might be partly out of frustration that I am so obsessed with the music of poetry," he repeats; "because I can't do the music of music."

So music matters to him in writing as it matters to him in place. And it occurs to me that the lyric essay is a mode that suits the project of the musical apprehension of a landscape and its people, perfectly. "We turn to the lyric essay," write the *Seneca Review* editors, D'Agata and Tall, "to give us a fresh way to make music of the world" (ibid., 8).

Galvin, schooled already in poetry, stumbled onto the lyric essay when he was looking for a way to get the landscape down on paper. The lyric essay asks a writer to ration his commentary, explanations, and interpretations. It calls on him to let the subject speak; it asks him to step to the back of the narrative, to give ground to what he witnesses, to its form and structure. It asks him to apprehend, in other words, lyrically and to write out of the heart of his experience, not to write *about* it or shape it into tale. It allows him, if he chooses, to order his prose by the kind of logic that runs through a geography, to disrupt the flow and arc, the dominion, of human time. It does not even have to tell a *story* as we understand a story.

The lyric essay suits places, which don't run along the narrative lines with which we tend to make sense of human lives. Places are concatenated, entangled storylines, intersecting causalities, a thousand plots on the edge of denouement, always falling short of resolution. Places are always in the process of writing and rewriting themselves, making themselves up out of pieces of the past and the future, the earth and the sky, the plants and the animals. Forsaking narrative line, as it does, taking off on excursions, meditating idiosyncratically, depending on (and therefore supplying) gaps, the lyric essay is well made for landscapes, those complex, multilayered, eclectic, yet coherent entities. Emphasizing musicality—the looser music that prose (like place) makes—it is well made for divining and joining the music of places.

Though it is made of prose, and its lines are not metrically broken like a poem's, the lyric essay is like poetry in its concern for shape and structure. A lyric essay is often made of pieces, each composed with the same attention to shape and structure that a poet dedicates to a stanza or a line of verse. There is plenty of space in it. "The lyric essay often accretes by fragments, taking shape mosaically—its import visible only when one stands back and sees it whole" (ibid., 7). This is a perfect description of the form of *The Meadow* and of my experience reading it. It is made of fragments of text, few of them more than one or two pages long, some of them a single paragraph. The book's discontinuities struck me first—its gaps, its jumps in time and place and character, in point of view. But the larger whole that these saturated sediments implied is what I was left with. The meadow, it turns out, was in the spaces between—in the gaps. And later, reading the book again, and again, I was struck not by the discontinuities, but by the book's elegant sequencing.

Landscapes accrete by fragments too, of course. At first it is the pieces that we see or think we see. But the story is never neatly told. A place is a mosaic of weather and geology and culture and fire and flood and birdsong. It requires a certain kind of being present (never still, but always attentive), a steady reading and rereading, to apprehend a suggestion of the whole that is made of the pieces. Yet it is a whole that lives through all time, and goes on each moment remaking itself. A place accretes by fragments, and never stops doing so; it plays in many time zones all at once, fast and slow, ancient and modern; and it comes to us in snatches. This may be why the form of the lyric essay serves so well the task of witnessing landscape: its pieces are not so randomly scattered as they seem, for each of them, being a part of the whole, carries the pattern of the whole. In the gaps between the jumbled fragments, the place itself may arise. In both place and lyric essay, storylines stop and start and intergrade.

In *The Meadow*, James Galvin includes a selection of entries from the journal of Lyle's sister, Clara, from the year 1949. Later he does the same with Lyle's jottings for 1974. Galvin tells me that he transcribed these entries verbatim into his book, though not all of them. Clara kept a journal all her life. Lyle took to writing one the year after his mother died and then left off. He hid the journal in the toe of an old boot. Lyle never threw anything out; he used the tongues of worn-out boots to resole newer ones. At his death, Jim and Lyle's relatives found a pile of leather carcasses, and among them was one with the journal hidden in it. "I don't think we were meant to find that journal," Galvin comments. Well, perhaps it found him.

The two journal sequences, Clara's for 1949 and Lyle's for 1974, struck Galvin's editor as too strange to include, but they stayed in the end. Galvin insisted on them. Each is a plainspoken, clipped recital of weather and work, of comings and goings. Here is Clara:

1/1 I started two new pictures. Lyle put up his stove in the cabin.

1/2 I cleaned up around the house. Tried to fix hole where packrat got in. Lyle went to ditch camp AM, worked in shop PM. It's cold and snowing all day.

1/3 Woke up this AM still blizzarding. 10 below. Willis won't get home today. (1992, 44)

And here is Lyle:

12/6 Snowing today—worked on grindstone shaft bearings.

12/7 Still snowing—have about 6". Jimmy Galvin and Julie came over in afternoon.

12/8 J. Galvin Sr. came today with his woman. Forgot her name.

12/9 Cleaned chicken house—shut off Marie's spring—put new wire glass on south side bay window—washed outside windows— charged light batteries.

12/10 Went to town then res for supper. Nice day but cold— −14 in morning. (ibid., 156)

And so on. These belong well in a lyric essay. They are fragments of a place, two voices and two lives within it. And they are there for their cadence and rhythm more than for their content. "I don't even know what makes a person keep such records," Galvin says. "But you can hear a rhythm in them, a music." That is why he put them in. They mark the rhythm of daily life and work, of solitude and community, of wind and snow, of continuity and persistence.

This is the vernacular of the meadow; this is the vernacular of two people native to it. In the entries, the cycle, pace, and meter of the place are transcribed. In them also are lodged the voices of two people— each voice formed in part by the place and their humble obedience to it. Like the music of the place the book gives voice to, the music of these fragments is found, not made. Unlike the music of the meadow itself—of beaver dam and grasses—the music of Clara and Lyle's texts is sampled, quoted, not imagined. Still, these passages speak as just two among the many notes and phrases that compose the landscape, and compose, also, this lyric essay.

Although he has written this book of prose—and a novel, to which I will come—James Galvin thinks of himself as a poet. To be known as a poet is important to him. It is a matter of temperament, he says. He doesn't feel prose is up to the tasks to which he wants to put language on the page. "Poetry has a kind of a snap to it," he says. "Getting back to horse terminology, poetry steps out so smart."

Prose, according to Galvin, is tethered to time and ordered by reason, whereas poetry, ruled by line breaks and shot through with gaps, runs to a beat. It is organized spatially, not temporally; it moves outside time—it is lyric. "If you sit down to write a prose work," Galvin says, "before you even touch the pen to the paper you have already addressed the idea of the passage of time. And if you sit down to write something that's in lines, you have already decided to resist that passage." A line of poetry depends on space; its very purpose is to fill a set space with a particular pattern of beats. A sentence, however, disregards space; it sets out to name something and to say something about that thing: subject and predicate—there is your sentence, no matter how long or short, regardless of its syllable count. Sentences and paragraphs are defined as units of thought. Of thought, you see; not of music, not of space.

I take Galvin to mean also that a work of prose, made of sentences, sets out to tell some stories, and those stories have to move through human time to make any sense to us. Narrative, steeped in and moving through time, from start to finish: that is the business, normally, of prose. Lyric, transcending time, existing in space—lively, auditory space: that is the work of poetry. "You can have a kind of simultaneity, a kind of suspension of time, at least for a little time, in poetry that you can't in prose," he says.

Oddly, despite his emphasis on the musical work of poetry, Galvin's own poems are marked by ideation, conceptual playfulness, shapely and economical aphorism. They are proselike in some ways—

rhythmic thought as much as they are rhythmic song. Critics often remark on the philosophical bent, as well as the swing and song, of his poems: "they dare to say what they mean," writes the *Virginia Quarterly Review* in its review of *Resurrection Update* (autumn 1997, 136); "Galvin sets the transcendentalism of Thoreau to the music of the lonely, magnificent, and taunting expanses of the West," comments Donna Seaman in *Booklist* (April 1997, 1277). A less sympathetic reader, Thomas Merrill, however, charges the poems with being "relentlessly gnomic" (*Library Journal*, February 1997, 84). In his review of *The Meadow*, Franklin Burroughs finds "a self-protective quality of cleverness" about the poems—the absence of which in *The Meadow* he greatly admires (1994, 153).

Some of Galvin's poems, such as "Small Countries" from *Lethal Frequencies* (1995), which appears also in *The Meadow*, and a number of the poems from *Imaginary Timber* (1980), actually take the form of prose paragraphs. But they are still poems. They still step out pretty smart.

And if his poems are sometimes like prose, his prose is always like a poem. As James Galvin speaks to me, with the same grace of phrase he uses in essay and poem, I hear in his voice his love of the poem, and I think of *The Meadow* and of his novel and how, despite the absence of line breaks in those, time is dislocated there, music of a loose kind plays, mystery is present. If prose is lyric, as Galvin's is, and if its storylines are discontinuous, if it is made of fragments, much like a poem, then time may well be suspended, and space—lively, dynamic, and musical—may prevail. Large-scale musical perceptions may be induced, just as though one were reading a poem, and in those perceptions we may discover the place, that large-scale musical form, to which the work is a response. Franklin Burroughs, for one, isn't buying the argument for the superiority of the poem. "The choice [of literary form] isn't absolute," he writes in his review of *The Meadow*. "It is a question of what takes the writer through the looking glass of self, to where worlds can be perceived and created" (1994, 153). As though he is reading my thoughts, Galvin picks up the copy of *The Meadow* that sits between us on the table, flicks through its pages, and makes a small concession to prose: "Well," he says, referring to the business of getting outside time's clutches, "you can try, by using these little vignettes and tableaux. But you can't pull it off."

Although prose, like poetry, makes the rhythm syntax makes, there is another kind of rhythm prose cannot make—the rhythm of the line. This is the point Galvin is making. Line brings meter to a work of words. And meter, writes Ellen Bryant Voigt in her essay "Syntax: Rhythm of Thought, Rhythm of Song" (2003), works in a poem like beat in a piece of music; and so it is music—and, through music, space—that orders poetry. Meter is pulse; a regular pattern of accentuated beats. Voigt quotes Robert Jourdain (1997, 123–24) as saying that meter "provides a sort of grid upon which music is drawn. . . . Meter organizes musical time on the small scale while phrasing [the kind of rhythm we speak and write prose in] organizes it on the large scale." Meter organizes a work of poetry, as it does a piece of music, according to a musical order that does not arise from the human voice, an order that is universal and transcendent of the human realm. So poems open out into that realm—the realm beyond human time, where the music of the spheres is audible—in a way that, in theory, prose cannot. For prose is not strung across a grid of regular beats. Prose is ordered by the rhythms that belong, and belong only, to human thought and speech. So prose remains soundly rooted in the human and upon the earth. Yet through the irregular rhythms of its phrasing and structure, a work of prose such as The Meadow can still make music; it becomes a large-scale choral work of loose form, capable of inspiring in a reader a perception of the musical order of the world it alludes to.

What Galvin says of prose—that it is tethered to time, to the merely human realm—may be true of the novel, perhaps, because the novel, operating as it must in narrative, telling stories of human lives and times, is premised on the arc of human existence, which moves forward through time. The novel is grounded in human time. Its dramas and comedies, its ironies and tragedies, its farces and its moral tales depend on the notion that life runs forward. Galvin mentions

William Faulkner, his favorite prose writer—specifically, his book of interlaced stories *Big Woods*. "He does everything he can to keep the story from ending," Galvin says. "All his weird forms and extreme formal structures, I believe, are intended to resist the passage of time—which passes anyway because he is writing a novel." In *The Meadow*, Galvin notes that Lyle, who read a lot, hated Faulkner. Once, speaking of Faulkner, Lyle says to Galvin, "If that sumbitch wants to tell me a story why don't he start it at the beginning and tell it through to the end?" (1992, 167).

But if a writer sets aside the ambition to narrate a story in human time; if he works in prose but aims neither to expound nor to tell but simply to delve, to make a mosaic; if he sings story as Faulkner did, or if he sits down to write a lyric essay, a book like *The Meadow*—what then? A prose writer is stuck with sentences, of course, which are disrespectful of space. But what if he pays particular attention to their rhythm and their tone, their sound effect? What if he shapes paragraphs with the kind of care for the pattern of sound, for the arrangements of their cadences—the kind of care Galvin takes in *The Meadow;* what then? I think a writer might manage, by these means, these lyric modes, to slough off most of the difficulties of time and logic almost as well as he might in a poem. For no form, not even a poem, escapes completely a career in time and logic. I think a lyric essay like *The Meadow* might take us about as close as we're going to get to the real world—to the order that organizes the broken fragments of perception and of country.

In 1999 James Galvin, "the author of *The Meadow,* an unconventional memoir, and three highly praised books of poetry," as the flyleaf puts it, published a novel called *Fencing the Sky,* dedicated to Lyle Van Waning. It has a plotline its author does everything he can think of to keep from running straight toward its end. It is another book of shining pieces, artfully made, its sentences beautifully turned, its paragraphs laconically lyric like the best of Galvin's poetry and nonfiction.

The country this novel moves in is the same, only there's more of it than we meet in the pages of *The Meadow*. The book is made, Galvin confesses, of horse stories, veterinary catastrophes, personal experiences, local folklore, and current events, reshaped and recostumed as fiction. Nearly every piece of it really happened. Yet, it works as fiction—as a tale of human drama and destiny, a modern cowboy fable. Lyle and his meadow appear, but not for long. Pat Sudeck, the man who homesteaded the Galvin property, gets a mention. A vet named Oscar, a man very like the real-life Clay whom we met in *The Meadow*, plays a supporting role to the book's hero. In Dr. Adkisson Trent there is more than a little of James Galvin, mixed perhaps with pieces of a neighbor or two on the ridge; and the outlook from Ad's verandah all the way to the Snowy Range sounds pretty much like the view from Galvin's place. Trent's love of climbing and his love of his only child, a daughter, also allude to aspects of the author's real life. This is a novel made, like many novels—*Moby-Dick*, for instance—from a world the author knows well. The spine of the novel is made of an escape on horseback, which runs through country intimately observed and named; and those names are the ones that appear on a good topographic map of the country spreading out around Boulder Ridge and the meadow. That journey grounds the novel in the actual world; you can follow the route, as Galvin did with his daughter in a four-wheel drive when he was writing the book (and as I did, for most of its length, in my hired truck on a snowy day in May). But while the book is set down in the material realm; while it explores real land-use issues at play right now in this country; and while this story runs in real time, the past keeps intruding. Memories, fables, anecdotes, and episodes in the recent life of the rangelands break the narrative line and complicate the journey, without lessening the suspense. Instead, they surround it with a context within which the drama of the rider and his friends becomes both small and mythic, as fleeting and moving as every event looks when seen in geologic time.

The novel starts with a murder and runs forward through time, with Mike Arans, a fat and endearing cowboy with a ponytail and a radical past, making off on Potatoes Browning toward the Great

Divide Basin and the Wind Range beyond, toward a place and a possible afterlife the author keeps dark until near the end. We start at the scene of the crime and spend the novel moving slowly, with Mike, away from it; at the same time, we wander among the fractured lines of causality that led to the murder. The novel's pieces, each dated, span a thirty-year period. Some of them—bits of folklore—are called "Once." Out of these fragments, Mike, even as he rides out of his life (he thinks), deepens into his past. We come to understand the anger, the grief, and the principles that led him to throw that deft and fatal loop of rope at the start—or is it the end?—of it all, back on page four. We get to know Oscar and Ad and the nature of the friendship the three men share, their bond to this place, their care for it. We learn steadily more about Merriweather Snipes, the man Mike murders, more about his schemes and devices. It is one of the small triumphs of the book that Snipes does not become a mere caricature of evil, even though we cheer at his downfall. And in poetic grabs, the place itself—its geological past, its pastoral traditions, its current dissection into marketable if unsustainable portions—grows around Mike's crime and flight. The more the book's multiple time frames and storylines spin toward order, the more its action—its human action, which starts with a bad man killed and a good man riding and riding away—spins toward chaos. "I was thinking about Yeats's gyre, you know," explains Galvin. "So that is my highfalutin explanation."

Fencing the Sky is a novel of a place and its people—in that order. Not that the people don't count, but their stories are folded into, are expressions of, the long life of the ranges and high valleys, the sinuous streams and rangelands that run like scar tissue across Wyoming from Fort Collins, Colorado, toward Jackson. The fates of the men and women of this kaleidoscopic tale come to matter deeply, but they are inseparable from the fate of the lands they love. They will go the way the land goes. Either they will be saved to carry on a tough, compromised, but loving stewardship of this country and to carry on the traditions that have sustained them, or they will go with the land, broken up and diminished. The land and these lives rest on a divide—and must run one way or another in the end. The novel's story holds your interest, but in the end it is the storied life of the place itself that concerns you most. What is happening to Mike, what may become of him, becomes part of a wider tragedy befalling the land; it becomes a part of the great cycles of the earth that make and remake places like this one; and it becomes an emblem of the edge that the West these people have loved teeters upon.

The men you meet here (for this is a book mostly of men) seem made of this high country, possessed by it, already grieving for the loss of this land that has loved them. For it is falling victim to smaller dreams than theirs—real estate dreams that diminish the land and parcel it out to consumers to possess. It is doomed, and they know it, yet they stay.

It is a novel about land and land use, in which the land itself breathes and plays its part. It carries Mike away, delivers him to his afterlife in the end. Its draws and willows, prairies and sky, its national forests and wide Red Desert are as intimately present and as lively in this book as the ridge and haymeadow of *The Meadow*.

And then there are moments when Oscar, Mike, or Ad reflects on the land about, thinking wryly about its form and habits—like this:

> Oscar riding behind his three bulls. After sky the thing we have most of here is grass, he thought. Sweet flag, cattail, timothy—it pulls the horizon away with it—bottlebrush, tickle grass, panic grass. Oceans of it, waves of wind spelling themselves out onto the prairie.
>
> To be grazed or burned. Grass has two fates, both of which it survives.
>
> He thought about the Wyoming grass dinosaurs ate, in a Wyoming we wouldn't recognize. How after the last ice age, woolly mammoths turned these prairies into themselves. Then the bison; now a commensurate number of cattle, sharing grasses with elk, deer, antelope, rabbits, chipmunks, blind moles, and sundry insects, transforming the blades into flesh, grooming it green.

For ten thousand years, people torched vast prairies to attract
the herds when the grass came back anew.

If there's nothing to eat it and no Indians around to burn the
big beige lawn, lightning is waiting in the wings. (1999, 78)

Or this, at the book's close—Ad is looking out at the Snowy Range,
thinking: "Something pushed the Rockies up, but at first they weren't
real mountains. It was just a big hill, six hundred miles of incline. Erosion made the granite faces, the river valleys, and left topsoil thirty feet
deep in Iowa. 'Nobody likes erosion anymore,' mused Ad, 'now that all
the scenery is made'" (ibid., 258).

At the center of the book is a scene in which a man called Marty
addresses a small crowd of ranchers, environmentalists, bleeding
hearts, and developers in Laramie. His speech is called "Losing It All,"
and it rehearses the ideas that the rest of the novel enacts. What the
West is at risk of losing, with the coming of men like Snipes and their
values, is two things at once: "its distinctive horse-based, non-progress-
oriented culture, and its natural history" (ibid., 100). Farmers like Lyle
and ranchers like Oscar's family, like Mike, have loved the land and husbanded it—sometimes damaged it, sometimes, inadvertently, improved
its health, but certainly changed it. Though stockmen and greenies
have seen each other as enemies, they both speak for the land. The
land's real enemies—the enemies also of the good, tough life local people have managed upon it—are the corporations, who run acreage
without living from it, and developers like Snipes, who sell the West off
in small lots, reducing it to a parody of itself.

"Marty," writes Galvin, "had belonged to every green group there
was from the Sierra Club to Earth First! until, one by one, they all
made him gag. Now he worked alone. He wrote books" (ibid., 101).
Marty, of course, is Galvin himself, who for a time went out and got the
kind of conversation going among the locals that follows in the book.

There is more argument and ideology in this scene alone than
there is in all of *The Meadow*. This is at odds with conventional under-
standings about fiction and nonfiction. Novels are supposed to show,

nonfiction to tell. As we have seen, Galvin's nonfiction elaborates mostly through music and image; here, his fiction, though always reined in and economical, speaks out its philosophy. Elsewhere it enacts his anger—especially in the death of Snipes, of course.

When I ask Galvin why he wrote *Fencing the Sky* as a novel, he replies that he wanted to "place some blame," and fiction is better for that. It has always been a moral enterprise. "In nonfiction," he says, "you are saying that you were there and saw these things. It is a work of witness. And it is dull when it is about you and your thoughts about things. Who wants to know about what you think about everything?" Fiction lets the author hide, and exact revenge because it claims to be an invention. In fact, only two parts of the novel are entirely made up, Galvin tells me—the killing of Snipes at the beginning and the deliverance of Mike Arans at the end. He invented nothing else. As for the murder, "I sure as hell wanted to rope the guy who became Snipes in the book."

"*The Meadow* was an elegy," says Galvin; "the novel is a pure lament. I wanted to say that bad things are happening." Timothy Foote, writing in the *New York Times Book Review,* commented that although it doesn't work as a story, "polemically speaking, this is a very successful novel" (31 October 1999, 22). While noting the "beautiful descriptive writing," Foote poked fun at the cowboying, and he entirely missed the larger role of the landscape in the book. None of the book's characters, he alleges, "can carry the freight of affection and significance that Galvin wants them to." Maybe. Maybe not.

Apart from laying some blame, Galvin wrote *Fencing the Sky* as a novel because it was what his publisher wanted next. People understand novels. Booksellers know which shelf to put them on. They sell in quantities that leave "an unconventional memoir" in the dust. So he wrote it as fiction.

"Fiction is a way of dealing with the problem of your own involvement," Galvin says. He has been talking about how hard it is to write about his own actions—particularly when they are things of some

accomplishment, like roping cattle and climbing mountains, or, perhaps, doing so well the kind of work Marty does in the novel. It is usually horrible to read such stuff, he thinks. He is a man schooled by his
father, by Lyle and his landscape, in modesty. In that place of sudden,
deep snow and the summer risk of fire, and all manner of other interesting ways to die, you would learn pretty early the price of hubris or
bravado. That land is a tough teacher, and humbling.

I agree that writing about the good things one has done is one of
the chief challenges of nonfiction writing. But I am aware too that this
is a man eager to keep himself—at least in the role of hero—off the
page. He will open up his soul, lay bare his grief, in the mythic time
and space a poem creates; but he won't put down his triumphs and
tragedies, his private thoughts and personal history, in ordinary time—
in prose. That would sound like boasting or complaining, and neither
has its place in the stoic ethic of the meadow and the prairie. Even in
The Meadow, Galvin's own life is very sparely gestured. He gives all the
lines to Lyle and the others. This is in keeping with the charter of the
lyric essay; but it is also his nature, shaped by that place.

So the novel is a device of a man who wants to write what he
grieves for and name men he disdains; who wants to talk about stuff
he loves and does well himself—roping and horsemanship, the care of
a daughter, for instance—without drawing attention to himself. It is
another defense against hubris.

James Galvin's landscapes are animated. They speak and persist and
pray: the meadow "wears a necklace of waterways"; "wildflowers still
joy in its swells and hollows"; "sage-choked irrigation channels"; "the
meadow is a green ear held up to listen to the sky's blue"; and "the
island never heard of states." His trees are a particularly lively lot,
yearning and longing—pining away. In *The Meadow*, for instance,
timbered ridges come down from Chambers Lake, then "suddenly
stop and bunch like patiently disappointed refugees" (1992, 3, 5). In
poems and prose the sky listens to the land, receives the prayers of the
pines. He ascribes will and desire to meadow flowers, wry admiration

to coyotes. His beavers are pretty thoughtful, too. Virga, with "sublime indifference," lets down its hair.

But all this is clearly no simpleminded anthropomorphism. We know that mostly from the tone of voice in which these images are sounded out. This is very knowing image-making, sincere but light-hearted and modest. Never grandiose. This writer is under no illusions. He knows he is using phrase and syllable and image to get at the life that moves through things other than himself, through the land itself and all its citizens. *These human terms are the best that I can do,* he seems to be saying. *These are images of the truth of other lives than mine. We know what I am talking about, don't we? Everything lives, in the real world, and this is a way of showing it.*

In his poem "Speaking Terms," from *Lethal Frequencies* (1995), Galvin has the pine boughs "lisping approval" in words that sound a lot like trees in wind: "Shh! This way! Shh! This way!" And then:

> Better to impersonate than to
> Personify, when it comes to nature.
> Shh! I tell them. This way!
> And start walking. (1997, 216)

He knows the rules and he breaks them knowingly, trying to let the living world live again on the page. He carries his witty critique of the rule against anthropomorphism one step further in the next poem, "Trespassers":

> A breeze tensely riffles the pond,
> Erasing the pond's attempt at representation
> Of treetops and sky—try again.
> It keeps doing that. (1997, 217)

In all his writing—particularly, of course, those passages dedicated to the land in its nonhuman aspects—Galvin works at uncentering his mind from himself. He attempts to write from inside other articulations of creation, but without trying to mimic them, and without imagining he can possibly leave his own voice and humanity behind while doing so. He sloughs off a little of his humankindness, his mere and separate self, without losing his perspective. He is at once the tree or the meadow or the rain and also utterly himself, its witness. We feel them both, world and witness, and the relationship reaching between them.

The Meadow, looked at this way, is a sustained exercise in uncentering. Galvin writes the life of the meadow from many points of view (including his own), entering for a time lives he has not actually lived and thoughts he has not thought. Because he imagines the actual from the inside, his writing preserves the liveliness of things that are not human. His imagination is able to make the stretch to touch the life that moves—quick as a horse's gait, slow as a mountain's rise and fall, patient as the sky—in all things, not merely the human ones.

Galvin's landscapes are holy too, sacred. His trees are prayerful. His skies are cut out for receiving prayer. Rain is God's mistress, a kind of angel. Trees aspire to become angels. Lyle, too, is a one-winged angel, a kind of feral saint. Galvin writes a landscape of prayer, blessing, miracle, but of little mercy; it is an unforgiving paradise. Yet it is not in the least effete. His world is substantial and tough and also hallowed, respected by its tenants. His diction of prayer and divinity is his way, I suspect, of expressing the mystery, eternity, and otherness of land, his wonder at it, his respect for those qualities in it, his love for what moves in and over it. It is his way of carrying on "harmonious and reverent conversation with his surroundings," as Lyle did. As with all of Galvin's writing, to read it literally would be to read it wrong. His poem "Still Here" makes all this clear:

> The horses drift in from pasture
> With their heads down.
> Since horses don't pray they must be grazing.
> Lost in tenderness,
> They could be, already, in another life. (1997, 131)

Prayer in Galvin's world is a metaphor, as these lines make clear, for being fully present, resigned to the moment and to the order of the place. Inhabiting a place as horses do makes it holy.

In James Galvin, we have a man who has lived in and prayed in, has listened to and conversed with, a particular place for most of his life. He is more indigenous, continuously, to his home place than any of the other writers I have studied. And his practice of belonging on Boulder Ridge has been perhaps the hardest. He has been schooled in it by a man, Lyle, who also knew that place all his life and expressed in every habit a deep fealty to it. Galvin is a man who points me to a mountain range he has looked at all his life for a picture of his soul. So, all things considered, it is not surprising to find some of the meadow, some of the ridge, the prairie and the Neversummers, Sheep Creek and beaver dams running through his work. How, specifically, is his writing harmonious with his country?

I may have quoted enough of Galvin's writing already to demonstrate its qualities of sound, form, line, structure, cadence, and rhythm. Let me offer one more piece to stand for it all:

> The meadow is under two feet of snow, which looks gray but not dirty in this light. Leafless willow branches make an orange streak down the middle. Each year the snow tries to memorize, blindly, the landscape, as if it were the landscape that was going to melt in spring.
>
> The wind has cleared a couple of the knobs above the meadow, and the silver-gray sage throbs out. Above that stands the front line of timber, where the trees begin, or end, depending, still dead black though the sky has brightened behind it, a willing blue. Nothing is moving across the meadow this morning. (*The Meadow*, 1992, 5)

All his writing has about it a quality of vast, deep passion, powerfully, elegantly reined in. It is, in this way, very like the oceanic prairies, reminders of the seabed this country once was. It is unadorned, unfussy, austere. It is lean, its phrases minimally made ("a willing blue"). It is angular, but its faces are eroded, its rises and falls fashioned as though by wind into smoothness. Everything curves; nothing juts high or gapes low, though you sense that, once, like this landscape, it did. Now its relief is low, much of what it was or might be barely hinted at. All its gestures are brief and restrained. It affects nothing but humility.

The musical, regular rise and fall of a sentence like the last one in this passage—I dare you not to hear its steady, unexcitable rhythm—moves as this eroded landscape moves, this terrain of long, shallow curves and modest yet hardy ridges.

Like the weather, Galvin's writing prevails steadily, and, for the most part, softly; slender utterances within a wide open space; and again like the weather, even when it changes and delivers tragedy or violence, it never raises its voice for very long. His sentences are clean of excess, sculpted until there is nothing left of them but what there must be to bear the music and the message they are made for. This is how the country looks and sounds—undemonstrative habitats, un-decorated places, angular, spare, abraded; just what they should be in this light and wind, and nothing, not a branch, more. In the same way, Galvin's words say more than they appear to. They are short and shapely, apt and resonant. They stay with you because nothing clutters them. Clutter is one thing the landscape of the meadow does not suffer from.

The tone of his writing is elegiac, tender, and reverent, yet gritty and witty. It puts you in a space where just such a mood prevails. It was prevailing in the meadow and the surrounding country the day I visited them. Those timbered hills and this pasture were utterly inde-pendent of the text that had fashioned them first in my mind, and they contained much that was not in the writing. Yet their line and form and tone were like those of the words and sentences that evoked them for me in the first place: similar terrains made of different mediums.

Galvin's writing, like the nature of this place of sky, prairie, meadow, range, and timber, is a play of toughness and softness—like granite or red sandstones, which make soils as fine as flour; like the sky and its weather, both ferocious and gentle; like grasses, which endure everything (fire, grazing, snow, wind) by balancing resistance with sur-render; like sagebrush, which grows where nothing should and puts out such a perfumed and proud flower; like Lyle; like coyote; like pines.

But this writing has a human voice, always. You are aware that this is speech and that a man is making it. This happens through small, vernacular turns of phrase (that word *depending* in the passage above, punctuated to mark the inflection of the speaker). Galvin makes no sharp distinction between the landscape and its people, and he too is part of the place. The more his prose carries a music like, or harmonious with, the place, the more it also sounds like him. This is conversation: which murmur is the land's and which the man's?

I set out on this exploration of land and language wondering in what ways a set of landscape-oriented writers imagined the land ecologically—not merely in human terms, but as though they could apprehend one place on earth as that place might see itself: in terms of geologic time, as sets of relationships, complexly, evocatively. So how ecological is James Galvin's imagining?

Profoundly ecological, I think. His writing, particularly *The Meadow*, but all of his prose and poetry, starts from the principle he learned from Lyle and from this place: that we are the land's, not the other way around. It was the meadow he set out to write about—through its human stories and the cadences of its weather—in *The Meadow*, and the very structure of that book embodies a conception of land in which the place contains, shapes, possesses its people, who also contribute to it, as weather does. In his prose works Galvin deliberately dislocates the passage of human time to suggest the otherness of time and causality that prevails in the land. And here is Marty addressing the locals: "From nature's point of view, if nature had a point of view (maybe nature is nothing but points of view?) . . ." (*Fencing the Sky*, 1999, 97). This idea that nature or a place is just the composite of the infinite points of view within it is deeply ecological—transhumanist. In both his works of prose, he tries to write from many points of view, some of them nonhuman; and *The Meadow* is a sustained piece of such imagination.

Landscape, scattered in its many pieces throughout his writing, is present in his books for its own sake, because its drama is the one that contains and surpasses and explains all others. All his writing, one way or another, is a self-confessed attempt to imagine things—especially places—"the way God sees them," as he puts it in "Trapper's Cabin" (1997, 190). He tries to look at a piece of creation in time lapse, as one would know it if one could transcend mere humanity and see how the place got to be what it is and how all its parts, including oneself, related. His work is an essay in ecological perspective.

All Galvin's writing arises from and expresses a musical engagement with the world. According to Zuckerkandl, music makes space lively, forceful, dynamic: "Space we *hear* flows; it is in motion, unlike visual space. It is the process of composing itself" (1956, 277–78). Just like a work of words—a thing that one hears, which composes itself aurally as one reads it. Music speaks what we cannot grasp with our eyes and thought. To imagine and therefore to experience a place musically is not just to hear its sounds; it is to understand it as animate and dynamic, and it is to sense the patterns of life at play within it, even those we cannot see. It is to grasp the whole of it—its ecology.

Places are not symphonies. They are places. Their "music" is a metaphor for the elements of their actual lives that animate them. The writer who imagines a place on earth musically begins to know that place as it actually is—dynamic, complex, much more than merely human, much more than meets the eye, richly and densely patterned. In actual music, listening—that is, musical apprehension—connects us to the source of sound, and to every other thing that is touched by that sound, because the song, once made, belongs everywhere within the space in which it occurs. "We are always at the edge of visual space looking into it with the eye," writes R. Murray Schafer in his essay "Acoustic Space"; but "we are always at the center of auditory space listening out with the ear. . . . Aural awareness is omnidirectionally centered" (2000, 94). Auditory awareness joins one to everything else (everything audible, I guess). It is weblike. As Paul Carter puts it, a writer who perceives a place in auditory mode "borrows from the facts of auditory perception in order to rescue seeing from the reductionist cast of 'visualist thinking,' reinserting [seeing] into its natural mobile setting" (1996, 303). Perceiving in this way disposes one ecocentrically.

To *see* a place is to stand separate from it: my seeing a tree or a meadow places it there and me here, seeing it. To write only of visible things would be to write a pointillist landscape, each part severed from each other and from me. Unlike, say, my seeing of Lyle's barn or the empty reservoir or the meadow flowers, the song of the bird I heard, like music, stood entire, separate from the bird, like a work of art—it was a thing made, expressive, of course, of the thing that made it and the space in which it resonated, but transcendent of them both and touching everything present in that place. So to imagine a place as though it were music, and to apprehend it so, would be to experience connection with all its parts and pieces, even those one did not notice, could never see; and then it might be to turn that experience into a lyric that sings in a pattern akin to some of the patterns at play in the place, representative as one or two notes of a chord are of the whole chord, and the whole chord is of the sonata, all its tempi and keys. To imagine a place musically is to stand in musical relationship with it: to see one's self and even one's work as part of it, as expressive of it as any of its pieces; and it is to seek to express not its parts so much as its rhythms, its patterns of connection. It is to want to do justice to that larger whole, in a way that transcends a simple enumeration of the pieces, histories, weathers, and waters of a place.

The imagined music of a place is the pattern or order of life it expresses; it is the symphony of all its parts, living, moving, playing— dissonantly and in a hundred key registers, yet all, somehow, of a piece. All of us, sometimes, somewhere, lean toward, yearn for what Paul Carter calls the metrical quality of the earth, its poetic; for space that flows, for the tonal world of a landscape—that is what we feel for in certain places of earth, a quality as ineffable and real as a chorus of song. The music of a place is a thing that, though real, has no body. In our words we find it one, for a while. The music of a place is the eternity of the place, its enduring genius from start to finish, its ecology-through-time.

"The human brain is avid for pattern," writes Ellen Bryant Voigt (2003, 147). We make meaning through language spoken and heard, written and read, by the expression and apprehension of patterns of sound, through rhythms. We are, as humans, avid for pattern in language—and in the world. Some of us are more avid for pattern in landscape than others, but all of us make sense of it, if we are the least bit concerned to know where we are, by sensing its structures. We find meaning in a text the way we find it in a landscape—not by imposing it upon the thing, but by listening and discerning the shapes and interconnections of things. And then out of all the words that compose the sentence, out of all the life forms, fast and slow, that compose the place, an order in which they all participate is suggested, a logic that could not be understood without the act of listening for pattern. The writer avid for a place's patterns (which is to say, avid for its ecology) attends to it musically, then; and she tries to sing the nature of what she has discerned there in the rhythms, the breaks and starts, the play of tones, within her own prose. To put it another way: ignore the patterns and rhythms, the dynamism, of a place (for which "music" is a good metaphor), and the place will elude you; ignore the rhythms and patterns of your prose (your written witness), and the place will elude your writing. The place does not elude James Galvin. He imagines and renders places ecologically because he witnesses them musically, taking care in his work to remember his metrics, his tones and rhythms, just as he felt for those qualities in the landscape. This is how James Galvin writes—of landscape music, in linguistic music.

"I wanted to paint the landscape-in-time," he writes in the reading guide notes to *The Meadow* (Holt 1998). The landscape begins and contains everything, and all his writing is, among other things, an attempt to see a particular landscape on its own terms—as something that has so long a heritage already that our human lives within it seem almost infinitesimal. "Grass is a long time and a big space," Oscar reflects in *Fencing the Sky*. "Your own life in it? A match going out" (1999, 79).

The novel ends with these words, shaping themselves into a mean-ingful pattern in the mind of Ad Trent, who sits in contemplation of the Snowy Range and imagines its rise and fall through time: "It's good to get a little perspective now and then" (ibid., 258). Galvin's per-spective is ecological. It is, like Ad's, lyric. It is nature's; it is that of the place.

I have driven, now and then walked, around all the country in the island made by the Poudre and the Laramie, the North and South Platte Rivers, and I sit here again in Lyle's meadow, an island within that island. I have traveled all this, and I sit here now, alone. Tomorrow I fly home. This is not how I planned it. I meant to walk here with James Galvin. But he was away in Iowa teaching and could not join me in the country he has blackened with his life and prayers. I sat with him in Iowa City instead, and we talked for hours about his writing, his life in this country, its life in him; and now I have come back here to reflect on what I learned. I think he is as present and as mysterious here as the "real" landscape he has spent his life in conversation with, on the ridge behind me and in the meadow on Sheep Creek.

The pasture is a little greener now than it was when I came up here before my pilgrimage across the prairie, but only because spring is a little further advanced. No rain has come, and as it turns out, a sum-mer of fire will follow, all around the mountains that offer up this meadow to the sky.

Mine has been a passage through a lyric landscape—of high meadow and range, of this writer's nature, of the terrain of his writ-ing. I carry away many things about all three. And since this has also been the last leg of my larger journey, I find myself able to pull together thoughts and ideas that arose earlier.

I have learned to think of this land-oriented writing as a kind of witness, in which music matters deeply. It is a kind of musical appre-hension of the world practiced first in respectful conversation with your surroundings—nine parts listening, one part a testing of phrases meant to ring harmoniously with what it was you heard of the fractured music of the place. And then it is a speaking forth—bearing personal and local witness to that landscape, to what you have learned in conversation with it (for the place is where you have tried your ideas and images, sounded them first for truth). Your writing is a kind of *evocation*—a calling up, with rhythm and voice, of your encounter with that place and, to the extent that you can manage it (for most of it will elude you), of the soul, the inmost nature within and beyond the forms, of the place itself.

In your listening and conversing, you discern the score(s) by which the place plays; in your writing you write down that score in words; in the sounding out of your writing that happens when a reader reads it, those scores play as a second music. If you have listened well and written truly, the musical quality of the place may reach the reader through your text. Music connects whoever hears it to the place from which the tone and rhythm seem to come, and allows, though disembodied in this case, an intimate engagement with the source of the music, such as the writer himself experienced. (Since it is the writer whose words make the music, the reader will also find herself connected intimately to the writer through the music of his words.) Your writing is not meant to be a re-creation—how could it be?—of the place. But it recalls the place, so that it arises imaginatively, true to its original nature, in the mind of a reader.

Your speaking forth is an act of love intended to honor the place and its people; or it is meant, as Galvin's has been, to catch the cadences of people and place, their dignified relations, against a looming future, when the place you have known, and which has stood in some sense intact—the landscape-in-time, as Galvin calls it—may be lost.

You will do justice to the piece of country if you work hard to give your words an order as elegant, as immaculate (though you will fail), as the order of relationships at play in that country—the tonal order of the space that holds there, the ecological order and the visual and the tangible order. It is not enough to explain it or to describe it. Your words converse with, they sing with and relate to that country, and they must aim to be as well made as it is, and as eloquent. It will take a lot of care to find patterns of words conversant with that place, adequate to speak with and for it.

Music matters in this relationship of text and place, because most of what you will want to catch about the place lies beyond the landscape's form and history and will escape the meaning-making and visual-image-making power of words. What you want to get at is the pattern of the place, its larger musical structures, the ones by which it keeps, characteristically, making itself up; its coherent tendencies; the poem to which the interconnected lives here amount.

The patterns of sound and rhythm that sentences make will be where much of the evoking happens—much of the echoing of the place's music, much of the response to its call. But most of this will happen with very little intention on the author's part. Your text's music will be, as it were, an accident of your close listening. You will simply try, as Galvin says he did, to paint a picture of that landscape, to catch the cycle and rhythm of its seasons, the cadences of its people's speech; and your words will make some music. You don't try to mimic it, for it does not actually sing; nor does it force your hand and fill your words with its notes and rhythms. But if you pay close attention to the land, and its mysteries begin to open to you, then, if they touch you and you attempt this kind of witness, you will find it, the land, there in your word choice and structures. Somehow. There it will be—that place, its music.

I learned that the prose form in which James Galvin composed *The Meadow*—the lyric essay—is particularly apt for this kind of work of witness, because it encourages musical engagement with and elaboration of the actual world. It asks you, the writer, to step back and let that world emerge through the music of your words and the silences between fragments of text. By encouraging evocation over exposition, it allows the world to stand clothed in your words, but not lost in your human conceptions of it. That piece of the world may speak, and survive, a little more in your sentences, the less you box it into categories of human thought, the more you let its body and music sing.

And the music of the place rings in the life of its people. A writer gets at the country through the vernacular cadences of folks grown native to it, who have shaped their inflections and turns of phrase in conversation with their home ground. The poetry of their lives, I learn from Lyle Van Waning and James Galvin, expresses some of what is most real about their home place. It is through listening to the rhythms of those lives—but listening and recording what one hears as though it took place by the landscape's calendar and played as notes in the landscape's score—that a writer can best hope to sing the place true.

The voice of a piece of writing—even such an ecologically imagined essay as *The Meadow*, made with utter reverence for the authentic music of the world it witnesses—will remain a human voice, and so it should, But not *merely* a human voice. Writing is steeped in the human, being made of words; and words have human histories, make human meaning, sound in a human voice. But if the writing is made with an ear for its own music—and for the fitness of its music to the music of the place—then the voice of the writing may catch the lyric of the place. The materiality of words—the fact that we see them and know them as things with form—along with the fact that they are products of a human intelligence, ground a text's music in the everyday world, in a world we can grasp in ordinary time. A lyric text like Galvin's may bring a reader an experience of the inmost musical nature of a place on earth and of one man's intimate connection with that place, while also conversing with the reader about that place and its human lives, in a voice absolutely its author's own. It accretes by fragments, like a landscape, like a long slow conversation.

I look about. James Galvin may not be in the meadow, but the meadow is in James Galvin. It plays in his words, which make a prayer for the place they come from.

Catching the Lyric of the Country

A CONCLUSION

Lavender Bay and the Blue Plateau,
New South Wales

The earth says have a place, be what that place
requires; hear the sound the birds imply
and see as deep as ridges go behind
each other. . . .
Listening, I think that's what the earth says.
                                William Stafford,
                        "In Response to a Question"

I am home. My apprenticeship—fragmentary and discursive—among
these writers is over. I set out with a question about the power of a
piece of prose to speak for a place on earth, to sway, in the reader's
mind, with sedge and grass, to run like a winter watercourse in orange
willow, to weep like a forest with rain, to moan like a high prairie with
wind, to sing with distance and regeneration like a shoreline, to glow
like a desert canyon with light. I have listened to these writers and their
home places, and I think I have heard some answers. I have returned,
at least, to this plateau, with a better, more complicated, notion of the
nature of places and of writing itself; and in that understanding, which
arose in conversation with country and writer, and over which I have
troubled myself long in the library and late at this keyboard, lie the

makings of an ecological theory of representation. The places sing; and the writing can catch them at it. Writing can carry the place—its musical nature—to the reader. The structures by which a piece of country composes itself, over and over, may reach the reader in the structures of the prose. That which makes the writing most artistic—most peculiar to the writer, the product of one human imagination—is what makes it capable of rendering the character of one place on earth, a more than merely human realm, the land-in-itself. The writing is not severable—if it is conducted with a lyric apprehension, with an ecological imagination, in the manner of a dance—from the place.

The Pond

And it turns out Henry David Thoreau knew this all along. Walden Pond lies at the center of this book, though I have let it lie silent. I took a visit there in the midst of my travels. I went there with some of the writers I have written about here. We took an excursion to the pond one day during a seminar on nature writing at Harvard University. "The Ecological Imagination," that event was called. There in Walden Pond—and in the ransacking of Thoreau's journals and the rereading of *Walden* that my visit there led me to—I caught a glimpse of what I set out, in this book, to find. In the pond's dark water, in its wind-affected portrait of the Concord sky, in its deep, still remembrance of long-gone times, in its ringing chorus of regrown oaks and hickories, and in the recitations of Thoreau's works I listened to there, I began to fathom how a work of words might sing its place and at the same time sing its writer. Wildness was the key.

How to write a literature of nature—how to allow nature to write through him—troubled and enticed Thoreau much of his life. In the years after his stay at the pond, he dedicated himself to a discipline of closer and closer observation and recording of the natural history of Concord, botanical in particular; but as he did so, he worried that his words left the life, the poetry, of Concord out. As Frank Stewart puts it, Thoreau's eternal project was to seek truth in nature "and a way to render it that would betray neither nature nor language" (1995, 11). And in his struggles with both ends of that project—with coming to know the nature of nature and with learning to express it without reducing nature to a mere object of appreciation—Thoreau pioneered a literature that became known as nature writing.

Witnessing and then bearing witness demand both proximity and distance—the microscope and the memory. It was and remains a problem of scale: how to keep hold, in both seeing and writing, of the essence or meaning—the poem, perhaps—of an encounter with the world, while attending minutely to the detail of the flower or the leaf or the fruit (ibid., 8). It is the challenge of letting the moment be what it is "without making a minute of it," as Thoreau put it on July 23, 1851. It is the challenge, as Thoreau put it on the same day, of giving yourself over to the "impression" while making sure you recall enough to give it truthful "expression." Poetry, he thought, puts an "interval" between the two; it waits "till the seed germinates naturally" (1927, 75). Although Thoreau does not elaborate on his metaphor, its implication is that the world sows a seed in one's body and mind, and that seed must stay there until it is ready to find expression in a way that is natural to the poet as well as true to that experience and its world. How does one learn not to spoil nature by one's reflection upon it, by one's work upon one's text? How does one let the world dawn on one, sow its seeds, without reducing the business of being-in-the-world to an exercise in chronicling creation here? Thoreau was again worrying away at this question of scale in writing and seeing in mid-August 1851: "I fear that the character of my knowledge is from year to year becoming more detailed and scientific; that, in exchange for views wide as heaven's scope, I am being narrowed down to the field of the microscope. I see details, not wholes nor the shadow of the whole. I count some parts, and say 'I know'" (ibid., 79).

Though he troubled himself about that balance, in the *Journals* in particular, he struck it very truly, brilliantly for the most part. Observation leads to reflection; image always accompanies idea. The solution to the problem that concerned him and should concern every nature writer—that he would, in his writing, reduce his engagement

with the world (the pond, in his case) to fastidious observation, to list-
ing and naming—did not come to him as a revelation that fell from the
sky. He did not find it lying upon the shore. The prose he needed came
out of his taking his thinking outside, out of his engagement in mind
and body with one place, and out of his determination to write, later,
as though he were always in the moment of his engagement in the
world. He arrived at his solution, then, from agonizing over the matter, from careful and endless exploration of the kind of looking one
must learn to do, and the kind of writing that would be adequate to
the expression of one's impressions. If the seed is to be sown, one
must walk out in the world as a poet and a naturalist. And then, later,
one must write as a poet, in whom the seed of the world has germinated. "The poet is more in the air than the naturalist," Thoreau wrote
on August 21, 1851, "though they may walk side by side. Granted that
you are out-of-doors; but what if the outer door *is* open, if the inner
door is shut! You must walk sometimes perfectly free, not prying nor
inquisitive, not bent on seeing things. Throw away a whole day for a
single expansion, a single inspiration of air" (ibid., 80).

And a writer who wants to do justice to what he or she has seen
in this way must do more, writes Thoreau the next day, than give a
"faithful, natural, and lifelike account of their sensations" (ibid.). A
writer must make a prose or poetry fresh, strange, and vivid enough
to touch and stir us, to change us, even. To report one's responses, to
give an account of what one saw and how one felt, would not do,
thinks Thoreau. What is needed, he suggests, is a work of words seeded
by the experience, by the place itself, but nourished in the writer's
mind by love and time, and given a form, by that gestation, that
"affects" both writer and (with luck and grace) reader with the same
force and originality and mystery as the experience in the place
affected the writer. What kind of writing will pull that off?

> Sentences which suggest far more than they say, which have an
> atmosphere about them, which do not merely report an old, but
> make a new impression; sentences which suggest as many things
> and are as durable as a Roman aqueduct; to frame these, that is
> the *art* of writing. Sentences which are expensive, towards which

so many volumes, so much life, went; which lie like boulders on
the page, up and down or across; which contain the seed of other
sentences, not mere repetition, but creation; which a man might
sell his grounds and castles to build. (ibid., August 22, 1851)

When other people write them, Thoreau calls such sentences—the
kind adequate to the challenge of writing nature—"nutty and concentrated," like nature herself. He does not say how one learns to write
them—but he learned, and I wonder if it was not largely from his
readiness to step outside convention, beyond literature and society,
and look to all of nature for lessons.

As with so much in Thoreau, there is a paradox in what he says
about writing. The more a writer tries humbly to give the reader the
place, by making a plain, transparent report of his bit of the world,
the less he will succeed, the less he will give us of the true nature of
the place. On the other hand, the more a writer works to give a reader
words that are themselves vivid and mysterious, shapely and fresh,
and therefore also patently the production of his own hand and heart
and head (hence disjunct from the world he is wishing to articulate),
the more the reader's experience will resemble that which the writer
knew in his own moments of intimacy with the place: it will be as
powerful, as authentic, as memorable. The more one's writing is one's
own and wild—patterned by many forces, not quite in control, a little dangerous, but limber and sufficient and original to his very
nature, the more it might serve to articulate the wildness of the earth,
and one's own place in that poetic order.

This is the kind of prose (see p. 81 above) Lawrence Buell may have
in mind when he speaks of how "stylization" allows a text to express a
place (1996, 86); the kind of writing Francis Ponge and Sherman Paul
had in mind when they spoke of *adéquation*—"an activity in words
that is literally comparable to the thing itself"(Paul 1992, 19). Such a
mode of expression might be the most fitting kind of engagement
with place, a dancing with it, a becoming part of it. "An activity in
words": a performance in rhythm and sound, an act of spatial creation
through words, a dynamic thing, alive and complex at the moment of

its writing and again at each moment of its being read, suggestive of a much larger world that has led to it and includes those words' arc, as the single moment-in-place is suggestive of a much larger local reality. As in love, one allows the other to express itself, herself, himself, the more one speaks of and with that other in one's own true voice. One never mimics, and one must be present.

Thoreau had an idea that the kind of writing nature demanded, the kind that might do it justice, needed to be imagined, and in a sense actually practiced, not as a sitting, but as a walking—as an activity or performance, made with the poet-writer's entire body. Frank Stewart finds this set of sentences in Thoreau's *Journals:* "How vain it is," he wrote on August 19, 1851, "to sit down to write when you have not stood up to live! Methinks that the moment my legs begin to move, my thoughts begin to flow, as if I had given vent to the stream at the lower end and consequently new fountains flowed into it at the upper. . . . Only while we are in action is the circulation perfect. The writing which consists with habitual sitting is mechanical, wooden, dull to read" (Stewart 1995, 4).

To write only what one has encountered in the flesh, out of a relationship constantly renewed with the rest of creation somewhere, and to write (even if one sat down to do it) as though one were at that moment "in action," fully engaged, body and mind—this is to write directly out of one's whole being's engagement with the world. It is to conceive of writing and practice it dynamically, befitting the nature of places, as Thoreau came to understand them: as enmeshed and fluid activities, as dynamic entities, always in the act of creation.

In September of this same year, 1851, Richardson tells us, Thoreau was reading Cato the Censor's *De Agri Cultura,* and was very taken with his careful and uncompromising attention to the practicalities of Roman farming, his advocacy of the virtues of the country life, and "the packed, severe style" of the prose. Cato admonishes a writer, *"rem tene, verba sequentur"* (grasp the thing, the words will follow), and the epigram seems to have spoken to Thoreau and helped him reconcile the tension he felt between fact and poetry (Richardson 1986, 250).

Writing well, making the things sing, demands attention to and loss of oneself within those things of the world. It also demands faith that the real things to which one gives oneself over will give rise later to words, a sequence of meaningful and shapely sounds—the truest poetry of fact. Cato and Thoreau may have imagined in the epigram a statement of the continuity that can hold between intimate encounter with the actual world and vascular expression of it: one activity of distinct parts, or movements, in which world generates word, and word becomes an expression of world—in which world is reenacted in word.

Attend closely to the place, go away, and then let the words, seeded by the intimate encounter, rise in your mind and express themselves in your prose—which is also, really, their prose, the essential prose of things. Let the words come, and let them stay wild so that they might speak of the wildness of things.

Rhythm Section

"So much of my writing is a matter of rhythm," said Barry Lopez.

He was speaking to me last week by phone, when I was deep in the long, long process of editing this book. I was in the workshop from which finished pieces of writing sometimes emerge. I was here in Lavender Bay, hammering and sawing. I was sitting and working my fingers into the right rhythms on these keys. I was standing and walking about, gathering ideas, letting my moving body form them right, and then sitting again to work them into the body of this piece. I was sounding each phrase and sentence for aptness—literally speaking every word. And he was in Finn Rock, Oregon, about to go to bed, spent from a day's work at the typewriter, the fifth draft of a new book nearly done. So much of the work of writing depends on rhythm. The larger part of writing is not the first inspiration or apprehension; it is the sustained and repetitive work of editing and rewriting. Particularly performed at a typewriter, when every new draft is a complete sounding out of the work from beginning to end, rewriting is a rhythmic practice—and for that matter, a sonic one. We concentrate on the finished piece of prose and call it an artifact, "the work"; but most of writing is the *work* of the making, and much of that depends on a rhythm the writer hears and tries to catch more truly in draft after draft. The remaking itself is rhythmic—a dance to a music begun in a landscape.

The rewriting—which is most of what writing consists of—is a drawn-out recitation; it is manual labor; it is a rehearsal of all one's lines in an empty hall; it is a readying for performance; but it is, itself, part of a performance that began, if one is a writer of this literature of place, in a dynamic space, outside somewhere, in a landscape. That place's rhythms, and one's own within it, are what you are trying to sustain. They are the meaning-laden music you are trying to make. You are working to let the writing ring true, sing true, move true to that rhythm.

Believe it or not, sometimes one is still months later at the keyboard, in the workshop, reverberating with the music of a place. The music, to be precise, of a moment—or even a lifetime of moments, within a dynamic space. That music, which one entered for a short time or a long time, and which animated one's whole body and mind, is what moves you still—your body and your thoughts. It is *that* one wants to sing out, sing about, continue in one's work. The hardest work of writing and rewriting goes into keeping the rhythm, the pitch, the timbre, the dynamics, all of it, true to all those qualities of the landscape. That music stirred the desire to write. But it is not a desire to make a thing separate from the place. It is a desire to make something that continues it, as the melody you whistle from the heart of a symphony continues that larger-scale music, which you still recall. But you must keep moving, for the place, like the work, lives in the movement. In the making and in the finished piece of prose—which, like the place, is never truly finished, for it is new and alive whenever it gets read—much depends on the rhythm, the shuffle of pieces and the intervals between them.

Land has lyric. One may enter it, for a moment or a lifetime; one remembers a music and spends months and years composing a work that re-sounds that lyric truly. You use words, of course, for you're a writer and otherwise no one would understand the thoughts and feelings the place woke in you; but you are making something that has its own sonic landscape, its own rhythm. When it is done, it will not be the landscape. It will be a work. But it will perhaps catch and continue the lyric qualities of the landscape and express them in its own sound-and-rhythm-scape. You will be pleased if it seems to. For you would like your work to touch a reader as the place touched and moved you. You would like that; and you would like a reader to be stirred by your work and the place that started it moving; and you would like a reader to be carried away by your work not so much to *your* place as to one of their own, and you would be thrilled if their part of the world were animated by this song. But you do not stop to think about any of that too often, either there in the landscape or here in some study, thrashing out a rhythm, dancing out a song, at the keyboard. You know that writing is good for such lyric reverberation of the land, for so much of writing is a matter of voice and interval and rise and fall; and only after that, and because of the patterns of sound it makes, is it also a matter of signification. Mostly, though, you just try to stay in the song, to sustain the vibrating air that is the chord.

Writing as though you were making a work of nature demands your whole body and most of your mind, and large regions also of that intelligence of a place, which is not yours but which you can share in sometimes—but only if you keep moving and keep listening and keep calling in response. Even in the fifth draft or the third, at the computer or on the typewriter, in some motel room in Nebraska or in your ex-wife's family's villa in Tuscany, or in the apartment at Lavender Bay, the converted toolshed on Long Island, the upstairs room in Finn Rock, the old container out the back of the house in Castle Valley, you've got to keep moving to the rhythm. Even cutting and tampering, polishing and throwing bits away. Even if you are long gone from the place where the song began.

I am thinking of Jim Galvin, blackening sheet after sheet of paper with the meadow, first in a rage and speedy with coffee, then slower, more spaciously, in a gentler kind of weather the meadow also knows. I am thinking of Peter Matthiessen, writing in a journal on a mountain and then coming home and smoothing and honing at a typewriter (now a computer), fashioning something in which the original moment rings, working at it until he begins to make it worse, and only then stopping, still not happy. I am thinking of Henry Thoreau writing outside at his table by the pond and by night in the cabin or back in Concord, cutting up pieces of his journal to make a poem of that pond, writing new sentences in white heat after walking far in Concord or climbing Ktaadn, hoping to sound not like a man writing at all, but like a place going about its life. I am thinking of Terry Tempest Williams at a laptop just like this one deleting words, eroding the larger landscape she has already laid down until what remains is fit to hold the space in which she danced in the desert. And I am thinking of Barry Lopez in his study upstairs, looking down toward the river where the chord he lives to is always sustained, and typing up a fifth and then a sixth and final draft of *Arctic Dreams,* each of them one hundred and fifty thousand words long and each of them a brand new thing, born of the one that came before it, sounded out sometimes in silence but always sounded, its entire topography traveled in his mind and stepped out, with four fingers at a typewriter, until the rhythm is right and the Arctic is there as he knew it in imagination and desire and in his body's long encounter.

And I am thinking of me, rewriting that last paragraph, particularly that last sentence, over and again, adding a preposition, inserting a comma, deleting a clause, adding another, killing off entire lines, in order to get the rhythm right, the rhythm, in this case, of the work of these writers in their writing places, sounding and stepping and typing out landscapes.

The philosopher John Dewey had a theory that "meaning is built into text as it is composed, step by step. Meaning is a function of all the choices made and problems solved in the act of creation, not of prior intentions or after-the-fact conclusions." Great artists, thought Dewey, "learn by their work as they proceed, to see and feel what had not been part of their original plan and purpose" (quoted in Shulevitz 2003, 31). Meaning is built into places, too, developed over time as they make themselves up to no particular purpose. Patterns develop, and in them we know the place for itself. The writer writes what arises out of immersing himself in country, stepping into the great wild unraveling of local meaning in one place on earth.

The World Is Music

All this talk of places and their rhythms is not so very far-fetched. The more that science teaches us about matter and the more we understand about the actual earth, the solid ground, the more like music they become.

"Matter," writes the physicist Willigis Jager, for instance, "is the domain of space in which the field is extremely dense" (quotations this paragraph are from Duncan 2002). Einstein said that "in the new physics, there is no place for both field and matter, because field is the only reality." And Rupert Sheldrake describes "morphogenic fields," forces beyond the material realm that cannot be seen or measured, yet can be intuited from everything science knows about the way things work. These fields "shape and direct the entire animate and inanimate creation." To describe a reality of this kind, whose dynamism, mystery, and amplitude strike us only occasionally, we are going to need a language that is more than merely rational. If reality is musical, poetic, spiritual—if landscapes, though physical and visible, are much more besides—we are going to need words and phrases that imply a whole lot more than they say, words freed from merely rational moorings. David James Duncan says in a recent essay: "The physical universe as we now understand it cannot be accurately described via static modes of thought, for that which enlivens all things is dynamic, imperceptible, and—I believe with all the science in my heart—*holy.*" It is a "symphony of forces woven through galaxies, unseen fields, synapses, ecosystems, subatomic particles and cells." And each of us (writers), he reminds us, is "steeped in and assailed" by that symphony of genera-tive and defining forces, the hum of things here, "even as we 'study it'" (2002, 79).

The more our scientists and philosophers discern about the nature of matter, the less it seems we should be trying to know it just by looking. "Matter," writes Fritjof Capra, "at the subatomic level, consists of energy patterns continually changing into one another—a continuous dance of energy" in which every atom is implicated and resonant in every other. The same musical reality holds in an ecosys-tem—within rocks and animals and among all the parts that make up a whole we call a place—and each separate part is implicated and sounded out in all the others. "To unify recent insights in physics and in the life sciences," Capra continues,

> into a coherent description of reality, a conceptual shift from structure to rhythm seems to be extremely useful. Rhythmic pat-terns appear throughout the universe, from the very small to the very large. Atoms are patterns of probability waves, molecules are vibrating structures, and living organisms manifest multiple, interdependent patterns of fluctuations. Plants, animals, and human beings undergo cycles of activity and rest, and all their physiological functions oscillate in rhythms of various periodic-ities. The components of ecosystems are interlinked through cyclical exchanges of matter and energy, and the planet as a whole has its rhythms and recurrences as it spins around its axis and moves around the sun.
>
> . . . It has been said since ancient times that the nature of real-ity is much closer to music than to a machine, and this is con-firmed by many discoveries in modern science. The essence of a melody does not lie in its notes; it lies in the relationships between the notes, in the intervals, frequencies, and rhythms. When a string is set vibrating we hear not only a single tone but also its overtones—an entire scale is sounded. Thus each note involves all the others, just as each sub-atomic particle involves all the others, according to current ideas in particle physics. (Capra, foreword to Berendt 1987, xi–xii)

The world is not a set of forms standing discrete, working like the parts of a machine. The world is a dance of matter and energy, a network of relationships, "intrinsically dynamic" (ibid., xi). It is going to need to be apprehended rhythmically if it is going to be understood and expressed in its essence. The lifeworld of a place is an impossibly elaborate musical form. And the whole may be apprehended, at least a little, in lyric engagement with a few parts, in the same way that a whole chord is heard in the one plucked note, a whole symphony in a single chord or musical phrase. Imagine a writer standing in—no, moving through—a place. She takes part in that symphony, even though she apprehends only snatches of it—the odd fragment of music James Galvin alludes to. Energy moves to and fro. Intervals rise and pass between witness and place, between footfalls, between breaths, on soundwave and wind. Nothing is still in these moments, in this place, in the relationship of human and land. The nature of this shared dance of form and energy moves the witness, energetically, imaginatively, at the level of the physiology of hearing, the pattern of brain activity, the imprint it registers in memory and body cell. By the process of composition I have described—all of it about movement and the elaboration of sound patterns, about listening and voicing, a dynamic process connected in rhythm and sound to the moment (or the lifetime) within that lively sphere, a place—the writer speaks *about* and relates something of that lyric encounter, yes; but equally, what she does is try to catch and carry in her phrasing, in the quality of the intervals between her syllables and words, her sentences and paragraphs, a quality of energy and rhythm, a quality of music, like the one she knew in that place. She will do her best to suggest the complex musical form she guessed at from the fragments she heard—the rhythms of geological and microscopic motion, the human and animal and vegetable tempi, all enfolded and singing together.

One wants echoes of the place's music to resonate in the sounds one's writing makes—the dance of energies and intervals it performs. What you write is just a bunch of individual notes, separated by intervals—a fragmented, less than fully musical form. And yet, since words and phrases sound, since typescript too is a dance of restless particles of matter, some resonance of the place and the encounter with that place—of the chord at the center of that lifeworld—may reach the reader. Although the writer heard only snatches of the whole song and dance that is the place, each fragment was alive with the whole shebang. And so is each lyric fragment she writes. In those fragments a reader may hear, may experience, the full and shifting complexity of the place.

I have come to imagine the work of the nature writer as something like the instrument's response to music that is played upon it. Let's imagine a cello. Let's imagine the sound of that cello playing the first movement of the first of Bach's Suites for Unaccompanied Cello. There is a score, which a player interprets as music and translates into movements of his right hand, pulling and pushing a bow across tuned strings, and into movements of the fingers on his left hand, stopping those strings high up on the neck of the instrument, and of his left wrist, rapidly oscillating to give the sounds color and shape. The strings vibrate—that is their part in this dance. But they need a bridge, the device over which the strings run, to carry those vibrations to the wooden and air-filled chamber of the instrument itself, held between the knees of the player—for it is the vibration of the air, amplified by the wood, that reaches us as music. It is resonance that we hear. What we hear is the response of the instrument's body to the physical sounding out of notes, their patterned intervals. Where is the music? Where is the entity we call the suite? Is it in the score, itself perfectly mute? Is it in the player's imagination of the music written in those notes? Is it in the movements his body makes in response? Is it in the strings' vibration? Is it in the sawing of the horsehair bow across the metal strings, setting them in motion? Is it in the bridge or the resonating chamber of the cello or the air within that wooden body? Is it in the air of the room into which the vibrations leap? Is it in the vibrations of the listener's eardrum and the pattern of waves that reaches the brain and registers as the first of Bach's cello suites? It is in all of them, I guess, and beyond all of them. It is something all these participants know and share and make. It is something that makes them all one.

In the same way, I imagine a place playing upon a writer, its lyric witness. Its music—read in the place's forms, felt as the place's dynamics—carries all the way through the witness's body and imagination, through all the rhythmic work of composition, into word and phrase, paragraph and chapter. The final piece of writing is the resonance of the encountered place, replete with the lifestory and voice of the witness, and it is this resonance that reaches the reader. Each time the work is read is a new performance of the work—and in it, the place's music. The place plays again and will be different each time, according to the mood of the reader, the tone of the space in which she perceives it. And so the place goes on; it surrounds and includes a reader, as Bach's first cello suite surrounds me now, playing out of speakers in the living room.

And so much of it depends upon rhythm.

Beyond Representation

"In contemporary literary theory," Lawrence Buell wrote, "the capacity of literary writers to render a faithful *mimesis* of the object world is reckoned indifferent at best, and their interest in doing so is thought to be a secondary concern" (1995, 84). All strains of literary theory, from "old-fashioned formalist theory," as Buell puts it, "of the literary work as artifact," to "the contemporary theory of writing as discourse," are skeptical or even disdainful of "the notion that literature does or even can represent physical reality, specifically the natural world in its self-existence as an assemblage or plenum or in the form of a gestalt that can impress itself on the mind or text" (ibid., 85–86).

Buell attempts to find a middle point between naive realism, in which the agency of nature and the capacity of texts to speak of it goes without theoretical explanation, and reductive poststructuralism, in which texts are held to be entirely closed off from the world. Buell has made perhaps the most theoretically compelling attempt at "a qualified version of literary representation as extratextual *mimesis*" (1999, 703). He makes an argument, he says, "for the importance of a poststructuralist account of environmental *mimesis:* for a critical practice that operates from a premise of bidirectionality, imagining texts as gesturing outward toward the material world notwithstanding their constitution as linguistic, ideological, cultural artifacts that inevitably filter and even in some respects grotesquify their renditions of the extratextual" (ibid., 704). Buell rests his argument on, as we've seen, the notion of *adéquation.* What he is doing is retheorizing nonfiction in order to make this argument for the capacity of texts, particularly nature writing texts, to represent the world.

But what I have described here as nature writing's enterprise is not really *mimesis.* It is something other, or more, than that. Representation is not what these writers are trying to do; they are not making facsimiles. They are taking part in the land, listening and being changed. And the way in which the land changes them is what we hear in their lyric essays. The rhythm we readers hear is an articulated listening— the reverberation of an intelligence to the life of a place. Their work is not dislocated from the land, but a kind of participation in and a continuation of it.

The idea of *mimesis* understands places and texts as finished things, as artifacts or material forms. Where one form is a body of words on paper and another is a landscape, it will always be hard to argue for the capacity of the first to look like or represent bodily the second. (It is less hard, of course, when the "text" is a photograph or a painting or a sculpture.) Understanding a certain kind of writing as "an activity" in words, as Ponge did, and after him, Paul and Buell, offers a way of getting over that difficulty; the work, in this conception, *enacts* itself or behaves in a similar way to the place. But if we reimagine a place as a *process* rather like music, and if we imagine a text, too, as a musical-rational *process,* not only does resemblance cease to be such a problem (the music of the text *resembles* the music of the place); it also becomes possible to understand a piece of writing as a *continuation* of what the place is—as *part* of the same process. In other words, following Paul Carter, I am not so much retheorizing representation, as describing in the work of Lopez, Matthiessen, Williams, and Galvin a different kind of relationship altogether between a text and its country.

Carter gives the name *methexis* to this kind of relationship, the writer's (metrical or lyric) engagement with country as dynamic space (1996, 301). That is the project of the place writer: an enactment or a performance of something—of witness, of celebration, of engagement with a stretch of ground. The work of the writers I have explored resembles the ground as a dancer resembles the music she moves to; as the sound of the cello resembles the movement of the player's fingers upon the strings. The same lifeworld animates them both. The work does not aim to set the country out before us, but to honor it, to ring true to it, to move with it, to communicate, in patterns of words worthy of the amplitude of the landscape, some ideas that arose, some stories that occurred there, which seem inseparable from the place itself—part of the very logic and structure of the place.

At its best, as in the work of Barry Lopez, Peter Matthiessen, Terry Tempest Williams, James Galvin, and Henry David Thoreau, this literature listens to the land and to those people intimate with its places. It puts words, patterned musically into shapely sentences, fragmented paragraphs, textured and cadenced lines of poetry and lyric prose, to work in service of that larger order—the land, natural history—hoping to animate it for a reader in the same way it was (and still is) animate for the writer. The poem or the piece of prose, at its best, is a choreography in words of an act of careful listening; and through it we, too, may hear the place express itself—much as we "hear" the music in a dance. We may catch the lyric of the country—or some of it, some scattered fragments. We will hear an echo of the world of a place somewhere, and feel that it is alive.

If a work of words by any of these writers resembles the place it engages with, it is because the same poetry patterns both the place and the piece of writing. It is because the work is a part of the place. If the writer succeeds in this—and it takes hard, rhythmic work, as well as a touch of grace—the work will move and animate the reader much as the place itself animated the teller. The music of the place—its coherent but wild structures of creation and recreation—carries in the structures, large and small, of the work, like a fractious continuo that roughly grounds and unifies all four parts of the whole: place, writer, work, and reader. A choir.

What I have discovered is that a writer rarely sits down with an ambition to offer up an impression of "here." It is not—or at least not mostly—an artifact one imagines oneself producing, which may or may not look or feel or work on a reader like the original. It is a process one engages in, like a dance to music that continues, in which most of one's ambition is to keep in time, and to stay in tune, if one is singing. It is the making that counts. To write with the land in mind is like sustaining a chord that one heard there—joining it, not copying it. And one sustains it by writing about all manner of ideas and stories, not just in depicting the actual landscape. It is the pattern of the place—its mind, if you like—one wants to discern and join, in the hope that by listening so actively for it, one may perpetuate it. One tries to let that pattern animate one's words; one tries to keep the place dancing in the work. But it is the *working* that catches the lyric—the hard labor of creating draft and redraft, of sounding out and editing over—not the *work,* not a produced text in itself, except to the extent that, in being read, the work sounds out the rhythm again, and again. It is the creating, not the creation—for a work, a place, creation itself, these are never done. Life is a process. One wants simply, impossibly, to take part for a time in an activity of creation as true and impeccable as that which the landscape performs on and on, daily, through the ages.

Lyrics, Line, and Sentence

Lyric writing, as the Greeks first spoke of it, was writing made to be sung to the accompaniment of the lyre. It was to be *sung.* Music—matters of rhythm, melody, rhyme: patterned sound, in other words—ordered it, and accompanied it. The lyric mode in poetry and prose has come to mean something more than this—but something, at its heart, still essentially musical. There is a lyric point of view, or disposition, as Ellen Bryant Voigt describes it, and it is characterized by a listening to the world. The writer in the lyric mode is witnessing the world and allowing herself to be moved. She becomes, in a sense, the lyre and lets her strings be played. The writer—the "I"—is the string vibrating, set in rhythmic motion by the place in which she stands. The work is the song that arises—the sound of how the place moves her; the music of the place in her. This is what witness, or listening, means. The writer allows herself to be *moved,* she opens herself up to what Rilke called "the gust in the god": the wind, the place-in-itself, its shifting amplitude. She is changed. Her work expresses that change— its source, its nature.

Although places find expression, musical *adéquation,* in all manner of writing, I have a feeling that prose, in particular the lyric essay, may be most apt for such expression. A paragraph is more like a stretch of country than a stanza is. A poem has architecture. It conforms to a poet's specific design, as a shed or a temple does, so that it takes just the form in the world that the poet intends. Poems are like sculptures. They are built environments. Paragraphs are more like meadows: half-wild places, looking the way they look because of the way they try to say what they mean. Sentences accrete in musical fragments, making and conforming to their own irregular music. So do places. The music of places is wild, like that of a lyric sentence—patterned, rhythmic, but irregular and unpredictable; self-sustaining, lively, old; obedient to structures that are organic somehow, not merely personal or cultural or instrumental. The wild order of the sentence is discovered, I believe (following Dewey), in the work of its creation—rhythmic work of mind and body, the interplay of phrasing, of song and dance. It makes itself up as it goes. It finds and manifests its structure on the run.

Prose, then, has a music wilder than poetry. The sentence is less orderly, more various, more changeful and irregular than the line. Its music, like a place's, is more full of holes, less orchestrated and arranged than the music of the line. And so the lyric sentence, in its wildness, may be better at catching the lyric of country, in its wildness, than the poetic line.

I have written these paragraphs after talking over breakfast with the poet and cultural theorist Martin Harrison, who has a foot in both camps (poetry and prose). I am making play with a thought of his, a conversation we shared. Perhaps, he suggested, the poetic line, because it is ordered according to a poet's musical scheme, because it is given beat, expresses "an individuated human voice" much more than the looser rhythms (the phrasing) of the prose sentence. For just that reason, he said—comparing a short-lined stanza of Jim Galvin's poem "Old Men on the Courthouse Lawn, Murray, Kentucky" to a stanza of Galvin's "Stringers for the Bridge," a poem written in paragraph form—perhaps prose is better at expressing that which is not merely the writer's voice; perhaps it is capable of belonging more to the country (if that is what it addresses) and the witness's encounter with it, than just to the writer and his thoughts. It may speak in what Carter calls the middle voice.

Neither Harrison nor I would want to push this argument too far. The point is not that a poem will not serve country well, but that a certain kind of shapely prose may do it sometimes better. As Thoreau wished to speak a word for wildness, since society had plenty of defenders, I wish to speak a word for the wildness of the lyric essay—for the sentence, since the line has so many defenders.

The Ecology of Imagination

I have proposed that nature writing is a practice of ecological imagination. But I have also, I notice, practiced a kind of ecological imagination myself. Not only have I reimagined and spoken of places as dynamic musical forms—never done, always composing themselves out of the impossibly varied and complex set of beings and energies at dance somewhere; I have also reimagined texts, the writing process, and authorship ecologically. I have come to understand writing, authorship, even self, as adaptations and responses to environment, as a dance between a body and mind (the author's) and the body and mind of the country. A text—this essay, that book, this poem—is an ecology of interrelated sound and rhythm, making music and making meaning out of its long elaboration of itself, and even then going on composing itself at every reading. As Paul Carter suggests, a text may be understood as a *performance*—the continuing rhythmic expression of the writer's relationship with a dynamic space. And in the same way, a place may be an ongoing, fragmentary, vibrant performance, never still, and never done. Place and text, for a time, shape the other and are part of the same musical reality.

And so I have imagined not only places and texts but also the relationship between them ecologically. Writing is a sustained and dynamic, if truncated, engagement with and within a musical order, the land as it is here. The author's self is an identity not finished at the skin, not reducible to ego, but shaped by what it shapes in its imagination, continuous with the place(s) where it knows itself best; and, moreover, made and remade daily out of its dance with the order of reality in the land that the nature writer wanders and wonders in. I have imagined cultures as caused and shaped by what is not merely cultural, writer's minds and ways of being touched and fashioned by what is not merely personal or cultural or social, and works of words as the products not just of individual cognitive processes, nor even of individual biologies, but of a complex of interrelationships, including one writer's body and mind and the lives and energies in which he or she works.

Places make themselves up, over and over, in the way they play, the way the relationships of form and energy express themselves just here. David Rothenberg (2002) calls this improvisation on a theme. For there is always a theme, it seems: coherence and identity. Works of words also make themselves up, find their form and make meaning, in the process of their composition, in the labor of question and answer, of making sense and making patterned sounds that ring true to that sense. In this way, texts and places are most similar; and because of the dynamic reality of both, a text that engages with a place may resonate it in the structure of its becoming, in its improvisations on the place's theme.

To the extent that writing is a purposive, artifact-making enterprise (which it also is), I have shown, I hope, how much of that work of fabrication, stylization, and artifice is about movement and music, in its processes and in its intentions. Just because a thing is made by a man or woman who puts all of his or her skill into making it a work of art does not mean it may not carry in its structure and nature the very essence of a world beyond the author's skin—in the case of a piece of nature writing, the place the author is trying to witness. Indeed, as Thoreau argued, also the critic Lawrence Buell and others, it may be through precisely those elements of a work—its most individual, human, and artifactual—that the piece of writing might best express a place. Writerly devices need not always be a kind of falsification of the world, nor are they merely explicable as self-expression. Much depends, as both theorists and ecological writers like Lopez would agree, on the intention of the writer, the way she approaches the world, and the craft of her writing. As SueEllen Campbell reminds us, both theorists and ecologists accept that each of us experiences the world through a filter formed of predisposition, personality type, gender, and intention (1996, 128–29). The world is not the same to all of us; what a stretch of land is to each of us depends on how we approach it, and that depends on who we are. If a writer goes somewhere to discern something of the identity of a landscape and then to speak of that—to let it speak through him—then perhaps something of its essential nature may speak through their work. Or at least, what his writing expresses will be the nature of how that place stirred him—the place-as-he-experienced-it. That will only happen if he manages not to turn the land into a mere object of his gaze, a thing separate from him entirely. If, on the other hand, he goes to the land disposed not to participate in its lifeworld so much as to extract from it something he can use to make a story, what he finds will have no life in his story.

The Real World, Mysticism, and Theory

Here we reach the impasse between most theorists of literature and most writers of nature. The nature writer attributes to the land an authority, an identity, that is quite independent, finally, of any perception of it. The theorist is equally convinced that nothing is true, independent of the mind that asserted it was so (Campbell 1989, 129–30). "What is it we witness," I asked at the start of this inquiry, "and how?" Even to call it witness is to presume the existence of an independent reality. Is there a "real world," as all the writers I have studied, one way or another, would assert, one that is there even when our backs are turned? And can any of us ever know *that* reality free of our interpreting reflex? For that, to answer my question, is what I think we try to witness. And we try to do it by casting our imaginations out into the landscape and understanding it as the concatenation of points of view and dynamic relationships it is, most of which escape my notice but will be hinted at in what I do notice. We try to do it by imagining a moment or a lifetime somewhere, as though we could set our human nature aside for a moment. We try to view reality from within a place, as though we were not merely one discrete human being bearing witness. That is, perhaps, never quite possible. We hear what we are capable of hearing, what we are disposed by our own mind and body's nature to discern and resonate with. But we sense that what we hear is part of a much larger musical order. Listening for that larger musical form, imagining one place, at least, on earth, in its wholeness—this is what the lyricist always attempts.

Remember those "morphogenic fields," those generative forces David James Duncan referred to; the energies that science cannot measure but which it knows animate everything it can? It may turn out that these are the real world, these are the generative, sustaining dynamic forces that make a place what it is and differentiate this bit of the real world from the next. It may be these that one picks up now and then—in the red desert, in the winter sky above the meadow, in a halo about the sun. Who knows? The world within the world may be known to science someday soon. Perhaps this is what we really tune our witness into.

Every one of my subjects here can report odd moments of numinous encounter, of inexplicable revelation, of magic, when the landscape rang and his or her body seemed to ring inseparably from it. This is what is called a mystical experience, and the world of reason, of theory, is skeptical of such reports.

But all of us lyricists of place are mystics, finally: we sense that the larger order we live within depends on us only to care, and occasionally it shows us a quality that nothing in our logical brains, our narrative instincts of cause and effect, can explain. We are mystics like Lyle Van Waning, who, much to his own embarrassment, could hear, now and then, "the tones emitted by different stars" (Galvin 1992, 221). We share intelligence with coyote; we are guided by a canyon wren. Sometimes we try to dismiss what we have experienced, but we have known the world to be like that from time to time, and so we are convinced that it has an order all its own. It is not magic we dabble in. It is just the world itself in its mundane particularity, as it makes itself known to our ears and eyes and body. We place faith in the "inexplicable coherence" of the land because we hear it expressed daily, in the undertone and overtone of the notes we actually hear; we experience it daily and feel for its poetic secret, which we know has inhered in the land, evolving, of course, for ever, whether we fathom it or not.

When we speak of the numinous, the elusive, the real, perhaps all we are saying is that we have learned that the world, a place, the land, everything, is never merely what it seems at a glance. There is always much more going on in a meadow or a river, an arch or an Arctic plain than we will ever perceive or understand. And yet that life, that reality, goes on, and it is possible to sense that it does. This is why some places and moments seem so impossibly alive and suggestive. These are moments and places in which, as for Lyle Van Waning looking to the Snowy Range at one day's end on Boulder Ridge, it occurs to us out of a sunset that we don't know the half of it. As writers we seek forms and structures fit to express the few notes we have heard somewhere and the wild, coherent order—the chord of the place—those few notes imply.

It is in rhythmic language, fragments of incantatory prose, essays written out of a feeling for the rhythms of places, that we come closest to true witness of what is real. We do it best in poems and in essays, if we keep them more or less lyric. To enter into lyric engagement with place is to allow ourselves to become wild—to let our mind be more than it sometimes is, to let our cells and synapses be stirred by what is beyond thought, to go down deep and fly up high, to sink and be unmade and made again. It is to become the green man, Nature's scribe, the shore bird, the dancing woman, the meadow's surrendered soul. To apprehend wildly is to allow ourselves to hear and see, as William Stafford puts it, what the bird's song, the line of ridges, *imply;* it is to be for a time, and then to resonate in our words' lyric, what these trees, this pond, this long shoreline, this animated canyon, this meadow and ridge, this blue plateau *imply* in what we know of them through witness. We write, still half wild, out of the voice, the dance of words, that belonged to our encounter with that dynamic, suggestive space—the middle voice, the wind's voice.

We experience the land poised in an interval of its long composition, between notes. Yet that interval is not silent or still. It is a note, and it is filled and made elaborate by other musics impossibly slow (like the geomorphology at work under our feet), impossibly fast (like that of the microbes and the birds' flight), and inconceivably varied— some of which we perceive and some of which eludes us. Everything, even the cliffs and ridges, is in motion, is in the process of remaking itself. And this life of the place is what the nature writer tries to imagine. This person's writing, if it is good, will become a harmonious part of the wild music of the place.

Yet it will be utterly that writer's own. For no two of us are built alike. No two of us witness quite the same thing; no two of us resonate quite the same way. In mind, in body, in life's experience, in "nature," each of us is unique. Still, the same place will sound true in my voice and in yours, if we are listening and singing in tune—just as the same piece of music, composed, for instance, by Thomas Tallis, will sound true in the voices of two choristers, each singing the same part (even singing different parts), though neither of us sounds exactly alike and each of us expresses everything we are in the singing. Singing in tune, resonating tunefully, though—this is hard work. It takes practice; it takes time; it takes love and grace.

I say we write "half wild" when we write out of the reverberation that our stepping out into the place sets off in us. But one is only *half* wild. For if the place moves us, if we catch its lyric, it takes an effort of will, the hard work of art, the labor of forming musical syntax, to sustain the rhythm, to keep it going in our sentences or lines. You can take your writing table outside; you can hear fragments of the place's endless improvisation on its theme; you can sit on the mountain and hear the blue peak opposite ring; you can open yourself to the stories that pass through stone; you can let revelations come to you; you can occasionally hear the voices of stars; you can see the country just for an instant as it is when your back is turned; you can wake up with a word from the prairie upon your tongue; you can stand avid for the numinous event—but you will have to go back inside and turn out some sentences that sustain and make sensible the land as you encountered it. You must never stop listening. You listen to the sentence as it finds itself, just as you listened to the place as it made itself clear to you. You listen and you articulate until text and place seem of a piece—in their musical form, their rhythm, the characteristic but ceaselessly unraveling structures that compose both.

What Is Nature Writing For?

A doubt has dogged me, writing this book. For you could look at it, if you were feeling ungenerous, as a narrowly aesthetic investigation into a distinctly minor genre. Why does it matter how a nature writer engages with a place? Why does it matter if one is able to let the patterns that make a place cohere pattern also one's awareness of it, one's memory of it, the work one shapes?

Back home in October 2003, I was part of the very first Australian festival of nature writing. And there, I heard Scott Slovic give a paper (2005) that helped me remember why the nature writer's practice of musical attention matters, and how an inquiry like mine might help by offering a renewed understanding of what places are, how they run, how prose might engage with them so that the place, the prose, the writer, and the reader are all animated again and embedded again in the world.

Scott's paper described the enterprise of nature writing as something profoundly political. Its task, he says, is to find new ways to reanimate the *language* we use for landscapes. And this matters because that is what it takes to reanimate *places*—nature itself—in human minds and in the discourses of politics, lawmaking, and everyday life, so that, in turn, we might be moved to preserve something of the dignity of the places we live in, in the face of the (often destructive) change we, in our human nature, continue to work upon them. Through this renovation of language we writers and readers may be returned to some lively intimacy with the rest of creation. And finding ourselves again embedded in the world, in its dynamic structures, we may know how and why to work to save it, and also ourselves.

This is the work of lyric apprehension. The poetics of listening and responding is vitally political. At the heart of the work of nature writing, this reanimation of language and landscape and the relations between them, is the work of discerning and recalling in our writing the larger order of reality in which we live our lives and practice our governance.

Falling Water

And now I'm home. This book is done. So, too, is my book of home, *The Blue Plateau*. It has been accreting in fragments all this time, voicing itself in irregular phrases, falling like sediment from streams, forming a bed that will harden and rise and erode into the form of the finished book—not that books, as I now know, are ever quite finished, any more than places are, or investigations such as this one. To learn how to make a book that makes a worthy witness of this Australian plateauland, that makes a space in which the plateau's wisdom may rise; to find structures and forms that will let the place reverberate; to let its chord sound—to do all this, I have traveled these North American landscapes, studied these North American writers and their being-in-the-world, explored the topography of their prose and poetry. To go so far away and read so widely in the literature of another continent is, at a glance, a strange apprenticeship for a witness of home. If it is true that landscape shapes language, that a work of lyric prose performs a dance with *here,* how did I expect to find *The Blue Plateau* in coniferous forest, in glacial pond, in Atlantic coastline, in red desert, or in mountain ridge and meadow?

Well, I didn't expect to discover my book there, of course, or a grammar or a voice suitable for resonating my own place. I hoped, like the pilgrim, to become the man I needed to be to write a book of home. I went to learn how to listen to land and how to write—as though in rhythmic response—the essential prose, the wild music, of where one is, which is also who one is. I was trying to enter the inner life of a practice of attention to country, and I went where I could find writers, in their own places, who follow such a practice. I went to find a tradition and to learn from it, from its practitioners themselves, from their work and country. If one wants to find what it means to live and sing inside one's own country, that is where one should end up— at home. And that is where I have ended up. But some people—I am one—need to leave home to find home. Here I am, though, returned to the plateau, more deeply at home in it than I would have been had I never left.

I began this book in the wind, and I end it in the rain—at Lavender Bay this morning. Out there in the falling water, the butcherbirds are taking a phrase of notes, toying with it, varying it, turning it, returning to the phrase with which they began. The birds' singing makes the morning's grace note. The whole morning is strung with music: the morning is music.

It is now another winter in another year. The plateau and the country all about it have been in drought between those winters, between those notes, and I—all of us here—have been in drought too. But drought is just one of the phrases, a movement perhaps, of the large musical form that is this land. It, too, is necessary. It has shaped this place—the plateau and the whole continent. It is one of the notes that always plays in the chord of the country I know, part of the poem of here. We have been, between these winters, between the wind and the rain, on fire, this sclerophyll woodland and I. Now and then we have been in danger. Often we have been in wind. And now we are in rain.

Up in the Place of Falling Water, Katoomba, the dry is over, but barely, uncertainly. Within the plateau, the creeks run thin. The land has known all this before, though. It knows rain will fall again. The rocks remember drier times by far, and the trees, which have been weeping leaves and putting out extraordinary blossoms, have suffered longer arid spells than this. The dry is part of the place, which goes on becoming itself. The place of falling water has gone on falling. And I, part of it when I am there and even when I am not, have gone on listening and—which is the same thing—writing. I have followed the phrases that come to mind, as the butcherbird does this morning, as though I did not make them but heard them, as though they belonged to the place and arrived like the rain, out of drought, a wild and necessary music. I have gone on falling into myself, coming—fragment by fragment, note by note, interval by interval—home.

Bibliography

Nature Writing, Other Prose, and Poetry

Abbey, Edward. 1971. *Desert Solitaire: A Season in the Wilderness*. New York: Ballantine.

———. 1979. *Abbey's Road*. New York: Penguin.

———. 1991. *The Journey Home*. New York: Penguin.

Agee, James. 1939. *Let Us Now Praise Famous Men*. New York: Houghton Mifflin.

Austin, Mary. 1903. *The Land of Little Rain*. Boston: Houghton Mifflin.

Bass, Rick. 1991. *Winter: Notes from Montana*. Boston: Houghton Mifflin.

Berry, Thomas. 1999. *The Great Work: Our Way into the Future*. New York: Bell Tower.

Berry, Wendell. 1996. *Recollected Essays, 1965–1980*. New York: Farrar, Straus & Giroux.

———. 1998. *The Selected Poems of Wendell Berry*. Washington, D.C.: Counterpoint.

Beston, Henry. 1928. *The Outermost House: A Year of Life on the Great Beach of Cape Cod*. New York: Henry Holt.

Blixen, Karen. 1937. *Out of Africa*. New York: Random House.

Burroughs, Franklin. 1992. *The River Home: A Return to the Carolina Low Country.* Boston: Houghton Mifflin.

———. 1998. *Billy Watson's Croker Sack.* Athens: University of Georgia Press.

Burroughs, John. 1895. *Riverby.* Boston: Houghton Mifflin.

Campbell, SueEllen. 1996. *Bringing the Mountain Home.* Tucson: University of Arizona Press.

———. 2003. *Even Mountains Vanish.* Salt Lake City: University of Utah Press.

Carson, Rachel. 1941. *Under the Sea Wind.* New York: Simon & Schuster.

———. 1951. *The Sea Around Us.* Oxford University Press, Boston: Houghton Mifflin.

———. 1955. *The Edge of the Sea.* Oxford University Press, Boston: Houghton Mifflin.

———. 1962. *Silent Spring.* Boston: Houghton Mifflin.

D'Agata, John. 1999. *Halls of Fame: Essays.* Saint Paul, Minn.: Graywolf.

———, ed. 2003. *The Next American Essay.* Saint Paul, Minn.: Graywolf.

Daniel, John. 1992. *The Trail Home: Essays.* New York: Pantheon Books.

———. 2002. *Winter Creek: One Writer's Natural History.* Minneapolis: Milkweed.

Dillard, Annie. 1974. *Pilgrim at Tinker Creek.* New York: Harper's Magazine Press.

———. 1982. *Teaching a Stone to Talk: Expeditions and Encounters.* New York: Harper & Row.

———. 1989. *The Writing Life.* New York: Harper & Row.

Duncan, David James. 1983. *The River Why.* San Francisco: Sierra Club Books.

———. 2001. *My Life as Told by Water.* San Francisco: Sierra Club Books.

Ehrlich, Gretel. 1985. *The Solace of Open Spaces.* New York: Penguin.

Eiseley, Loren. 1957. *The Immense Journey: An Imaginative Naturalist Explores the Mysteries of Man and Nature.* New York: Random House.

———. 1960. *The Firmament of Time.* New York: Charles Scribner's Sons.

———. 1971. *The Night Country.* New York: Charles Scribner's Sons.

———. 1978. *The Star Thrower.* New York: Times Books.

Elder, John. 1998. *Reading the Mountains of Home.* Cambridge, Mass.: Harvard University Press.

Emerson, Ralph Waldo. 1836. *Nature.* Boston: J. Monroe.

Faulkner, William. 1946. *The Portable Faulkner,* edited by Malcolm Cowley. New York: Viking.

———. 1955a. "The Bear." In *Big Woods: The Hunting Stories,* 11–112. New York: Random House.

———. 1955b. *Big Woods: The Hunting Stories.* New York: Random House.

Finch, Robert, and John Elder, eds. 1990. *The Norton Book of Nature Writing.* New York: W. W. Norton.

———, eds. 2002. *The Norton Book of Nature Writing,* 2nd edition. New York: W. W. Norton.

Fowles, John. 1979. *The Tree.* Boston: Little, Brown.

Galvin, James. 1980. *Imaginary Timber: Poems.* Garden City, N.Y.: Doubleday.

———. 1984. *God's Mistress: Poems.* New York: Harper & Row.

———. 1988. *Elements: Poems.* Port Townsend, Wash.: Copper Canyon.

———. 1992. *The Meadow.* New York: Henry Holt.

———. 1995. *Lethal Frequencies: Poems.* Port Townsend, Wash.: Copper Canyon.

———. 1997. *Resurrection Update: Collected Poems, 1975–97.* Port Townsend, Wash.: Copper Canyon.

———. 1999. *Fencing the Sky.* New York: Henry Holt.

———. 2003. *X: Poems.* Port Townsend, Wash.: Copper Canyon.

Griffiths, Tom. 1992. *Secrets of the Forest: Discovering History in Melbourne's Ash Range.* Sydney: Allen & Unwin.

Haines, John. 1981. *Living Off the Country: Essays on Poetry and Place.* Ann Arbor: University of Michigan Press.

———. 1989. *The Stars, The Snow, The Fire: Twenty-five Years in the Northern Wilderness.* Saint Paul, Minn.: Graywolf.

———. 1993. *The Owl in the Mask of the Dreamer: Collected Poems.* Saint Paul, Minn.: Graywolf.

———. 1996. *Fables and Distances: New and Selected Essays.* Saint Paul, Minn.: Graywolf.

Halpern, Daniel, and Dan Frank. 1996. *The Nature Reader.* Hopewell, N.J.: Ecco.

———. 2001. *The Picador Nature Reader.* London: Macmillan.

Harrison, Martin. 1997. *The Kangaroo Farm: Poems.* Brooklyn, N.S.W.: Paperbark.

———. 2001. *Summer: Poems.* Brooklyn, N.S.W.: Paperbark.

Haruf, Kent. 1999. *Plainsong.* New York: Knopf.

Hay, John. 1969. *In Defense of Nature.* Boston: Little, Brown.

Hoagland, Edward. 1973. *Walking the Dead Diamond River.* New York: Random House.

Hogan, Linda. 1995. *Dwellings: A Spiritual History of the Living World.* New York: W. W. Norton.

Jeffers, Robinson. 2001. *The Selected Poetry of Robinson Jeffers,* edited by Tim Hunt. Stanford: Stanford University Press.

Kingsolver, Barbara. 1995. *High Tide in Tucson: Essays from Now or Never.* New York: HarperCollins.

———. 2000. *Prodigal Summer.* New York: HarperCollins.

———. 2002. *Small Wonder.* New York: HarperCollins.

Kittredge, William. 1992. *Hole in the Sky.* New York: Alfred A. Knopf.

———. 2000. *The Nature of Generosity.* New York: Alfred A. Knopf.

Krutch, Joseph Wood. 1952. *The Desert Year.* New York: William Sloane.

———. 1957. *The Great Chain of Life.* Boston: Houghton Mifflin.

Kutchins, Laurie. 1993. *Between Towns: Poems.* Lubbock: Texas Tech University Press.

———. 1997. *The Night Path: Poems.* Rochester, N.Y.: BOA Editions.

———. 2003. "Wind Ensemble." In *A Place on Earth,* edited by Mark Tredinnick, 135–45. Sydney: University of New South Wales Press; Lincoln: University of Nebraska Press.

Least Heat-Moon, William. 1991. *PrairyErth: A Deep Map.* Boston: Houghton Mifflin.

Leopold, Aldo. 1949. *A Sand County Almanac, and Sketches Here and There*. New York: Oxford University Press.

———. 1953. *Round River*. New York: Oxford University Press.

Lines, William J. 1991. *Taming the Great South Land: A History of the Conquest of Nature in Australia*. Sydney: Allen & Unwin.

———. 1998. *A Long Walk in the Australian Bush*. Sydney: University of New South Wales Press.

———. 2001. *Open Air: Essays*. French's Forest, N.S.W.: New Holland.

Lopate, Phillip, ed. 1994. *The Art of the Personal Essay: An Anthology from the Classical Era to the Present*. New York: Doubleday.

Lopez, Barry. 1976. *Desert Notes: Reflections in the Eye of a Raven*. Kansas City: Andrews & McMeel.

———. 1978. *Of Wolves and Men*. New York: Charles Scribner's Sons.

———. 1979. *River Notes: The Dance of Herons*. Kansas City: Andrews & McMeel.

———. 1986. *Arctic Dreams: Imagination and Desire in a Northern Landscape*. New York: Charles Scribner's Sons.

———. 1988. *Crossing Open Ground*. New York: Charles Scribner's Sons.

———. 1990. *Crow and Weasel*. San Francisco: North Point.

———. 1992a. *The Rediscovery of North America*. New York: Vintage Books.

———. 1992b. "Natural History Writing." *Mānoa* 4, no. 2: 89–90.

———. 1993. *Winter Count*. New York: Avon.

———. 1994. *Field Notes: The Grace Note of the Canyon Wren*. New York: Alfred A. Knopf.

———. 1997. *Lessons from the Wolverine*. Athens: University of Georgia Press.

———. 1998. *About This Life: Journeys on the Threshold of Memory*. New York: Alfred A. Knopf

———. 2000. *Light Action in the Caribbean*. New York: Alfred A. Knopf.

———. 2002. "A Scary Abundance of Water." *L.A. Weekly*, January 11–17.

———. 2003. "The Language of Animals" (1999). In *A Place on Earth: An Anthology of Nature Writing from Australia and North America*, edited by Mark Tredinnick, 159–66. Sydney: University of New South Wales Press; Lincoln: University of Nebraska Press.

Mabey, Richard. 1991. *A Nature Journal.* London: Chatto & Windus.

Maclean, Norman. 1976. *A River Runs Through It.* Chicago: University of Chicago Press.

MacLeish, Archibald. 1985. *Collected Poems, 1917–1982.* Boston: Houghton Mifflin.

Mahood, Kim. 2000. *Craft for a Dry Lake.* Milsons Point, N.S.W.: Anchor.

Marsh, George Perkins. 1864. *Man and Nature; or, Physical Geography as Modified by Human Action.* Cambridge, Mass.: Harvard University Press.

Matthiessen, Peter. 1959. *Wildlife in America.* New York: Viking.

———. 1961. *The Cloud Forest: A Chronicle of the South American Wilderness.* New York: Viking.

———. 1962. *Under the Mountain Wall: A Chronicle of Two Seasons in the Stone Age.* New York: Viking.

———. 1965. *At Play in the Fields of the Lord.* New York: Random House.

———. 1966. *Blue Meridian: The Search for the Great White Shark.* New York: Random House.

———. 1969. *Sal Si Puedes: Cesar Chavez and the New American Revolution.* New York: Random House.

———. 1972. *The Tree Where Man Was Born.* New York: Dutton.

———. 1973. *The Wind Birds: Shorebirds of North America.* New York: Random House.

———. 1975. *Far Tortuga.* New York: Random House.

———. 1978. *The Snow Leopard.* New York: Viking.

———. 1983. *In the Spirit of Crazy Horse.* New York: Viking.

———. 1984. *Indian Country.* New York: Viking.

———. 1986. *Men's Lives.* New York: Random House.

———. 1989. *On the River Styx and Other Stories.* New York: Random House.

———. 1990. *Killing Mister Watson.* New York: Random House.

———. 1991. *African Silences.* New York: Random House.

———. 1997. *Lost Man's River.* New York: Random House.

———. 1998. *Nine-Headed Dragon River: Zen Journals.* Boston: Shambhala.

———. 1999a. *Bone by Bone.* New York: Random House.

———. 1999b. *The Peter Matthiessen Reader,* edited by McKay Jenkins. New York: Vintage.

———. 2000. *Tigers in the Snow.* New York: North Point.

———. 2001. *The Birds of Heaven: Travels with Cranes.* New York: North Point.

Maxwell, Gavin. 1960. *Ring of Bright Water.* London: Longmans.

McCarthy, Cormac. 1985. *Blood Meridian: Or, the Evening Redness in the West.* New York: Random House.

———. 1992. *All the Pretty Horses.* New York: Alfred A. Knopf.

McDonald, Roger. 1992. *Shearers' Motel.* Sydney: Random House.

———. 2001. *The Tree in Changing Light.* Milsons Point, N.S.W.: Knopf.

McKenna, Mark. 2002. *Looking for Blackfellas' Point.* Sydney: University of New South Wales Press.

McPhee, John. 1977. *Coming into the Country.* New York: Farrar, Straus & Giroux.

———. 1981. *Basin and Range.* New York: Farrar, Straus & Giroux.

———. 1986. *Rising from the Plains.* New York: Farrar, Straus & Giroux.

———. 1998. *Annals of the Former World.* New York: Farrar, Straus & Giroux.

Melville, Herman. 1851. *Moby-Dick; or, the Whale.* New York: Modern Library.

Momaday, M. Scott. 1969. *The Way to Rainy Mountain.* Albuquerque: University of New Mexico Press.

Montaigne, Michel de. 1958. *The Complete Essays of Montaigne.* Translated by Donald M. Frame. Stanford: Stanford University Press.

Muir, John. 1894. *The Mountains of California.* New York: Century.

Nabhan, Gary Paul. 1982. *The Desert Smells Like Rain: A Naturalist in Papago Indian Country.* San Francisco: North Point.

Nelson, Richard. 1969. *Hunters of the Northern Ice.* Chicago: University of Chicago Press.

———. 1989. *The Island Within.* San Francisco: North Point.

———. 1997. *Heart & Blood: Living with Deer in America*. New York: Alfred A. Knopf.

Nelson, Richard, Barry Lopez, and Terry Tempest Williams. 2002. *Patriotism and the American Land*. Great Barrington, Mass.: Orion Society.

Newell, Patrice. 2003. *The River*. Ringwood, Vic.: Penguin.

Norris, Kathleen. 1993. *Dakota: A Spiritual Geography*. New York: Ticknor & Fields.

Oliver, Mary. 1992. *New & Selected Poems*. Boston: Beacon.

———. 1995. *Blue Pastures*. New York: Harcourt Brace.

Pyle, Robert Michael. 1988. *Wintergreen: Listening to the Land's Heart*. Boston: Houghton Mifflin.

Quammen, David. 1996. *The Flight of the Dodo: Island Biogeography in an Age of Extinctions*. New York: Charles Scribner's Sons.

———. 1998. *Wild Thoughts from Wild Places*. New York: Charles Scribner's Sons.

Rilke, Rainer Maria. 1923. *The Sonnets to Orpheus*. Translated by Stephen Mitchell. New York: Modern Library.

Robinson, Tim. 1986. *Stones of Aran: Pilgrimage*. Dublin: Lilliput.

———. 1995. *Stones of Aran: Labyrinth*. Dublin: Lilliput.

———. 1996. *Setting Foot on the Shores of the Connemara*. Dublin: Lilliput.

———. 2001. *My Time in Space*. Dublin: Lilliput.

Rogers, Pattiann. 1994. *Firekeeper: New & Selected Poems*. Minneapolis: Milkweed.

———. 1997. *Eating Bread and Honey*. Minneapolis: Milkweed.

———. 1999. *The Dream of the Marsh Wren: Writing as Reciprocal Creation*. Minneapolis: Milkweed.

Rolls, Eric C. 1969. *They All Ran Wild*. Sydney: Angus & Robertson.

———. 1981. *A Million Wild Acres*. Melbourne: Nelson.

———. 1984. *Celebration of the Senses*. Ringwood, Vic: Penguin.

Sanders, Scott R. 1993. *Staying Put: Making a Home in a Restless World*. Boston: Beacon.

———. 1999. *The Country of Language*. Minneapolis: Milkweed

Seddon, George. 1994. *Searching for the Snowy: An Environmental History.* Sydney: Allen & Unwin.

———. 1997. *Landprints: Reflections on Place and Landscape.* Melbourne: Cambridge University Press.

Servid, Carolyn. 2000. *Of Landscape and Longing: Finding a Home at the Water's Edge.* Minneapolis: Milkweed.

Silko, Leslie Marmon. 1977. *Ceremony.* New York: Viking.

Slovic, Scott, ed. 2001. *Getting Over the Color Green: Contemporary Environmental Literature of the Southwest.* Tucson: University of Arizona Press.

Slovic, Scott, and Terrell F. Dixon, eds. 1993. *Being in the World: An Environmental Reader for Writers.* New York: Macmillan.

Smith, Annick. 1995. *Homestead.* Minneapolis: Milkweed.

Snyder, Gary. 1990. *The Practice of the Wild.* San Francisco: North Point.

———. 1995. *A Place in Space: Ethics, Aesthetics, and Watersheds.* Washington, D.C.: Counterpoint.

———. 2000. *The Gary Snyder Reader: Prose, Poetry, and Translation.* Washington, D.C.: Counterpoint.

Spragg, Mark. 1999. *Where Rivers Change Direction.* Salt Lake City: University of Utah Press.

Stafford, Kim Robert. 1987. *Having Everything Right: Essays of Place.* New York: Penguin.

Stafford, William. 1998. *The Way It Is: New & Selected Poems.* Saint Paul, Minn.: Graywolf.

Stegner, Wallace. 1962. *Wolf Willow: A History, a Story, and a Memory of the Last Plains Frontier.* New York: Viking.

———. 1969. *The Sound of Mountain Water: The Changing American West.* New York: Doubleday.

———. 1998. *Marking the Sparrow's Fall: Wallace Stegner's American West.* Edited by Page Stegner. New York: Henry Holt.

———. [1987] 2001. *Crossing to Safety.* New York: Modern Library.

Strehlow, T. G. H. 1969. *Journey to Horseshoe Bend.* Sydney: Angus & Robertson.

Tall, Deborah. 1993. *From Where We Stand: Recovering a Sense of Place.* New York: Alfred A. Knopf.

Tallmadge, John. 2003. "A Matter of Scale." In *A Place on Earth,* edited by Mark Tredinnick, 239–44. Sydney: University of New South Wales Press; Lincoln: University of Nebraska Press.

———. 2004. *The Cincinnati Arch: Learning from Nature in the City.* Athens: University of Georgia Press.

Thoreau, Henry David. 1854. *Walden: Or, A Life in the Woods.* London: Everyman-Dent.

———. 1864. *The Maine Woods.* Boston: Ticknor & Fields.

———. 1927. *The Heart of Thoreau's Journals* (1881–92). Edited by Odell Shepard. Boston: Houghton Mifflin.

———. 1992a. "Civil Disobedience" (1849). In *Henry David Thoreau: "Walden" and Other Writings,* edited by B. Atkinson, 665–94. New York: Modern Library.

———. 1992b. *A Week on the Concord and Merrimack Rivers* (1849). In *Henry David Thoreau: "Walden" and Other Writings,* edited by B. Atkinson, 313–456. New York: Modern Library.

———. 1992c. "Walking" (1862). In *Henry David Thoreau: "Walden" and Other Writings,* edited by B. Atkinson, 625–63. New York: Modern Library.

———. 1992d. *Cape Cod* (1865). In *Henry David Thoreau: "Walden" and Other Writings,* edited by B. Atkinson, 457–526. New York: Modern Library.

Timms, Peter. 2001. *Making Nature: Six Walks in the Bush.* Sydney: Allen & Unwin.

Tredinnick, Mark, ed. 2003. *A Place on Earth: An Anthology of Nature Writing from Australia and North America.* Sydney: University of New South Wales Press; Lincoln: University of Nebraska Press.

Van Dyke, John C. 1898. *Nature for Its Own Sake.* New York: Charles Scribner's Sons.

———. 1918. *The Desert: Further Studies in Natural Appearances.* New York: Charles Scribner's Sons.

Viney, Michael. 1996. *A Year's Turning.* Belfast: Blackstaff.

Wallace, David Rains. 1983. *The Klamath Knot: Explorations of Myth and Evolution.* San Francisco: Sierra Club Books.

White, E. B. 1977. *Essays of E. B. White.* New York: Harper & Row.

———. 1997. *One Man's Meat.* Gardiner, Me.: Tilbury House.

White, Gilbert. 1789. *The Natural History and Antiquities of Selborne.* London: B. White & Son.

Williams, Terry Tempest, with Ted Major. 1984a. *The Secret Language of Snow.* San Francisco: Sierra Club Books/Pantheon.

Williams, Terry Tempest. 1984b. *Pieces of White Shell: A Journey to Navajoland.* New York: Charles Scribner's Sons.

———. 1985. *Between Cattails.* New York: Charles Scribner's Sons.

———. 1989. *Coyote's Canyon.* Salt Lake City: Peregrine Smith.

———. 1991. *Refuge: An Unnatural History of Family and Place.* New York: Pantheon.

———. 1994. *An Unspoken Hunger.* New York: Pantheon.

———. 1995. *Desert Quartet: An Erotic Landscape.* New York: Pantheon.

———. 2000. *Leap.* New York: Pantheon.

———. 2001. *Red: Passion and Patience in the Desert.* New York: Pantheon.

Winton, Tim. 1999. "Strange Passion: A Landscape Memoir." In Richard Woldendorp and Tim Winton, *Down to Earth: Australian Landscapes.* North Fremantle, W.A.: Fremantle Arts Centre Press.

Wright, Judith. 1959. *The Generations of Men.* Melbourne: Oxford University Press.

———. 1981. *The Cry for the Dead.* Melbourne: Oxford University Press.

———. 1991. *Born of the Conquerors.* Canberra: Aboriginal Studies Press.

———. 1994. *Collected Poems.* Sydney: Angus & Robertson.

Zwinger, Ann. 1975. *Run, River, Run: A Naturalist's Journey Down One of the Great Rivers of the West.* New York: Harper & Row.

Scholarly Works, Texts, Guides, and References

Abram, David. 1996. *The Spell of the Sensuous: Perception and Language in a More-Than-Human World.* New York: Vintage.

Adams, William M., and Martin Mulligan, eds. 2003. *Decolonizing Nature: Strategies for Conservation in a Post-Colonial Era*. London: Sterling.

Anderson, Lorraine. 1996. "Terry Tempest Williams." In *American Nature Writers*, edited by John Elder, 973–88. New York: Charles Scribner's Sons.

Anderson, Lorraine, Scott Slovic, and John P. O'Grady, eds. 1999. *Literature and the Environment: A Reader on Nature and Culture*. New York: Longman.

Arthur, Jay M. 2003. *The Default Country: A Lexical Cartography of Twentieth-Century Australia*. Sydney: University of New South Wales Press.

Auden, W. H. 1962. *The Dyer's Hand*. New York: Vintage.

Bate, Jonathan. 1991. *Romantic Ecology: Wordsworth and the Environmental Tradition*. New York: Routledge.

———. 2000. *The Song of the Earth*. Cambridge, Mass.: Harvard University Press

Berendt, Joachim-Ernst. 1987. *The World Is Sound: Nada Brahma— Music and the Landscape of Consciousness*. Rochester, Vt.: Inner Traditions.

Berry, Wendell. 1994. "A Few Words in Defense of Edward Abbey" (1985). In *Earthly Words: Essays on Contemporary American Nature and Environmental Writers*, edited by John Cooley, 19–28. Ann Arbor: University of Michigan Press.

Blainey, Geoffrey. 1975. *The Triumph of the Nomads*. Melbourne: Macmillan.

———. 1980. *A Land Half Won*. Melbourne: Macmillan.

Bolton, Geoffrey. 1981. *Spoils and Spoilers: A History of Australians Shaping Their Environment*. Sydney: Allen & Unwin.

Bonyhady, Tim, and Tom Griffiths, eds. 2002. *Words for Country: Landscape and Language in Australia*. Sydney: University of New South Wales Press.

Boorstin, Daniel J. 1966. *The Americans: The National Experience*. London: Weidenfeld & Nicolson.

Branch, Michael P. 1996. "Indexing American Possibilities: The Natural History Writing of Bartram, Wilson, and Audubon." In *The Ecocriticism Reader: Landmarks in Literary Ecology*, edited by Cheryll Glotfelty and Harold Fromm, 282–302. Athens: University of Georgia Press.

Branch, Michael P., Rochelle Johnson, Daniel Patterson, and Scott Slovic, eds. 1998. *Reading the Earth: New Directions in the Study of Literature and Environment.* Moscow: University of Idaho Press.

Branch, Michael P., and Scott Slovic, eds. 2003. *ISLE Reader: Ecocriticism, 1993–2003.* Athens: University of Georgia Press.

Buell, Lawrence. 1995. *The Environmental Imagination: Thoreau, Nature Writing, and the Formation of American Culture.* Cambridge, Mass.: Harvard University Press.

———. 1999. "The Ecocritical Insurgency." *New Literary History* 30, no. 3: 699–712.

———. 2001. *Writing for an Endangered World: Literature, Culture, and Environment in the U.S. and Beyond.* Cambridge, Mass.: Harvard University Press.

Burroughs, Franklin. 1994. "Landscapes of the Alternate Self." *Southern Review* 30, no. 1 (winter): 143–56.

Burroughs, John. 1896. *The Writings of John Burroughs: Walt Whitman—A Study.* New York: Houghton Mifflin.

———. 2001. "Notes on Walt Whitman as Poet and Person" (1867). In *A Century of Early Ecocriticism*, edited by D. Mazel, 34–39. Athens: University of Georgia Press.

Cameron, John, ed. 2001. *Changing Places: Reimagining Sense of Place in Australia.* Richmond, N.S.W.: University of Western Sydney.

Cameron, Sharon. 1985. *Writing Nature: Henry Thoreau's Journal.* New York: Oxford University Press.

Campbell, SueEllen. 1996. "The Land and Language of Desire: Where Deep Ecology and Poststructuralism Meet" (1989). In *The Ecocriticism Reader: Landmarks in Literary Ecology*, edited by Cheryll Glotfelty and Harold Fromm, 124–36. Athens: University of Georgia Press.

Carroll, Joseph. 1995. *Evolution and Literary Theory.* Columbia: University of Missouri Press.

———. 2002. "Organism, Environment, and Literary Representation." *ISLE*, summer, 27–46.

Carter, Paul. 1987. *The Road to Botany Bay: An Exploration of Landscape and History.* New York: Alfred A. Knopf.

———. 1996. *The Lie of the Land.* London: Faber & Faber.

Cooley, John, ed. 1994. *Earthly Words: Essays on Contemporary American Nature and Environmental Writers.* Ann Arbor: University of Michigan Press.

Crotty, Michael. 1996. "Doing Phenomenology." In *Qualitative Research Practice in Adult Education*, edited by Peter Willis and Bernie Neville, 272–82. Ringwood, Vic.: David Lovell.

D'Agata, John, and Deborah Tall. 1997. "New Terrain: The Lyric Essay." *Seneca Review* 27, no. 2 (fall): 7–8.

De Voto, Bernard. 1943. *The Year of Decision, 1846.* Boston: Little, Brown.

———. 1943. *The Western Paradox.* Boston: Little, Brown.

Duncan, David James. 2002. "Assailed: Improvisations in the Key of Cosmology." *Orion* 21, no. 3 (summer): 79–90.

Eckersley, Robyn. 1992. *Environmentalism and Political Theory: Toward an Ecocentric Approach.* London: University College of London Press.

Elder, John, ed. 1996a. *American Nature Writers.* 2 volumes. New York: Charles Scribner's Sons.

———. 1996b. *Imagining the Earth: Poetry and the Vision of Nature.* Athens: University of Georgia Press.

———. 1999. "The Poetry of Experience." *New Literary History* 30, no. 3: 649–59.

Evans, Howard, and Mary Alice Evans. 1991. *Cache La Poudre: The Natural History of a Rocky Mountain River.* Niwot: University of Colorado Press.

Evernden, Neil. 1992. *The Social Creation of Nature.* Baltimore: Johns Hopkins University Press.

———. 1996. "Beyond Ecology: Self, Place, and the Pathetic Fallacy" (1978). In *The Ecocriticism Reader: Landmarks in Literary Ecology*, edited by Cheryll Glotfelty and Harold Fromm, 92–104. Athens: University of Georgia Press.

Fritzell, P. 1990. *Nature Writing and America: Essays upon a Cultural Type*. Ames: Iowa State University Press.

Gifford, Terry. 1999. *Pastoralism*. London: Routledge.

Glotfelty, Cheryll, and Harold Fromm, eds. 1996. *The Ecocriticism Reader: Landmarks in Literary Ecology*. Athens: University of Georgia Press.

Griffiths, Tom, and Libby Robin, eds. 1997. *Ecology and Empire: Environmental History of Settler Societies*. Edinburgh: Keele University Press.

Haar, Michael. 1986. *The Song of the Earth: Heidegger and the Grounds of the History of Being*. Bloomington: Indiana University Press.

Harrison, Martin. 2005a. *Who Wants to Create Australia? Essays on Poetry and Ideas in Contemporary Australia*. Sydney: Halstead.

———. 2005b. "The Degradation of Land and the Position of Poetry." Paper presented at "Be True to the Earth," inaugural conference of the Association for the Study of Literature and the Environment— Australia and New Zealand, Monash University, April.

Hay, Pete. 2002. *Main Currents in Environmental Thought*. Sydney: University of New South Wales Press.

Heaney, Seamus. 1980. *Preoccupations: Selected Prose 1968–1978*. London: Faber & Faber.

Heidegger, Martin. 1928. *Being and Time*. New York: Harper & Row.

———. 1935. "The Origin of the Work of Art." In *Heidegger Gesamtausgabe*, vol. 5: *Holzwege*, edited by F.-W. von Hermann and Vittorio Klostermann. Frankfurt am Main.

———. 1979. *Underway to Language*. Pfullingen: Noske.

Hirsch, Edward. 1999. *How to Read a Poem and Fall in Love with Poetry*. New York: Harcourt.

Hitt, Christopher. 1999. "Toward an Ecological Sublime." *New Literary History* 30, no. 3: 603–23.

Hollander, John. 1981. *Rhyme's Reason: A Guide to English Verse.* New Haven, Conn.: Yale University Press.

Holt, Henry. 1998. "Henry Holt Reading Group Guides—James Galvin's *The Meadow.*" www.henryholt.com/readingguides/galvin.htm.

Howarth, William. 1996. "Some Principles of Ecocriticism." In *The Ecocriticism Reader: Landmarks in Literary Ecology,* edited by Cheryll Glotfelty and Harold Fromm, 69–91. Athens: University of Georgia Press.

———. 1999. "Imagined Territory: The Writing of Wetlands." *New Literary History* 30, no. 3: 509–39.

Husserl, Edmund. 1970. *The Idea of Phenomenology.* The Hague: Martinus Nijhoff.

Huxley, Aldous. 1946. *The Perennial Philosophy.* London: Chatto & Windus.

Ihde, Don. 1977. *Listening and Voice: A Phenomenology of Sound.* Athens: Ohio University Press.

Jefferson, Margo. 2002. "Writers and Writing: An Instructor in How to See." *New York Times Book Review,* 12 May, 31.

Jenkins, McKay. 1999. "Introduction." In *The Peter Matthiessen Reader,* edited by McKay Jenkins, xi–xxix. New York: Vintage.

Jourdain, Robert. 1997. *Music, the Brain, and Ecstasy.* New York: Morrow.

Knight, Dennis H. 1994. *Mountains and Plains: The Ecology of Wyoming Landscapes.* New Haven, Conn.: Yale University Press.

Leuders, Edward, ed. 1989. *Writing Natural History: Dialogues with Authors.* Salt Lake City: University of Utah Press.

Love, Glen A. 1972. "Ecology in Arcadia." *Colorado Quarterly,* no. 21 (autumn): 175–85.

———. 1996. "Revaluing Nature: Toward an Ecological Criticism" (1990). In *The Ecocriticism Reader: Landmarks in Literary Ecology,* edited by Cheryll Glotfelty and Harold Fromm, 225–40. Athens: University of Georgia Press.

———. 1999. "Ecocriticism and Science: Toward Consilience?" *New Literary History* 30, no. 3: 561–76.

———. 2003. *Practical Ecocriticism: Literature, Biology, and the Environment.* Charlottesville: University of Virginia Press.

Love, Glen A., and R. M. Love, eds. 1970. *Ecological Crisis: Readings for Survival.* New York: Farrar, Straus & Giroux.

Lyon, Thomas J., ed. 1997. *Updating the American West.* Fort Worth: Texas Christian University Press.

———, ed. 2001. *This Incomparable Land: A Guide to American Nature Writing.* Rev. ed. Minneapolis: Milkweed.

Macy, Joanna. 1991. *World as Lover, World as Self.* Berkeley: Parallax.

Malpas, Jeff E. 1999. *Place and Experience: A Philosophical Topography.* Cambridge: Cambridge University Press.

Marshall, Ian. 1998. *Story Line: Exploring the Literature of the Appalachian Trail.* Charlottesville: University Press of Virginia.

Marx, Leo. 1964. *The Machine in the Garden: Technology and the Pastoral Ideal in America.* New York: Oxford University Press.

Mathews, Freya. 1991. *The Ecological Self.* London: Routledge.

Mazel, David, ed. 2001. *A Century of Early Ecocriticism.* Athens: University of Georgia Press

Meeker, Joseph W. 1997. *The Comedy of Survival: Literary Ecology and a Play Ethic.* Tucson: University of Arizona Press.

Merleau-Ponty, Maurice. 1962. *Phenomenology of Perception.* London: Routledge.

Moran, Dermot, and Timothy Mooney, eds. 2002. *The Phenomenology Reader.* London: Routledge.

Mulligan, Martin, and Stuart Hill. 2001. *Ecological Pioneers: A Social History of Australian Ecological Thought and Action.* Cambridge: Cambridge University Press.

Nash, Roderick. 1982. *Wilderness and the American Mind.* New Haven: Yale University Press.

Oelschlaeger, Max. 1991. *The Idea of Wilderness: From Prehistory to the Age of Ecology.* New Haven: Yale University Press.

Oliver, Mary. 1994. *A Poetry Handbook.* San Diego: Harcourt Brace.

———. 1998. *Rules for the Dance: A Handbook for Writing and Reading Metrical Verse.* New York: Houghton Mifflin.

Packard, William. 1992. *The Art of Poetry Writing: A Guide for Poets, Students, and Readers.* New York: St. Martin's.

Paul, Sherman. 1992. *For Love of the World: Essays on Nature Writers.* Iowa City: University of Iowa Press.

Peck, H. Daniel. 1990. *Thoreau's Morning Work: Memory and Perception in "A Week on the Concord and Merrimack Rivers," the "Journal," and "Walden."* New Haven: Yale University Press.

Phillips, Dana. 1999. "Ecocriticism, Literary Theory, and the Truth of Ecology." *New Literary History* 30, no. 3: 577–602.

Plumwood, Val. 2002. *Environmental Culture: The Ecological Crisis of Reason.* New York: Routledge.

Ransom, John Crowe. 1984. "Criticism as Pure Speculation." In *Selected Essays of John Crowe Ransom,* edited by Thomas Daniel Young and John Hindle, 128–46. Baton Rouge: Louisiana State University Press.

Relph, Edward. 1976. *Place and Placelessness.* London: Pion.

Richardson, Robert D. 1986. *Henry Thoreau: A Life of the Mind.* Berkeley: University of California Press.

Rigby, Kate. 2002. "Ecocriticism." In *Introducing Criticism at the Twenty-first Century,* edited by J. Wolfreys, 151–78. Edinburgh: Edinburgh University Press.

———. 2004. "Earth, World, Text: On the (Im)possibility of Ecopoiesis." *New Literary History* 35, no. 3 (summer): 427–42.

Rose, Deborah Bird. 1996. *Nourishing Terrains: Australian Aboriginal Views of Landscape and Wilderness.* Canberra: Australian Heritage Commission.

Rothenberg, David. 2002. *Sudden Music: Improvisation, Sound, Nature.* Athens: University of Georgia Press.

Rueckert, William. 1996. "Literature and Ecology: An Experiment in Ecocriticism" (1978). In *The Ecocriticism Reader: Landmarks in Literary Ecology,* edited by C. Glotfelty and H. Fromm, 69–91. Athens: University of Georgia Press.

Sales, Roger. 1983. *English Literature in History, 1780–1830: Pastoral and Politics.* London: Hutchinson.

Sanders, Scott R. 1991. "The Singular First Person." In *Secrets of the Universe: Scenes from the Journey Home.* Boston: Beacon.

———. 1996. "Speaking a Word for Nature." In *The Ecocriticism Reader: Landmarks in Literary Ecology,* edited by C. Glotfelty and H. Fromm, 182–94. Athens: University of Georgia Press.

Schafer, R. Murray. 2000. "Acoustic Space." In *Dwelling, Place, and Environment: Toward a Phenomenology of Person and World,* edited by David Seamon and Robert Mugerauer, 87–98. Malabar, Fla.: Krieger.

Seamon, David, and Robert Mugerauer, eds. 2000. *Dwelling, Place, and Environment: Toward a Phenomenology of Person and World.* Malabar, Fla.: Krieger.

Seddon, George, ed. 1976. *Man and Landscape in Australia: Towards an Ecological Vision.* Canberra: Australian Government Publishing Service.

———. 2003. "Getting Off the Sheep's Back: Farewell to Arcady." Photocopy.

Shulevitz, Judith. 2003. "Get Me Rewrite." *New York Times Book Review,* April 6, 31.

Silko, Leslie Marmon. 1986. "Landscape, History, and the Pueblo Imagination." *Antaeus,* no. 57 (autumn): 882–94.

Slovic, Scott. 1992. *Seeking Awareness in American Nature Writing.* Salt Lake City: University of Utah Press.

———. 1996. "Nature Writing and Environmental Psychology" (1992). In *The Ecocriticism Reader: Landmarks in Literary Ecology,* edited by Cheryll Glotfelty and Harold Fromm, 351–70. Athens: University of Georgia Press.

———. 1999. "Seeking the Language of Solid Ground: Reflections on Ecocriticism and Narrative." *Fourth Genre* 1, no. 2 (fall 1999): 34–38.

———. 2005. "There's Something About Your Voice I Cannot Hear: Environmental Literature, Public Policy, and Ecocriticism." *Southerly* 64, no. 2: 59–68.

Smith, F. Joseph. 1979. *The Experiencing of Musical Sound: A Prelude to a Phenomenology of Music.* New York: Gordon & Breach.

Spiegelberg, Herbert. 1982. *The Phenomenological Movement.* The Hague: Martinus Nijhoff.

Stegner, Wallace. 1953. *Beyond the Hundredth Meridian: John Wesley Powell and the Second Opening of the West.* Boston: Houghton Mifflin.

Stewart, David, and Algis Mickunas. 1974. *Exploring Phenomenology: A Guide to the Field and Its Literature.* Athens: Ohio University Press.

Stewart, Frank. 1995. *A Natural History of Nature Writing.* Washington, D.C.: Island.

Tacey, David. 1995. *Edge of the Sacred: Transformation in Australia.* Melbourne: HarperCollins.

———. 2000. *Reenchantment: The New Australian Spirituality.* Melbourne: HarperCollins.

Tallmadge, John. 1997. *Meeting the Tree of Life: A Teacher's Path.* Salt Lake City: University of Utah Press.

Taylor, J. Golden, ed. 1987. *A Literary History of the American West.* Fort Worth: Texas Christian University Press.

Thomas, Keith. 1983. *Man and the Natural World.* London: Allen Lane.

Tredinnick, Mark. 1998. "Nothing but the Truth." *Quadrant* 42, no. 9: 61–64.

———. 2003. "Belonging to Here: An Introduction." In *A Place on Earth,* edited by Mark Tredinnick, 25–47. Sydney: University of New South Wales Press; Lincoln: University of Nebraska Press.

———. 2004. "Editorial." *Southerly* 64, no. 2: 5–6

Tuan, Yi-Fu. 1974. *Topophilia: A Study of Environmental Perception, Attitudes, and Values.* Englewood Cliffs, N.J.: Prentice-Hall.

———. 1977. *Space and Place: The Perspective of Experience.* Minneapolis: University of Minnesota Press.

Van Manen, Max. 1990. *Researching Lived Experience: Human Science for an Action-Sensitive Pedagogy.* Albany: State University of New York Press.

Voigt, Ellen Bryant. 1999. *The Flexible Lyric.* Athens: University of Georgia Press.

———. 2003. "Syntax: Rhythm of Thought, Rhythm of Song." *Kenyon Review* 25, no. 1 (winter): 144–63.

West, Herbert Faulkner. 1939. *The Nature Writers: A Guide to Richer Reading.* Brattleboro, Vt.: Stephen Daye.

Wilson, Edward O. 1992. *The Diversity of Life.* Cambridge, Mass.: Harvard University Press.

Wilson, Edward O., et al. 1973. *Life on Earth.* Stamford, Conn.: Sinauer Associates.

Wolfreys, Julian. 2002. *Introducing Criticism at the Twenty-first Century.* Edinburgh: Edinburgh University Press.

Worster, Donald. 1994. *Nature's Economy: A History of Ecological Ideas.* 2nd ed. New York: Cambridge University Press.

Wright, Judith. 1976. "Biological Man." In *Man and Landscape in Australia: Towards an Ecological Vision,* edited by George Seddon, 167–72. Canberra: Australian Government Publishing Service.

Zuckerkandl, Victor. 1956. *Sound and Symbol: Music and the External World.* New York: Pantheon.

Index